UNDERSTANDING THE PRIMARY SCHOOL

A SOCIOLOGICAL ANALYSIS

David Hartley

CROOM HELM
London ● Sydney ● Dover, New Hampshire

© 1985 David Hartley
Croom Helm Ltd, Provident House, Burrell Row,
Beckenham, Kent BR3 1AT
Croom Helm Australia Pty Ltd, Suite 4, 6th Floor,
64-76 Kippax Street, Surry Hills, NSW 2010, Australia

British Library Cataloguing in Publication Data

Hartley, David
    Understanding the primary school : a sociological
    analysis.
    1. Elementary schools — Scotland — Sociological
    aspects
    I. Title
    372.9411   LC191.8.G72S3
    ISBN 0-7099-3742-3

Croom Helm, 51 Washington Street, Dover,
New Hampshire 03820, USA

Library of Congress Cataloging in Publication Data

Hartley, David, 1945-
    Understanding the primary school.

    Bibliography: p.
    Includes indexes.
    1. Education, Elementary — Social aspects — Great
Britain — Case studies. 2. Elementary school students'
socioeconomic status — Great Britain — Case studies.
3. Education, Urban — Great Britain — Case studies.
4. School integration — Great Britain — Case studies.
I. Title.
LA633.H37   1985   370.19   85-11369
ISBN 0-7099-3742-3

Printed and bound in Great Britain by
Biddles Ltd, Guildford and King's Lynn

CONTENTS

CONTENTS

LIST OF FIGURES

LIST OF FIGURES

LIST OF TABLES

LIST OF TABLES

ACKNOWLEDGEMENTS

In undertaking this study I came to meet many people.
In different ways, each of them contributed to it,
though I doubt that they were always aware of doing
so at the time. My thanks go to all of them,
particularly the teachers, children and parents
whose identities must remain undisclosed. There
are, however, others whom I can name and thank. I
am especially indebted to Felicity Merchant and
Sharon Lowe for collecting factual material and
administering objective tests. To Sarah Fell and
Moira Stewart, whose typing skills far surpass mine,
I am equally thankful, not only for their secretarial
efforts, but also for their candid comments on my
use of English. In discussion with colleagues and
students I have learnt much, and I am grateful to
Barbara Meyer, Hector Montiel and the late Jim Smith
for their insights. I wish to thank the editors of
Research in Education for permission to reproduce
from No.28 of that journal some data which appears
in Chapter 9 of this book. Finally, I should like
to express my deep appreciation to my wife Linda who,
in the middle of a very busy schedule, took time to
read and comment upon the various drafts.

INTRODUCTION

The designs of educational policy makers are rarely
realised as intended. When the words of curriculum
innovators are translated into action in the classroom, the outcome is often at odds with what the
innovators had in mind (Shipman, 1974). When
legislation is enacted for well-intentioned motives,
the consequences may be to the very detriment of
those who were meant to be helped, as witnessed, for
example, by the unintended consequences of the famous
'Brown Decision' in 1954 on racial desegregation in
American schools (Rist, 1979). What intervenes
between the carefully reasoned thoughts of policy-
makers and the deeds of teachers is the latter's
interpretation of what the new policy means to them in
practical terms. It is they who must weigh the
possible consequences in the light of the exigencies
of their classroom situation. Not surprisingly, the
educational landscape is strewn with spent 'projects',
nurtured in the minds of idealistic policy-makers,
but withering away in the face of teacher realism.
     The inner-city school which forms the research
here was influenced by the policy of "positive discrimination" advocated in the Plowden Report on primary
education in England and Wales (Plowden, 1967). That
is to say, the school sought to compensate for the
presumed material and emotional difficulties which
beset its pupils in and around their homes. As part
of its recommendations, the Plowden Report called for
policies which would better the cognitive performance
of such children. Nevertheless, it is not axiomatic
that the actual practice in inner-city schools in
deprived areas would accord with that policy. For
different reasons, teachers may interpret the term
"compensation" to mean something other than an academic compensation. It is one of the purposes of this
case-study of an urban primary school to discover how
teachers interpreted compensation: to discover how

its pupils, who had spent their entire primary education being compensated, fared at the end of it.

Our first major concern will be with the
interpretation of the term 'compensation'. What did
it mean to individual teachers? What classroom
consequences followed from their interpretations?
For example, one of the teachers likened the school
to a 'black comedy'. The metaphor constituted an
off-the-cuff remark made by a teacher to depict, for
her, life in this inner city school. It is a statement which implies the frustration she felt when
doing her job and which further hints at the
difficulties which beset her pupils doing theirs.
For her, the lives at home which many of her pupils
led were 'tragic'. What compounded the tragedy was
that so few of them would eventually acquire the
educational credentials which might pave their way
to better things. Yet she did not foresake her
intention to instruct her pupils as best she could
in the circumstances which limited her endeavour to
do so. She interpreted 'compensation' to mean
academic compensation - to push her pupils, against
the odds, towards marketable credentials.
Occasionally her frustration was expressed in the
unguarded moments of the staffroom. It was done by
rendering everything about the school as comical:
although it was tragic and frustrating, it was also
funny. Other teachers, however, confronted by the
same kinds of pupil and the same formal goal of
compensation, did not feel the need to ease their
dilemma and frustration. This was because they felt
no such frustration; they had simply intended it
away. That is, 'compensation' did not mean academic
compensation; it meant the less onerous provision
of a therapeutic environment for their children so
that they might shelter in the school from the
trials of growing up in the inner city. We are
concerned, therefore, with a school whose teachers
defined their pupils as in need of very different
kinds of education, but who still defined their
respective goals as 'compensating', as 'positively
discriminating' and, above all, as well-intentioned,
in the best interests of their pupils.

The major concern of this book, therefore, is
with the construction of educational ideologies:
the reasons which underpinned them; the extent to
which they were shared; the extent to which attempts
were made to impose ideologies on others. For
Keddie (1971) these ideologies constitute what she
calls the Educationist Context, or what teachers say
they would do. Here the term 'professed', as opposed

INTRODUCTION

to 'practised', ideologies is adopted. In arriving
at what counts as a teacher's ideology we rely upon
the first-hand observation of the primary school
staffroom, and upon the observation of the teacher
in the classroom by myself and by the pupils. We
are also concerned with changes in the teacher's
ideology and practice, and the reasons for them.
This requires something of a long-term perspective
which the three-year span of the study permitted.
More importantly, we are concerned with the 'politics'
of education within the school; that is, the extent
to which the head teacher, as the bureaucratic
authority in the school, sought to impose his own
views. Finally, the issue of teacher ideologies
raises the further matter of the degree to which
teachers see themselves as possessing professional
autonomy. Is this autonomy or is it 'autonomy'?
    We turn now to the second and minor theme of
the book. The sociology of education has become
somewhat obsessed with 'social class', be it from a
functionalist or neoMarxist perspective. Whilst it
is arguable that a class-based analysis of school
and society yields many insights, it runs the risk
of excluding other issues. It may be too simplistic.
That is to say, from a neoMarxist perspective, the
basis of social differentiation is seen, ultimately,
as being rooted in a conflict of interests between
labour and capital. Cultural phenomena are,
ultimately, rooted in class. The proletariat will
eventually become a class in itself, and for itself.
A pre-revolutionary consciousness within the
proletariat will emerge. Following Weber, the
approach here, whilst not denying the importance of
an affinity between material existence and
consciousness, does not agree that it wholly explains
cultural phenomena. This is illustrated by the
cultural differences and conflicts within the
working class. Differences which are rooted in
'status group' membership marked by a common
ethnicity, language, religion or gender will serve
to fragment the cohesion of the working class. To
argue for the homogeneity of the working class is
to ignore the manifestation of these status
differences. Moreover, these status differences,
though exploited by capitalism, are not derivative
of it. Ethnic cleavages, for example, pre-date
capitalism; they will not necessarily disappear
when capitalism ceases to be. Sociology of education
has paid scant attention to status differentiation
within the education of the working class. Our
second concern, therefore, is with an exploratory

endeavour to point up the educational consequences
of ethnic and gender status group membership within
a working class school.

In exploring these two themes, I employed an
eclectic methodology: that is, one which uses qualitative and quantitative methods in a complementary
manner, a procedure advocated by Weber. By the term
qualitative research, I refer to that process whereby
the meanings which teachers and pupils assign to their
school can be imputed, either through observation or
through conversation. Quantitative methodology
requires us to find out the extent to which these
meanings are shared - that is, the extent to which
they are social. It follows from this that we should
also seek to provide reasons why some meanings are
socially shared, whilst others are not. I do not
pretend to have observed all events which occurred
during the period of the research. Schools are not
laboratories, and teachers and children should not
be regarded as 'subjects' to be 'controlled' and
'manipulated'. Those events which I observed constitute a selection, a partial view of school reality.
Given that, I tried to ensure that the meaning of
those events which I did observe was checked, as far
as was possible. I do not claim that I had an
immaculate perception of those events, but I sought
to impute that meaning which was most adequate on the
basis of the evidence which I could adduce.

The school which was investigated was in Scotland.
Scotland's education system is administered by the
Scottish Education Department, not by the Department
of Education and Science. The organisation of
Scottish education is different from that in England
and Wales: it is more centralised, and the breadth
of the curriculum is wider in the secondary school.
At primary level, however, the educational ideology is
similar to that in England and Wales. Both the
Scottish 'Primary Memorandum' (SED, 1965) and the
Plowden Report (1967) in Engand and Wales, espouse
'child-centred' education. Moreover, recent research
on the extent to which 'child-centred' education has
been realised in both countries has drawn similar
conclusions (Galton et al, 1980; SED, 1980). The
school here should not, however, be seen as a typical
Scottish school - its very inner-city status sets it
apart as being different from other schools in "good,
middle class areas" - but it may share similar aspects
with other schools in deprived areas. Those who
teach in the inner city may find much that they
recognise; those who teach in 'normal' schools
might realise why their schools are so defined.

INTRODUCTION

The book is intended for teachers, both those in training and those in practice. By implication, those who train teachers and those who analyse education may find it of interest. Rather than give a very detailed exposition of my theoretical position at the beginning of the book, I make do in Chapter 1 with a brief excursion through the recent history of the sociology of the primary school, leading to a short statement of the theoretical approach to be followed here. Further elaboration of the theoretical perspective will be undertaken as deemed necessary in the text. Some readers may find that parts of Chapter 7 tax their statistical knowledge but, whenever possible, I have tried to show the findings graphically and/or with detailed verbal comment. When dealing with large numbers of people, some quantification is necessary. Finally, I have preserved the anonymity of the school, its teachers and its pupils.

CHAPTER 1

THE SOCIOLOGY OF THE PRIMARY SCHOOL

The sociology of the primary school, as opposed to
the sociology of primary education, is quite recent.
It was not until the 1960s that sociologists
entered schools and classrooms. The reason for this
stems largely from the fact that educational sociologists had previously been concerned with education
as an institution of society. Their concern with
the inputs and outputs of education, guided by
structural functionalism, had caused them to ignore
the process of schooling itself. However, after 1971
attention turned to the classroom and to the teacher-
pupil relationship. New theory guided this endeavour
and new methodologies were employed, mainly of an
inferential, qualitative kind. Whilst this 'new'
sociology of the primary school and classroom took
hold, it did not wholly predominate. Of late there
has been some sign of a resurgence of interest in
structural accounts of the school, though not from a
functionalist perspective. That is to say, there
has been some misgiving about the mere description
of the teacher-pupil classroom relationship, interesting though it is. What is required, so this
argument goes, is a structuralist explanation of
observed classroom events. There is a need,
therefore, to ask not just the 'how' question of
classroom life, but the 'why' question as well.
There is a need to reconcile the microsociological
with the macrosociological. In this chapter I shall
give a brief account of these theoretical 'shifts'
which have informed the sociology of primary schools
and this exercise will serve as the basis for the
statement of the theory which will guide the study
at hand. [1]

Structural Functionalism and Primary Education

The essence of the functionalist explanation is that
society may be thought of as a machine, or as a
biological organism, wherein the component
institutions, such as education, the economy and the
family, act in concert with a view to realising
society's needs (Parsons, 1951). Within these
component social institutions there are component
organizations, each of which contributes to the
overall effectiveness of each institution. And,
within individual institutions, there are
arrangements of social roles which incumbents fill
in the manner prescribed. What enables society to
cohere is an assumed and expected consensus of
purpose among all role incumbents in all institutions. It was this functionalist paradigm which
held sway during the immediate post-war period until
about 1971. Its emphasis was very much upon the
relationship among social institutions and not upon
the relationships among individuals within organizations. This is well illustrated if the title of
the best-known anthology within educational
sociology within Britain in this period is
considered: Education, Economy and Society (Floud
and Anderson, 1961).
   Within it the reader is informed that its
purpose will be to study the 'links' among education
and other social institutions, of which the economy
is paramount:

>   In modern society, the major link of
>   education to social structure is through the
>   economy and this is a linkage of both stimulus
>   and response. (Floud and Halsey, 1962:12)

In contributing to the realization of society's
needs, educational organizations were required to
fill a dual purpose: to socialize and, on the basis
of a fair competition, to select. In Parsonian terms,
schools must satisfy 'expressive' and 'instrumental'
needs, the former corresponding to the socialization
purpose, the latter to the function of teaching
technical skills and of selection (Parsons, 1961).
   It is this second function, especially that of
selection, which most concerned researchers in
primary education during the 1950s and 1960s. The nub
of the matter was that primary education was not as
'meritocratic' as had been predicted by functionalist

theory. That is to say, many 'talented' pupils in primary schools were being 'missed', their talents 'wasted'. Teachers had been unable to identify correctly the talent of many pupils, many of whom were working class and many of whom 'underachieved'. Instead of 'talent' being the predictor of educational achievement, 'social class' factors seemed the more sensitive indicators.[2] Despite the good intentions of the 1944 Education Act:

> Widespread social amelioration since World War II has not removed persistent class and ethnic inequalities in the distribution of ability (potential) and attainment (performance). (Floud and Halsey, 1961:7)

This conclusion pointed up two 'dysfunctions' in the social system. Firstly, it implied that the working class family, as a social agency, was being somewhat deficient in its pre-school socialization patterns. Working class children had not been socialised in a manner desired by the education system. Secondly, this 'underachievement' by talented working class pupils meant a 'wastage' of talent that the economy could ill afford to lose during a period of technological advancement and change.

The first of these 'dysfunctions' was assumed to be the cause of the second. That is, if the school could somehow make up the cultural deficiencies of the talented working class child, then he would not underachieve and the economy would not be deprived of his skills. Thus it was that the government sponsored a number of ameliorative and interventionist 'action' research programmes to 'compensate' for the dysfunctional outcomes of working class families. With the establishment of 'educational priority areas', not educational priority individuals, as in America, it was hoped that working class underachievement would end. But it did not and the E.P.A. programme has largely been regarded as unsuccessful (Shipman, 1980) although Halsey still avers the policy of positive discrimination, albeit on a more grand scale (Halsey, 1980). The other corrective practice aimed at ameliorating social class differences - the comprehensive school - has also not fulfilled its purpose (Ford, 1969; Gray, McPherson and Raffe, 1983). The failure, therefore, of these largely organisational arrangements prompted attention to be focussed on the classroom itself, and it did so informed by the 'new' approach provided in M.F.D. Young's (1971) anthology

Knowledge and Control which, despite early criticism
(Shipman, 1973), undermind functionalism's claim to
be the dominant paradigm.

The 'new' Sociology of the Primary School

The sociological study of the school before 1970 had
been virtually ignored. Only Waller's (1932) classic
and the pioneer works of Becker (1953), Lacey (1970),
Hargreaves (1967) and King (1969) were available. There
were other studies of the clasroom but these tended
to be drawn from social psychology and were used in a
diagnostic manner by teacher training institutions to
improve the classroom management techniques of student
teachers. Perhaps the best known work in this respect
is that by Flanders (1970). The approach taken was to
describe and to record the incidence of particular,
pre-specified categories of event. No attention was
paid to their context or to their meaning (although
Kounin's (1970) work began to move away from mere
description). Description, not explanation, was the
convention.[3] Even Jackson's (1968) perceptive study
Life in Classrooms which highlighted the patience,
toleration and boredom required of pupils was not
rooted in any explicit theoretical perspective, and
his work with Henrietta Lahaderne (Jackson and
Lahaderne, 1967) again employs the use of pre-
structured behavioural categories through which the
flow of classroom life was filtered. What was needed
was a theory which would not simply 'atomise' classroom life, but which would contextualise and interpret
it. That theory was available in the work of Schutz
and his disciples, to which we now turn.
A theory of society should be able to explain
how and why society coheres. In the strict sense,
structural functionalism is not an explanatory
theory; it is a model, based on the metaphors of
machine or biological organism. Whilst this model
may account for social consensus, it does not allow
for social conflict. Nor does it explain how society
has become the way it seems to be - the 'theory'
lacks an historical component. More importantly, for
our purposes here, it has little to say about the
individual, preferring to regard individuals as
mere incumbents who passively act out their
prescribed roles. If, for example, we take a school
as a component organisation within education, from
a functionalist perspective we can simply 'read off'
the actions of pupils and teachers from the official
descriptions of the formal roles which they fill.
There is a need to ask the question, 'How do they,

as individuals, interpret that role', or, at a deeper level, 'Why do we have or need pupils and teachers in classrooms in the first place?' Thus the need for schools is assumed and it is also assumed that pupils and teachers will not deviate from their roles. Such a perspective, therefore, ignores the discretion of individuals and their ability and willingness to respond passively to society, as given.

This was not the view of Berger and Luckmann (1966) and their symbolic interactionist approach. For them society is both a social construction and a constraint upon the individual. It is a social construction in that men subjectively make sense of the objective world and may come to share or impose their definitions of it upon others. It is a constraint because, over a period of time, the initial social construction may come to take on a fixed, reified form which is perceived to be beyond the power of men to change – the social construction becomes 'objectified'. But although this kind of constraint may occur, it need not occur. That is, society can be remade if sufficient numbers agree upon the reconstruction and have the power to make their endeavour prevail in the face of convention. However, for most symbolic interactionists, the socially constructed structure does place limits upon the individual in that it provides a framework, a set of parameters, within which the individual can make mental space for himself and within which he may negotiate with others (Rose, 1962). Much of the classroom-based 'new' sociology of education adopts this framework. Put another way, symbolic interactionist studies of the school take it for granted that schools, classrooms, teachers and pupils are 'given'. Although this framework had evolved historically, it is so entrenched and 'objectified' that its existence is rarely questioned. It is within that framework that the 'new' sociology of the classroom operates: it considers how teachers and pupils interpret their roles; it considers what their 'perspectives' of the school are; it allows for the practice of negotiation of order, knowledge and assessment within the classroom; it considers the authority of the teacher in the face of the power of the pupil.

Before we consider some specific studies of the primary school it is necessary to dwell briefly upon a theoretical concomitant of symbolic interactionism known as social phenomenology (Schutz, 1967).[4] We need to do so because phenomenology provides insights

into a crucial aspect of classroom research: how we
understand each other. That is, the classroom
researcher is required to impute the meanings which
those whom he observes assign to their actions. It
is not sufficient to observe classroom actions at
face value - we need to look behind the surface
phenomenon of the action and impute the reason why
it was performed.

This process whereby we come to understand each
other, which Schutz calls 'intersubjectivity', need
not conern us too much here (it will be developed
later). Suffice it to say that 'motivational'
understanding of the classroom participants by the
observer requires a methodology quite distinct from
the heavily statistical one employed by functionalists. It is said to be a 'soft' methodology which
lacks the 'rigour' of 'hard' data which can be
analysed using 'robust' statistical tests. It
requires the observer to empathise with the observed
and to infer the latter's meanings, which may be
subsequently checked through face-to-face interview.
It may require the observer to enlist the views of
others, pupils for example, who witnessed the same
event. It may require the inspection of documents
such as pupil record cards and written work, both
of which may throw light upon first-hand observations.
All this is with a view to interpreting the complexities of the process of schooling. It is to go
beyond official statements of what is said to happen
in classrooms and to find out what does happen, as
defined by the observer.

'New' sociological studies of the primary
school are relatively few, despite the great
interest which the 'new' sociology generated at the
theoretical and methodological levels. At the risk
of inviting accusations of incorrectly categorising
these classroom-based studies, I shall suggest four
by no means mutually exclusive categories into
which these studies may fall. Firstly, there are
those of an anthropological nature which do not
admit to any theoretical perspective; secondly,
there are those which emphasise the negotiation of
pupil identities within the classroom and which are
informed by a symbolic interactionism akin to that
which underpins the work of Strauss et al (1964) in
hospital settings; thirdly, are those microsociological studies informed by ethnomethodology;
fourthly, are those which seek to explain classroom
meanings and identities within a wider structural
framework (Sharp and Green, 1975).

Among the most well-known anthropological

studies of the primary school are those by Rist at
Attucks School in St. Louis (Rist, 1970; 1973) and
at Brush School in Oregon (Rist, 1978).[5] In the
first school, Rist observed the children from their
first day in kindergarten until Christmas in the
second grade, although little observation was undertaken during the second year of the study. One of
the most interesting aspects of his study was his
approach to 'working his way in' to the school, to
becoming accepted (not an easy task: he was the
only white person in the school). His careful
attention to the preservation of confidentiality, to
not being too distant, and to putting himself
mentally in the place of the teacher being observed
greatly contributed to the richness of his insights
into the all-too-ready typifications which the
infant teacher makes on the basis of a brief
experience of the perceived social characteristics
of her pupils. Rist's later study of a programme in
Oregon whereby black working class pupils were bussed
into a white, middle class area school looks behind
the well-intentioned motives of a school which wants
to help but can only do so by having the black
children assimilated into its normal regime, one
which they cannot relate to. The black children had
to sink or swim academically: most sank into
oblivion, ignored by a teacher bent on pushing the
highly motivated white children. Although Rist's
studies do not admit to a particular sociological
approach, there is much evidence generated within
them supportive of a Weberian conflict model
incorporating class and status analyses of school
and society.

Central to symbolic interactionism is the
notion that actors can assign meaning to institutional structures. They are not passive in the face of
those structures, as functionalism implies. On
occasions, meanings assigned to the 'same'
circumstances may differ. The element of power then
comes into play as a way of resolving different
definitions of the situation. A classroom is a good
example of an institutional setting where different
groups can assign different and competing interpretations of it.[6] Sociological studies of these
settings have yielded evidence on the process
whereby the typification of pupil identities arises
out of negotiations. For example, Martin's (1975)
study of Canadian elementary schools actually
typifies pupils on the basis of their imputed
willingness to negotiate with the teacher. Three
ideal types are generated: 'non-negotiable' pupils;

'intermittently negotiable' pupils and 'continuously negotiable' pupils. Symbolic interactionist studies also focus upon the teacher, permitting the researcher to observe teachers teaching and to impute their ideologies. These individual teacher ideologies may then be categorized. In this way it is possible to indicate that the ideology of the teacher is not always reducible to that of the institutional head of the organisation (Sharp and Green, 1975). Or it may be possible to point up the ideological and practical dilemmas which beset teachers. Berlak and Berlak (1981), for example, have generated three sets of dilemmas to allow them to make sense of the observations which they made of teachers in English primary schools.

A third element of the 'new' sociology of the primary school arises from a further theoretical strand within the interpretive paradigm, namely ethnomethodology (Garfinkel, 1967). The main difference between symbolic interactionism and ethnomethodology is that the latter eschews the notion of permanent social structures. Everything is in process, or on-going. The normative structure is continuously re-normed. The social order has no independent existence apart from its 'members'. The nature of reality is never fixed and nothing should be taken for granted. 'Social structures are social accomplishments' (Mehan, 1978:36). What is of concern to ethnomethodologists is the process whereby actors produce a shared reality no matter how ephemeral it might be. The observation of this process is best undertaken by placing individuals in an 'absurd' situation (Lyman and Scott, 1970); that is, a situation which makes no sense to those who are part of it as when, say, a classroom full of pupils is expecting a lesson on trigonometry but in comes a 'teacher' in a kilt and playing the bagpipes. The ethnomethodologist, therefore, seeks to 'unsituate', people, rendering their initial definition of the situation absurd. He then watches them re-build meaning or reconstruct reality (McHugh, 1968). Ethnomethodological studies of the classroom are, therefore, necessarily focussing upon very small social gatherings and the most well-known are those by Cicourel et al (1974), which are largely given over to revealing the hidden subjective considerations which affect the 'objective' assessment of pupils' performance.

These three approaches within the 'new' sociology of the primary school have provoked a number of criticisms: they have been seen as 'trendy', as

revealing an ignorance of the 'founding fathers'
(Szreter, 1975); they have been seen as too
subjective, by-passing the canons of validity and
reliability; as too psychologistic; as concentra-
ting upon the 'how' and not the 'why' of social life -
that is, although it offers various perspectives and
definitions of the situation, it does not explain
those perspectives; as ideologically conservative,
operating largely within capitalist parameters which
were taken for granted.

The New Synthesis?

Sharp and Green (1975) sought to meet some of these
criticisms. Theirs was a case study of a
'progressive', working class primary school. Using
a methodology derivative of Schutzian phenomenology,
the authors generated qualitative data, mainly from
interviews with the head teacher and three teachers,
which they sought to explain structurally, but not
from a functionalist perspective. Their Marxist
analysis interpreted the data to mean that the
teacher in a progressive, child-centred classroom
was constrained to typify her pupils against some
notion of an 'ideal pupil'. In other words, she
was constrained to stratify them and not, as the
rhetoric suggested, to define them as unique
individuals. This stratification of pupils at this
early age was seen as an institutionalization of
hierarchy and the beginnings of a selection process
whereby pupils were differentially allocated into
the class structure. Although Sharp and Green's
structuralist analysis has been questioned
(Hargreaves, 1978; King, 1978), it nevertheless
marked a departure from the 'new' interpretive
sociology by seeking to link its micro data with
macro-structural explanation. A further study
which calls into question the failure of social
phenomenology to pay heed to external constraints
on social action is King's (1978) study of three
infant schools in England. His theoretical approach
is based on 'Weberian action theory' which stresses
the dubiety of Marxist and functionalist accounts
which render the individual passive in the face of
false consciousness or role constraints. For King,
and for Weber, action is not wholly reducible to the
effects of social forces. Social structure can be
interpreted in different and often competing ways.
Within the context of a school, this theoretical
approach allows for the social construction of
teacher ideologies which, in turn, structure the

actions of teachers and have consequences for those
whom they teach:

> The ideologies of infant teachers are human
> products, the acceptance of which constrained
> teachers and through them the children they
> taught. (King, 1978:132)

Much of this comes close to the symbolic interactionist perspective which regards the ideologies of
teachers to be expressed within a range of opinion
bounded by a given, largely unquestioned set of
parameters which mark a liberal democratic perspective within capitalism. It is within this
institutionalised arrangement that different teacher
ideologies are constructed and compete with each
other, as in the case of junior school versus infant
school ideologies. The reportedly shared ideologies
within the infant school permit us to regard infant
school teachers as a separate status group - one
which has a shared sense of subjectivity - within
the teaching profession. A further example of the
structural constraints upon the infant teachers
which King investigated arises out of their 'theory'
of pupil performance, a theory defined as the 'family-
home background' theory. King states that this is
part of the functionalist approach outlined earlier
whereby the working class family socialization
process is seen as wanting. But this theory is
contained within a view of social structure which
does not allow the teachers to pose the question,
'What are the structural explanations of this
allegedly deficient family socialization pattern?'
If these teachers had pondered this question, they
did not inform King about it. Finally, King departs
from previous sociological studies of the school by
incorporating the Weberian concept of 'status group'
into his analysis, not only by regarding infant
teachers as a status group within the teaching
profession, but also by raising the neglected status
consideration of sex differences within a social
class group. By so doing, King raises an important
element in Weber's sociology which is that Marxist
accounts of society tend to ignore the social
differentiation which arises within social classes
on the basis of status factors involving ethnicity,
gender, religion and language.
    The theoretical perspective of this study also
owes much to Weber, particularly through his concepts
of ideology, domination, social class and status
group. It is not my intention to offer a thorough

10

account of Weber's sociology. Those who wish to begin with Weber are referred to the very comprehensive Economy and Society, vols 1 and 2 (Weber, 1978 - original 1922). Those who require a readable introduction to his ideas would profit from the following: Aron (1967); Freund, J. (1968); MacRae (1974) and Parkin (1982). Our central concern here will be with the Weberian perspective and education.[7]

Weber offers a conflict approach to understanding education. Competing groups will seek to legitimate their claims to higher status by pointing to the 'objective' indicators, namely credentials, which justify that status. Educational credentials, therefore, are a resource, an element of power which groups employ to maximise their goals vis-a-vis others. This is an explanation of education which is grossly at odds with that offered by functionalists who argue that there is a 'fit' between the needs of the economy and the output of the education system: as the economy expands so does the education 'service'. From this perspective, the surge in the demand for educational credentials - variously known as the 'diploma disease' and the 'paper chase' - is the necessary consequence of the demands of the economy. Weberians doubt this view. They do so because the available evidence does not fit the functionalist model; that is, once the transition from an illiterate to a literate society has been made, there is no necessary nor observed association between education and economic development. Indeed, in the Third World there is often an educated elite whose levels and type of education are at odds with the needs of the economy (Hoselitz, 1968). In the USA, Collins (1979) has concluded that although the level of education required for particular occupations has markedly increased, the technical demands of those jobs has not always proceeded apace. For Collins (1979) the association between the technical needs of the economy and the output of education systems is no more than the 'myth of technocracy'. In an analysis of the relationship between education and economy in a wide range of countries, Anderson (1961) concludes that within countries at a similar stage of economic development the observed rates of attendance in higher education varied considerably - they were not similar, as the functionalist model would have predicted. Anderson concludes:

... the underlying factors explaining national contrasts must be sought in values, customs and

> public educational policies - each of which may
> be different in its effects on males and
> females. (Anderson, 1961:255)

Finally, Ringer, in an historical analysis of the
education systems and economies of England, France
and Germany, reached a similar conclusion. Whilst
technological demands may partly account for
educational change, they do not wholly explain it:

> Even today, social conventions have at least as
> much to do with the demand for education as any
> supposedly objective requirements of the
> economy. (Ringer, 1979:261)

The Weberian view, therefore, rejects that of the
'technical-functional' model and regards the nature
and availability of education as being the outcome
of a contest among competing groups within society.
This point was long since made by Weber who saw the
'patent of education' (Weber, 1978:1000) as the
replacement of 'proof of ancestry' whereby groups
sought to legitimate their social status. An
increase in the desire for education was not, for
Weber, a 'sudden awakened thirst for education', but
the desire to limit the supply of candidates who
aspired to elite positions, thereby enabling the
elite to control their 'monopoly'. Weber's point
is supported by his investigations of the _literati_
in Confucian China. They were the mandarins who had
qualified for their positions on the basis of
examinations on classical literature. Examination
success certified their status as the cultivated
gentlemen of the bureaucratic elite. But, notes
Weber, these examinations did not test any 'special
skills', rather:

> The examinations of China tested whether or not
> the candidate's mind was thoroughly steeped in
> literature and whether or not he possessed the
> ways of thought suitable to a cultured man and
> resulting from cultivation in literature.
> (Weber, 1951:121).

Not only does a Weberian analysis question the
functionalist relationship between education and
economy, so also does it question those Marxist
analyses which regard the education system as
adapting to the needs of capitalism (Bowles and
Gintis, 1976). Both views offer an over-determined
analysis of the school which allows for no intervening

influences to be exerted between the needs of
capitalism and the nature of schooling. For
functionalists, those in school act in accordance
with 'society's' role prescriptions; for Marxists,
those in school go about their activities saturated
in an ideology which allows them to think that they
are acting in the interests of the pupils when in
'reality' they are acting in the interests of
capitalism (Harris, 1979). All this seems to obviate
the need for, and existence of, political action
within institutional arrangements. However, one of
the concerns of this study will be to suggest that
political action is found within schools and that it
arises from educational ideologies which are both
different and implicitly or explicitly in conflict
with each other. It is realised, however, that the
range of expressed ideologies is itself contained
within the possibilities permitted by the 'iron cage'
of bureaucracy and by a capitalist mode of production,
the 'spirit' of which Weber sought to understand, but
the existence of which he did not seek to terminate,
as did Marx. Although Weber was well aware of the
'alienation' of man under capitalism, he was also
aware that under socialism man would forever be
trapped in the 'iron cage' of bureaucratic
rationality.

Weber should not, however, be thought of as
refuting Marx.[8] He was indebted to Marx's insights
into the relationship between material existence and
consciousness. Yet he did not regard class position
as the sole 'cause' of consciousness. Nor for Weber
was class the 'ultimate' basis of social differentation. That is, he argued that, in addition to
class-based social differentiation, there were other
bases for it. These derived from status groups
marked by a common ethnicity, religion or gender.
This concept of status group will be dealt with more
fully later. It is sufficient here to argue that
within the proletariat there were competing status
groups whose ideologies and interests differed. Far
from the working class being an homogeneous, pre-
revolutionary group, for Weber it was marked by
cultural heterogeneity, and this weakened the
possibility for revolutionary change arising out of
concerted action against the bourgeoisie.

The analysis of status group differentiation
within the working class school - a major concern of
this study - has been neglected by both functionalists and Marxists, as well as by phenomenologists
whose micro-sociological focus does not allow them
to take elements of social structure in any permanent

way (Mehan, 1978). According to the functionalist sociology of the school, these class and status considerations should not arise: it is 'talent', not social attributes arising from class and status group membership, which schools claim to be able to identify and to convert into academic credentials. In this way, education acts as an agency of selection whereby individuals are allocated to the occupational structure according to the kinds of credentials they have earned through meritorious behaviour (Davis and Moore, 1945).

Implied in this meritocratic perspective is that the education system selects the winners and losers of society on the basis of a fair competition. The competition is fair because most children are said to be exposed to the same pedagogy and sit the same examinations. The criteria for assessment are common to all and subjective bias in examinations is eliminated. But this leaves aside the matter of what selection from culture shall be included in the curriculum, and what modes of communication shall be used to transmit it. The decision to include this or that aspect of 'common' culture is a political one since those in elite positions will seek to define curriculum and pedagogy in a manner accordant with their interests. Curricular knowledge and the form of its transmission is not reducible to a philo- sophical absolute but is what Bourdieu calls the 'cultural arbitrary' (Bourdieu and Passeron, 1977) of a particular society.[9] What remains hidden is that pupils will differ not just in their talent but in the kind of 'cultural capital' which they bring to the school. The closer that cultural capital is to that of the cultural arbitrary, the greater will be the academic recognition given to it. The school, therefore, confers academic recognition upon socially transmitted attributes as well as upon genetically transmitted talent. It should be emphasised, however, that a Weberian approach regards the struggle among economic, bureaucratic and intellectual interests over what education shall comprise, and who shall receive it, as a struggle among competing status groups and not as the mere consequence of the 'needs of the economy', nor of the needs of capitalism (Salter and Tapper, 1981).

Finally, we turn to the methodology advocated by Weber (and its subsequent refinement by Schutz (1967) to be elaborated upon in Chapter 3).[10] A sociology of the school must attend to the meanings which its members assign to their situation. Weber rejected the view that action was reducible either

14

to social forces or to innate mental properties. A
social determinism or a psychological reductionism
implicitly emphasises behaviour rather than purposive
action. Weber did not take this view. For him,
individuals attach a subjective meaning to their
behaviour - they orientate it to the action of
others, thereby rendering it social (Weber, 1978:4).
The task of sociology is, firstly, to observe the
phenomenon itself and, secondly, to impute the
subjective meaning which the action had for the
individual who performed it. This second procedure
of empathetic understanding, or what Schutz (1967)
calls 'motivational understanding', constitutes
Weber's method known as 'verstehen'.[11] All this,
however, does not tell us anything about social
structures, or patterns of regular action. In order
to bridge the gap between the explanatory understanding of individual action and social structures, it
is necessary to find out the extent to which
individual actions and meanings are repeated. Moreover, these patterned regularities are amenable to
statistical categorization and as such constitute
'sociological generalizations', but 'only when they
can be regarded as manifestations of the understan-
dable subjective meaning of a course of social
action' (Weber, 1978:12). That is, the basis of
statistical artefacts must always be the subjective
meanings behind those actions which support the
quantitative data. In short, therefore, the
empirical realities of social structures arise out
of repetitive actions at the micro level.[12]

   Such then is the background to the study, the
purpose of which is now formally defined. Informed
by Weber's sociology, we shall be concerned with
two broad themes. The major theme draws upon Weber's
concepts of ideology and domination, and considers
the following matters: to understand, to typify and
to explain the ideologies of the teachers within an
urban primary school whose remit is to provide
'positive discrimination' in the education of its
pupils; to indicate the extent to which these
ideologies are shared by, or imposed upon, others;
to consider the correspondence between the 'professed'
and 'practised' ideologies of the teachers by
observing the teachers in the classroom and by
obtaining the views which their pupils hold of them.
The minor theme draws upon Weber's concepts of
'social class' and 'status group'. It raises the
hitherto largely unexamined issue of status
differentiation within working class education and
addresses the following: does the ethnic, gender

and social class background of the pupil have
consequences for the ways in which teachers define
his ability and performance? Do pupils who share
common 'objective', physiological characteristics -
namely race and sex - appear to define themselves
as subjectively at one, or, in Weberian terminology,
as a 'status' group? These two themes, therefore,
represent the main purposes of the study. Before
considering them more fully, we turn to the school
itself and its social setting.

Chapter 2

THE PUPILS AND THEIR SOCIAL BACKGROUND

Educational sociologists in the 1950s and 1960s
defined the working class child as an under-achiever;
that is, given similar measured ability to his
middle class counterpart, he was more likely to be
destined for a secondary modern school than for a
grammar school. He was therefore less likely to
proceed to higher education. The generally accepted
thesis posed at the time to explain this turned on
the view that there was a discontinuity between the
working class home and the middle class orientation
of the school. Thus it was that working class
children, when they reached adulthood, found themselves no higher up the class structure. There
appeared almost to be an inevitability about the
causal associations between a 'deficient' working
class sociali ation, a relatively poor academic
record and an occupation within the working class.
The remedy for this under-achievement was to argue
that the consequences of the class structure in the
form of an inadequate (for school) socialization
could be mitigated and ameliorated by providing in
the school what was lacking in the home. Poor educational facilities in the home were compensated for by
better-than-average educational facilities in the
school: an improved pupil-teacher ratio; provision
for links with the community; a salary supplement
for teachers to reduce staff turnover; and physical
and material resources in the school which were
better than average. In the wake of the Educational
Priority Areas project, local authorities were able
to direct funds to provide additional resources to
schools which were thought to warrant them, although
there was no nationally agreed set of criteria
against which the characteristics of individual
schools could be measured. Our concern here is with
one such school, a school in a working class area

enmeshed in social problems. But, even within such an area, deprivation is not a state which all its inhabitants equally share, and in what follows I shall try to indicate that, within this working class and deprived part of an inner city, there are forms of intra-class differences. These differences present themselves to the school in the form of the social characteristics of the pupils. We shall not be concerned yet with the ways in which teachers inter-pret these differences in their pupils; that is, little will be done to discuss the educational impli-cations of these social differences – we shall merely be indicating what the differences are.

Rockfield School catered to many children who were defined as deprived, both materially and/or emotionally. This implies something of a cultural homogeneity, but it does not inform us that the area here is also culturally mixed, a mix derived from its ethnic diversity. About one-third of the pupils were of an Asian background, whilst the remainder were of a white Scottish (or, if you prefer, British) back-ground. Thus the presumed material homogeneity must be set against this ethnic heterogeneity.

The teachers at Rockfield referred to those children of Asian background as 'immigrants'. The great majority of them, however, had been born in Britain. Technically they were not immigrants. In other words, the teachers differentiated their pupils by stating that some were 'immigrants' (that is, all non-white children, regardless of their birthplace) and others were, in the parlance of some teachers, 'our children' (that is, all white children). A similar error is also implicit in the title of the Rampton Commission's interim report: <u>West Indian Children in Our Schools</u> (Rampton, 1981). That is to say, the title implies that these children are West Indian, not British (which most of them are) and that they are in 'our schools' not theirs. There is, therefore, clearly a need to stress the uncon-scious racism in the usage of the term 'immigrant' when referring to children who are black, but British-born. Accordingly, the research here distances itself from this possibly inferential racism and, forthwith, will refer to children in the school who are defined by their teachers as 'immigrants' as ethnic minority children. I shall, however, preserve the term 'immigrant' when I am quoting the actual words of a pupil or a teacher, and I shall place the term in quotation marks. It should also be indicated that ninety per cent of the ethnic minority pupils in the school were of Asian ancestry, and particularly of Bangladeshi background.

In addition to this matter of nomenclature, there is an argument which says that, by the very act of treating ethnic minority groups as units of analysis in a research undertaking, the researcher may be culpable of unconscious racism. That is, he may actually create a difference associated with ethnicity that might not have occurred to those whom he is researching. He may make an issue out of something that hitherto had not been perceived as such by the participants in the situation he observes. This is a dilemma which is difficult to overcome. My stance here is to state that it was the teachers themselves who offered the 'immigrant'/white dichotomy. Further, their categorizations had real consequences for their practice. There was, for example, the 'Immigrant Department', and there were 'immigrant meals' and 'immigrant parents'. Our purpose is neither to condone the teachers' inaccurate nomenclature nor their use of the ethnicity of the pupil as a basis for differentiation: rather it is to see what consequences these had for the school experience of the children who were labelled in this way. We shall return to the status 'factor' of ethnicity in Chapter 7. Meanwhile, we turn to our description of the school and its locality, and, in so doing, will attempt to offer both quantitative and qualitative data. We begin with some of the latter.

The school is an imposing grey-brick, three-storey Victorian building set amidst an area of demolished, decaying or renovated tenements. A main road from the nearby city centre passes the school. Towers of high-rise flats have replaced some of the demolished tenements. Where the existing tenements have been deemed to be structurally sound, they have been renovated. A spatial analysis of the homes of the pupils reveals no discernible clustering on ethnic lines. Virtually all of the parents were tenants of the local council. Trees are scarce; grass is virtually absent; graffiti abounds. Demolition sites and some small playgrounds provide play areas for the children.

Appendix B provides details on the number of teachers and pupils in the school during the period of the research. The names of the teachers are pseudonyms. It will be seen from Appendix B that the numbers of pupils and teachers fluctuated within and between years, and this explains discrepancies in the number of pupils and teachers in the statistical tables. As is normal in Scotland,

primary education begins at the age of five, when
children enter Primary 1, and continues until
children reach Primary 7 at the age of twelve. When
the research began, each of these seven levels had
two classes, except for Primary 2, which had only
one. There was also an 'Immigrant Department'
comprising three teachers, one of whom was of ethnic
minority status. (I shall give details of this
department later.)

There are many pupils at the school who live
beyond the boundary of the catchment area. This is
so for 38 per cent of the ethnic minority children
and for 26 per cent of the white. The former figure
is best explained by the fact that not all of the
schools in the city were able to offer facilities
for the teaching of English as a second language.
The parents of ethnic minority children were advised
to send their children to schools like Rockfield if
distances were not too great. Rockfield also catered
to the special diets which some ethnic minority
parents wished their children to have, these being
termed 'immigrant meals' by the teachers. Thus,
distance permitting, it was to Rockfield that ethnic
minority children were advised to go. The latter
figure is less easy to explain. As industry near
the school declined, and as housing near the school
was demolished, replaced or renovated, so people
moved to their new jobs and homes. Those whose
move took them beyond the catchment area, but still
within travelling distance of the school, were
permitted to remain at Rockfield. Another explanation may hold. Some of the teachers referred to
the school as 'Skid Row' or 'The End of the Line',
the implication being that Rockfield was a school
which would take pupils other schools would not -
children, for example, who had been placed in a
school for the 'maladjusted' would, after treatment,
sometimes re-enter the system through Rockfield.
When I asked Mrs. Watt about the number of outsiders
in the school, she admitted to some 'grey areas'
along the boundary and joked:

>   If they look slightly odd or are coloured, Jim
>   (the head of a nearby school) sends them to us!

This perceived terminal status was often bemoaned by
the teachers. At times, however, it gave them some
cause for self-congratulation: no-one else would
have these problems; few could cope with them.
But dealing with it all was an effort, an effort
made more tolerable through humour. Mrs. Letham,

for example, having inspected the school's poor
showing in the city-wide hierarchy of reading scores,
quipped:

> We're not bottom of the league – we're running
> for promotion. Imagine what it's like at the
> bottom!

A sign hung on the wall of the staffroom. It stated
'You must be crazy to work here'. Perhaps Mrs. French
summed it up best by declaring,

> It's like living in a black comedy. (No racial
> pun intended.)

A pupil's-eye view of the locality was made
available by the children in Mrs. Preece's Primary 3
class who had responded to the question, 'What I saw
on the way to school today'. This is an amalgamation
of what eight children saw:

> Hill, book, cars, lorry, chip-shop, mummy,
> houses, swings in the park, a shed, a 'DON'T
> PLAY FOOTBALL' sign, railings, a football
> ground, textile mill, phone, paper shops, fish
> shop, nursery, lamp-post, tree, big hills, a
> rocket monkey-bar, a 'VOTE FOR NELSON' sign,
> workmen, brick-dust machine, pub, butcher, a
> broken house, Safeway, a very big old school,
> workmen building.

Compared to what it had been, the area was said to
be 'improving' and some of the 'problem families'
were moving out. Mrs. Findlay's new Primary 1 class
provided the evidence:

> The standard of families is improving. None of
> the children are dirty – never had such a good
> (that is, clean) intake.

Perhaps, for her, cleanliness was next to 'readiness',
for she continued:

> They are ready. No point in waiting when I've
> got thirty-two to get through.

She was going to 'start' some of the ethnic minority
children to read and the 'others' had said to her,

> Mrs. Findlay, when are we getting reading
> books?

TABLE 1

Ethnic minority and white home backgrounds:
parental occupation, car ownership, garden access, family size and 'free meals'

	Father's occupation(1)			Working mothers		Single parents	Car ownership	Mean Family size	Garden access	Free Meals
	NonMan.	Manual	Unem-ployed	F/T	P/T					
	%	%	%	%	%	%	%		%	%
Ethnic minority (n=83)	27.0	62.0	11.0	36.9	7.1	0.0	39.3	3.67	75.0	11.9
White (n=206)	9.0	80.0	11.0	35.7	7.4	11.6	35.8	2.24	47.4	39.5

(1) Occupational class according to the Registrar General's classification.

'Stable' and 'Deprived' Backgrounds

Mrs. Findlay's comments introduce a more detailed
consideration of the children themselves. By
inference, most of the children could be said to be
deprived because the area in which they lived was
widely regarded as being one of urban deprivation.
Nevertheless, it cannot be assumed, as Smith (1977)
has indicated with reference to Educational Priority
Areas, that all such children are facing deprivation,
however defined. Nor, even if they are deprived,
are they necessarily facing the same degree of deprivation. To impute the particular from the aggregate
is to perpetrate the aggregative fallacy. Smith's
critique of the Educational Priority Areas argues
that not all children within an E.P.A. required
"positive discrimination", and that many children
beyond the boundaries of the E.P.A.s may themselves
have needed compensation, but could not obtain it.
In the subsequent discussion of the pupils and their
home backgrounds, we shall see that, despite the
'working class' label which was assigned to Rockfield's
catchment area, there are, within this occupationally-
defined 'working class', certain degrees of material
well-being and it is to these that we now turn.
    A number of indicators provide evidence of the
material condition of the children. These are:
parents' occupation; incidence of car ownership;
access to a garden; the size of the family and the
incidence of 'free meals'. Table 1 summarises these
facts for ethnic minority and white pupils alike.
It reveals an essentially 'manual' occupational
group - the higher levels of occupational group II
among ethnic minority families is accounted for by
small shop-owners. Of note is the absence of
single-parent families among the ethnic minority
group, an indicator of 'stability' as far as the
teachers were concerned. As for the white popula-
tion, the staff agreed that the figures for single-
parent families were undoubtedly an under-estimation
and to be treated cautiously. All of the personal
data provided in Table 1 were obtained from
individual interviews with the pupils, not from
record cards which are sometimes not up-to-date.
One-to-one interviews with the pupils, however, pose
problems of nomenclature: when, for example, is a
father not a father? The concepts of 'father',
'mum's friend' or 'uncle' may not be readily
distinguishable by the children, especially the
younger ones. The real father may be absent and
the surrogate simply referred to as 'dad'.
Mrs. Findlay covered all possibilities when she was

announcing a change in school hours:

> You leave school tomorrow at three o'clock -
> the same time as when we were in the babies'.
> Don't forget to tell your parents, grannies,
> aunties and uncles.

Table 1 also notes the provision of 'free meals',
the need for which is often regarded as an indicator
of material deprivation in the home. Very few,
about one in eleven, ethnic minority pupils took
'free meals', as opposed to nearly three times as
many white pupils. In both cases, these figures
may be low in relation to the numbers eligible. In
the case of ethnic minority children, as will be
argued in more detail later, parents may wish to
provide for the child at home to ensure he receives
the diet appropriate to his religion, despite the
fact that the school offers 'immigrant meals'. Thus,
though eligible for 'free meals', these parents may
not claim them, or, if they wish to claim them, they
may be deterred from doing so because the application form is written in English and requires answers
in English. Finally, some parents may not wish to
avail themselves of free meals for their children
because they regard them as tantamount to taking
charity:

> DH: How can some pupils get free meals?
> Pat: Well, if your mum and dad don't work.
> Laura: If your mum works and your dad doesn't
>   you can get free dinners like ... my
>   mum works but my dad doesn't, but my
>   mum doesn't want us to get free dinners.

The data in Table 1 offer some objective
indications of the material and social conditions
under which the children live. A further measure
of the 'stability' of the pupils' homes was derived
from teachers who rated each pupil in their class on
a seven-point rating scale, the dimensions of which
were STABLE HOME BACKGROUND - UNSTABLE HOME BACK-
GROUND. Some 45 per cent of both ethnic minority and
white homes were rated as falling within the STABLE
half of the continuum, but 22 per cent of the pupils
attracted a non-response on the grounds that the
teacher had no knowledge of the pupil's background.
This is a very crude quantification of a subjective
inference on the teachers' part. The degree of
uncertainty is emphasised by the high percentage of
'don't know' responses and by the fact that not all

teachers wished to make a judgement on the matter.
The basis of the teacher's inference is not personal
visits to the home, except in very few cases.
Rather, the teacher's rating of the home is her
view of the manifestation of the home background in
the pupil. That is, the teacher bases her judgement
on the appearance and behaviour of the pupil, the
attendance of the parents on Parents' Day, the
submission of notes from home to explain the absence
of the pupil, 'news time' in the classroom, and the
pupil's 'diary'. In a number of cases the teacher
will be informed of 'children at risk' in the home
by the school's social worker or by the police.
Seven of the children in the school, for example,
were on probation. The data derived from the
rating scale require cautious interpretation for
another reason. For example, if two teachers assign,
say, a '2' rating, it suggests that they assign the
same subjective meaning, but the identical and
'objective' numerical rating only makes it appear
that there is a shared subjective meaning. Furthermore, teachers from a 'good school with nice
children' may, as a group, define 'stability' in
quite different ways from the staff at Rockfield.
Finally, staffroom discourse at Rockfield was
replete with discussion about the home backgrounds
of individual pupils. Few of the pupils who were
the subject of discussion were said to enjoy stable
home lives. In other words, the staffroom banter
on this matter did not square with the mainly 'stable'
numerical ratings. A balance between the two may
be sought by turning to the individual teachers and
their general views of the domestic conditions of
the pupils in their respective classrooms.
What was the staff's interpretation of the
'stable home'? What proportion of the pupils came
from 'unstable homes', or, to use a further term
common to the staff, from 'deprived homes'? To
Mr. Houston, the stable home was:

> ... a two-parent family, a situation with the
> parent and children, and an environment which
> makes them happy and keeps them well-adjusted.

Mrs. French used the term 'normal home' which was:

> ... a fairly stable background of mother,
> father, both in the home - possibly a granny.

DH: About what percentage of the homes would be
    normal?

It wouldn't even be twenty per cent that would
be normal. I would say 'immigrant' families in
the school tended to have more stable backgrounds.

These proportions of normal and deprived homes were
confirmed by Mrs. Letham's comments:

DH: How many children in your class would you put
in this 'deprived' category?

For one reason or another, I would say about
seventy-five percent.

DH: That much. What sorts of reasons are they?

Well, we have children who come from one-parent
families. I'm not saying necessarily that's a
bad thing, but children who come from broken
homes; children who come from homes where
there are maybe five in a bed - no toilet
facilities. Things like that. We have
children with parents who have a drink problem,
economic problems, social problems in the sense
that they're maybe in jail (which was the case
with the father of one pupil in her class) -
that kind of deprivation.

The incidence of single-parent families was, in
Mrs. Findlay's view, 'about half'. Mrs. Stewart
recalled a previous Primary 1 class:

... and I think of twenty-six or twenty-seven
children, fifteen single-parent families. I
think it was the highest in the school at that
particular time when we did the survey.

'Deprived Children': Some Individual Cases

The statistics in Table 1 reduce the data on the
home background of the children to numerical
abstractions. Behind the numbers are the children
themselves, and in order to have a more realistic
idea of their home lives we return to the teachers'
knowledge of them. Here, however, the teachers are
not being requested to estimate degrees of deprivation in their school at a general level, but to
refer to what they know about particular children,
especially those who find themselves in difficult
and sometimes tragic home circumstances. In doing
so, we turn to two teachers, Mrs. Carter and

THE PUPILS AND THEIR SOCIAL BACKGROUND

Mrs. Findlay, both of whom had been at Rockfield since the beginning of their teaching careers. First Mrs. Carter.

Mrs. Carter, along with other teachers, often remarked upon the surface normality of the children who faced severe domestic circumstances:

> They seem on the whole a happy and well-integrated lot, in spite of difficulties at home, and in many cases, deprivation.

Some of her pupils are discussed here. Perhaps most tragic of all is the life of Parvaz, eldest of five children born to a Scottish mother and a Pakistani father. When the marriage failed, the father had taken custody of the children but the arrangement had not been a good one. Parvaz and his brothers and sisters had found themselves thrown onto the streets, after which he had taken them all to the Children's Shelter. After the children had been returned home, the father went to Pakistan, only to be apprehended on his return to Britain for drug-smuggling, an offence which brought him a sentence in prison from where he would occasionally telephone the children whilst they were at school. The mother had re-married and the children's cultural emphasis switched from Moslem to Western.

Two other children in Mrs. Carter's class, again of mixed marriages, had faced disruption associated with having to cope with Moslem and Western influences at home. Isobel's parents had divorced, her white mother being replaced by a Pakistani step-mother who was allegedly more in the care of her children than they were of her. Isobel's education had also been interrupted by a year's stay in Pakistan. Similar problems faced Susi, as Mrs. Carter's written notes about her show:

> Susi: Pakistani father and Scottish mother. Fourth of six children. Special school recommended. There is a malaise in this family set-up. Financial worries are absent, the marriage in itself is a happy one, but the trouble seems to arise from the mother's attitude to her own and to her children's situation. She wears saris, trousers - wants to be a Moslem - likes life in Pakistan where her colour gives her special position - but here she resents her children being referred to as Pakistanis. Her instructions are to 'hit children who say and do things to you'.

THE PUPILS AND THEIR SOCIAL BACKGROUND

Another girl, Asha, had arrived at Rockfield from
Pakistan with no schooling and no English. At home
were two other children, a baby and a five-year-old,
both of whom were handicapped or disabled. She
became used to days off school to go with the mother
to the doctor, the launderette or simply to 'jaunt'.
Her progress was poor.
 Illness afflicted some of Mrs. Carter's pupils.
Asif was asthmatic, Prinita had suspected kidney
illness - her mother, having become seriously ill,
had needed to have Prinita taken into a foster home.
Tina had a history of bed-wetting and ear, throat
and kidney infection. Janice was prone to bronchitis,
causing her to have many absences from school. Neil,
a 'miracle baby', had begun school still wearing
nappies. In Primary 5 he was still frail, had poor
co-ordination and a speech defect. Other children
had disruptions of other types: Roy had not started
school until the age of seven; Donna, the youngest
of five children, had been cared for in her early
years by relatives and had only recently been
returned to her parents. George's parents' marriage
had failed. Willy's mother was a widow, his father
having been killed in a road crash in America.
John's father was absent, and Saleem had seen his
parents' mixed marriage break up.
 These details of the backgrounds of some of
Mrs. Carter's children were given scant mention in
the pupils' record cards. There appeared to be a
tacit agreement among the staff to avoid committing
to paper matters other than medical and academic
details. Staffroom conversation 'filled in' what
the record cards omitted. The reason for these
omissions was that such issues could constitute
gossip which 'we're not supposed to know about',
such as, for example, the fact that the mother of
one of the children was a prostitute. The case of
Mohammed in Mrs. Findlay's Primary 2 class is also
appropriate. His mother was an alcoholic:

 I once saw her sleeping outside my room. Dad's
 a shop-owner and is very aggressive to the
 mother who has twice stabbed him.

Continuing with Mrs. Findlay's class, another
alcoholic was John's father, a one-time undertaker
whose career came to an end when he crashed a hearse
whilst he was drunk. John's real father lives away
from him, as does Karen's who lives in the flat
below that which she, her mother and her 'uncle'
inhabit. Tom's father is dead. As in Mrs. Carter's

28

class, child-neglect and illness affect some
children. Ann, for example, has got scabies, is
'completely neglected' and has to be washed daily at
school. Angie has 'a dreadful background'. The
previous year she had been absent for 132 days out
of 192. Her father is unemployed, one brother is in
a borstal, another is on probation; 'she needs
periodic de-lousing and is uncared for'. As for
Sinka, she, according to Mrs. Findlay, 'is of poor
stock' and, although cared for, is 'underfed, as so
many of them are'. Rakesh is a 'nice wee soul but
all his family are ill'. Larry has both parents in
a mental home. Hector is the son of political
refugees who had been interrogated whilst separated
from their son: 'When he entered the school he
screamed for three weeks'. Steve came from Rhodesia
without any English, and, being the only black in the
school, continually had his hair touched and
attracted the distressing nickname of 'carpet head'.
        Mrs. Carter proferred that,

>   I would say one in six in Scotland is deprived. [1]
>   It's not being deprived of money; they're
>   deprived in other ways. Three children here
>   were thrown out of the house and the eldest boy
>   (aged 9) took them to the Children's Shelter.
>   At nine years old he knew what to do so it's
>   not the first time that's happened.

The teachers felt it difficult to convey to other
teachers outside of the school the kind of child
with which they had to deal. Mr. Lane, for example,
had met a teacher on a course who was 'obviously
middle class' and who 'couldn't believe we have kids
with lice, or that we have a stock of clothes for
kids to change into'.
        I have already quoted Mrs. French's definition
of the school as like 'living in a black comedy'.
'You can't help laughing at it' was an oft-quoted aside,
a quip which helped the teachers to cope in the face
of their pupils' adversity. Occasionally the comedy
in the tragedy was overdone, as the comments about
Alan reveal. Alan was the product of a mixed
marriage which had failed. Afterwards matters had
gone from bad to worse: the mother was told she had
cancer; a relationship with a Pakistani boyfriend
had met with problems; a social worker had been
called in. To make matters worse, Alan broke his
leg in three places whilst 'hitching a lift' at the
speedway. On hearing this Mr. Houston joked:

>   Pity it wasn't his head.

In another exchange, Mrs. Watt recounted the occasion
when she had been covering for Mrs. Scott, Alan's
teacher. During a conversation, Alan had told
Mrs. Watt that he thought he would commit suicide.
When Mrs. Watt repeated this in the staffroom, a few
comments suggested that Alan's suicide might be no
bad thing. The peripatetic music teacher, who was
sat beside me, was not amused:

> I find that rather sad. I'm afraid I don't
> think it's amusing.

Mr. McLean, the head teacher, could reel off stories
at will which underlined Mrs. French's 'black comedy'
analysis. He referred to a section of the area as a
'whole substratum that no-one knows about', a group
whose bizarre, but sad capers seemed naive and bound
to fail. Take, for example, the case of the plaster
angels. These had been lifted from a grave in a
nearby cemetery, only to be taken to the main gate
and advertised for sale. Or consider the case where
two Rockfield pupils had stolen a handbag from an
old lady which had contained £300. The children
took the money home, said they had found it, and
accompanied their parents on a spending spree before
they were apprehended. I observed a similar incident
myself when walking back to the university through
a covered shopping precinct. A focal point within it
was an attractive fountain into which people would
toss a coin for charity. As I approached the fountain a boy with a saturated right arm dashed past me,
hotly pursued by a security guard. The boy was in
Mrs. Scott's class. He got away. Next day he told
me that he had been trawling for coins in the
fountain. He had done it before with impunity and
to his profit, and he would do it again. An equally
dishonest incident, not without its humour, centred
on one of the boy's classmates who had decided to
impress his girlfriend by giving her some jewellery
which had come his way. I asked if he was worried
about being caught if he continued to steal. His
confidence was disarming. He shrugged his shoulders:

> Nah. Ah'm a professional!

This professionalism in crime was echoed in an
exchange between Miss Darby and Mr. McPhail whose
family had, he told Miss Darby, just moved into a
squat 'with two bathrooms'. To his annoyance his
wife had been complaining because 'there was no nice
furniture to go with it'. The point of his meeting

with Miss Darby, however, was to talk about his
daughter Jane, 'a compulsive liar' according to her
father. Miss Darby and Jane's father proceeded to
discuss the matter of 'honesty', a topic close to
Mr. McPhail's heart:

> In ma profession (by all accounts he was a
> thief) ya have tae be honest ...

Miss Darby's conversation with Mr. McPhail introduces
the wider issue of contact between the home and the
school. Teachers communicate with parents either
orally, as at Parents' Day, or in writing, as in the
submission of notes from parents to teachers, or in
the issue of reports and notices from teacher to
parents. How well parents attend Parents' Day and
how correctly they write notes to the teacher are
important indicators of the competence of the parent
and of the interest they take in their children's
education. It was a school rule that when a child
was absent an explanation was required from the
parent in the form of a telephone message or a letter.
Teachers set great store on these letters and were
at pains to tell the children just what was required:

> I hold up. a letter with envelope and paper and
> say, 'This is the kind of letter'.

The request was rarely complied with in the manner
expected. Indeed, the varieties of 'notes'
received by the teachers provided some small amusement. Mrs. Findlay recalled cases where notes had
been written on cigarette packets, pages torn from
library books, and toilet tissue. She also stated
to the children her preference that notes be written
with 'no fish, chips or jam on them'. 'Very rarely',
said Mrs. Carter, 'do we get a note in an envelope'.
A matching note and envelope was a mark of high
status. All of these types of note were from parents
who had actually written a note; many did not. I
was invited to peruse Mrs. Reid's archive of notes
from parents and some are transcribed below. In the
transcription they lose much of their character -
the type of paper and the handwriting, for example -
but they convey something about the standard of
literacy obtaining in different homes. The
following three notes might have indicated to
Mrs. Reid that appropriate literacy skills were
perhaps lacking:

> (1) Please excuse John for being off school as

he had a tuch of the Cold.

P. Barclay

(2) Jim was off school because he had a cold
in the head because he had a hole in his
foot.

(3) Tommy was off school because I was not
well we had to do things.

McMillan

None of these notes came in an envelope. None used
the correct form of address to the teacher. None is
free of misspellings or grammatical errors. The note
from Tommy's mother was written on a piece of paper
about two inches square and with its edges frayed.
His mother was poor and might well have been unable
to afford proper paper. That Tommy lived in somewhat impoverished surroundings is indicated by the
fact that he took 'free meals' and, as Bobby, who
was a classmate of Tommy, informed me:

I mean there's a little boy called Tommy - his
second name is McMillan - he's got no carpets
in his house.

The note below provides us with the clue that Jim's
mother can afford, and wants him to have, music
lessons. She addresses Mrs. Reid in the correct way
and she informs her of her son's absence before he
returns to school:

Dear Mrs. Reid
Jim will not be at school today, as he was
leaving his music lesson last night, some body
threw bricks, and Jim was hit on the head. He
is alright he had to be stiched.

This letter introduces a prominent reason why parents
wrote to teachers: that of asking them to prevent
fights and bullying. The following letter from
Mrs. Strong provides another example of this and it
conforms most closely to what counted as an accept-
able note from a parent. It was the only one in
Mrs. Reid's collection that came in an envelope:

Dears Mrs. Reid,
Could you please have a few words with
Jim Smith, as he is giving Paul a terrible time,
he stole Paul's football last night, and he was

32

> throwing stones at him. And a few weeks ago I
> caught him with Paul on the ground. And this
> Jim was hitting him with a stick. My son is
> really scared of him   And has anyone handed in
> a green body warmer. Paul lost his yesterday
>
>   Yours faithfully,
>   Mrs. Jean Strong

All of these parents, no matter how deficient their
literary skills, have attempted to comply with a
school rule. Some parents did not make the attempt
and they were most likely to be the parents of
ethnic minority children. That they lacked sufficient English to write a note was, for some teachers,
no excuse:

> It's very difficult to get the 'immigrants' to
> bring notes in. We've said to the children that
> they should write notes and 'get your dad to
> sign it'.

And just as the child could write a note on behalf of
his parent, so too was the child expected to read
his report from the school to his parents. I asked
Mrs. Preece about this:

DH: How do the 'immigrant' parents know how their
     children are doing in school if they don't
     come, and if they don't read English as well?

     There are report cards.

DH: But do they read them? Can they read them?

     Well, I've often wondered about that ...

For teachers, the preferred way of communicating
with parents was to talk to them at Parents' Day.
The presence of a parent was a sign of her interest,
a sign that she cared. But the majority of parents
did not attend these meetings, as Table 2 reveals.
The Table indicates that the pupils' claims for
their parents' attendance were exaggerated for all
four groups of pupil. These data are, however,
drawn from only one meeting - other meetings may
have been better attended. The teachers did not
seem surprised at the low turnout of parents,
especially of ethnic minority parents. Mrs. Scott
said they usually saw 'just a sprinkling of them';
Mrs. Letham admitted they 'did not see many of the

TABLE 2

Claimed and actual attendance at
one parent-teacher meeting, by sex and ethnicity

	% of pupils saying their parents normally attended	% actually attending in Primary 1 to 3	% actually attending in Primary 4 to 7
ethnic minority boys	36.6	3.9	11.4
ethnic minority girls	33.3	5.3	23.1
white boys	56.6	41.1	23.2
white girls	50.0	29.7	21.6

Note: pupils questioned: n=272

34

'immigrant' parents at all - in fact, we didn't see
any last Parents' Day'. Why did they stay away?

> Some of them I suppose don't like coming in.
> Others can't make themselves understood when
> they do come in. I may be wrong, but they give
> me the impression that really they couldn't
> care less.

As with the matter of notes, deficiency in English
when meeting a teacher was not seen as a problem
since there were two teachers at the school who
could and would interpret. Although the teachers
knew this, I do not know if the parents did. When
the note to parents advising them (in English) of
Parents' Day was sent out, no mention of these
facilities for translation was made:

> An evening for meeting the Staff will take
> place on Thursday, 14 June, from 7 to 9 p.m.
> Light refreshments will be served. It is
> hoped there will be a good turn out.

The evidence so far has sought to elaborate upon the
social characteristics of an inner-city school
within a deprived area. Whilst there is a virtual
homogeneity in the occupational structure of the
area, there are, within it, differences in the
material and emotional circumstances of the
children. Teachers argued that, of itself, material
deprivation was not necessarily a cause of 'instabi-
lity' in the home, though in many cases it was. In
any event, the consensus among the staff was that
anything upwards of sixty per cent of the children
were 'deprived' in one way or another, some
children tragically so. In constructing this view
of the children's home background, we have resorted
to both quantitative and qualitative data. These
data suggest that the socialisation of the children,
and the material and cultural conditions which
influence it, is not always at one with what a
school expects. The child as pupil is a bearer of
what his home stands for, and, for the teacher, must
be taken as a 'given'. The analysis thus far has
concentrated on differences in the material and, in
some cases, psychological circumstances of the
children in this inner-city school. Cutting
across this material factor is that of ethnicity,
and this provides the basis of a type of differentiation which requires the apparent cultural homogeneity
of the locale to be viewed as being more diverse.

THE PUPILS AND THEIR SOCIAL BACKGROUND

We turn, therefore, to the ethnic differences within the schools' catchment area and discuss, in far more detail than hitherto, the interpretation which the teachers hold of those children they refer to as 'immigrants'.

The 'Immigrants'

Nearly a third of the children at Rockfield were classified by teachers as 'immigrants', but very few had not been born in Britain. In the teachers' eyes their homes were more 'stable' than those of the white children:

> In the 'immigrants' it is always a two-parent family situation. Where there are parents of different race then there are problems. But speaking about the 'true blue' ones, where it is a good background, these children learn very quickly to read, write and communicate orally, although now we are finding that the ones who come in are usually one up on their older brothers and sisters. They came from Pakistan five or six years ago; they had no English. But these youngsters that we have now have benefited from their older brothers and sisters. They are able to communicate orally as soon as they come to school, which is a big advantage. It's no problem; it's just like one of our own white children in class. In fact, they're so well cared for -- they're very much a family unit. I mean as far as health goes ... We have an awful lot who suffer from asthma, chest troubles, incontinence -- now where you have that, you have to push them a lot whether they can communicate with you or not. So you have the same situation as you have in the white family; if there's trouble at home it shows in the pupil at school.

That said, although the home was seen as stable, it was not always seen as educogenic: parental interest in their children's schooling was regarded as low, as indicated by their reluctance (or what was perceived as such) to provide notes and to attend Parents' Day.

Some of the ethnic minority parents did not ingratiate themselves to teachers for another reason. In short, teachers felt they were asked too often to intervene in disciplining a child whose misdemeanour had been perpetrated in the home, not the school.

Wrongdoings committed in the home were the
responsibility of the parent, not the teacher:

> Sometimes you get external pressures or problems
> that seem to involve the school - they don't
> happen a lot to white children. Things, for
> instance, like parents having little squabbles.
> These things seem to be magnified out of all
> proportion and they're quite often carried
> throughout the school. One of my children quite
> often says, 'Can I go and see my brother's
> teacher?' And it usually transpires that the
> reason he wants to go is that his mum said,
> 'You tell your brother's teacher to give him a
> ticking off because he did something bad in the
> house'. Now that sort of thing you would never
> get with a white kid - having that sort of
> feedback coming in.

> What I don't like about the 'immigrant parent'
> is that they put too much responsibility on the
> teacher, you know. Now it's a little better
> than before. I mean the troubles at home are
> automatically brought to you. A mother says,
> 'Can you attend to this', or 'Can you check
> him - he's very rude, this, that and the other'.
> They don't themselves take this responsibility
> of disciplining them.

But there were exceptions; that is, parents who
conformed to the teachers' model of the 'good parent':

DH: What about the parents of 'immigrant' children?
      Do they come to the school much?

> Not a lot. Some do. Some take part. Some
> take part all the time. Mrs. T is always in and
> out, although she doesn't speak much English.
> Some are really super, and some will support
> certain things and some ... all they want you
> to do is to sort out themselves. I've never
> seen mother, but I'm aware of her presence
> because she tells one brother to tell me how
> bad the other brother is ...

These criticisms of ethnic minority parents must be
weighed against the stability which they allegedly
provided their children. This stability was often
lacking in the white child's home and this was said
to have had detrimental consequences for his
performance and behaviour in school. There is,

therefore, something of a paradox in all this: for the white pupil a stable home background associates with a preferred mode of child socialisation in the eyes of the teacher; for an ethnic minority pupil, a stable home where the child is socialized into his own cultural heritage may be counterproductive. The teachers took the view that the child should adapt to the school, not the other way, except in matters of diet and, to a lesser degree, dress code. Parents who failed to 'co-operate' by failing to provide notes, attend meetings and contain family feuds were regarded by some teachers as manifesting a 'lack of interest' in the school and in their child's education:

> It's their parents' outlook: I mean they don't see the importance ... they don't have the same emphasis that we do on education.

It was decided to attempt some contact with the parents of ethnic minority children in order to obtain some first-hand knowledge of their material circumstances, their cultural habits and their views of the school. The attempt proved too difficult for myself: I could not speak the language; I was a man who would not be made welcome by unaccompanied mothers; I was regarded as a government official seeking illegal residents. To some extent these problems were surmounted. A female research assistant managed to accompany a local ethnic community worker on visits to seven families. No tape-recordings were advised, and this was agreed to. The research assistant wrote up her notes immediately on leaving the parents' home and she discussed each visit with me on the day that it took place. A second visit was made to one family where it was agreed that I could accompany her and tape-record the conversation.

The first household which the research assistant visited accommodated two families. In all there were nine children, six of whom attended Rockfield; a further two were at secondary school and there was a nine-month-old baby. Mr. Y, the occupant, was a bus-driver who spoke good English and had lived in Britain for fourteen years. He was pleased with his children's education and had visited the school, at the head teacher's request, to help curb his son's unruly behaviour. His brother, whose family also lived in the flat, spoke no English and was unemployed. The flat had four rooms. Paint peeled from the wall, plaster hung from the ceiling, three long sofas served as beds in the living room.

Mr. H's eight-room top-floor flat was luxury by comparison. It was inhabited by himself and his wife, his sister-in-law and his four daughters. Mr. H made a good living as a shop-owner and his home furnishings reflected this: a good Axminster carpet, bright gold wallpaper, vases of real flowers, a modern suite covered in pink chiffon material, a wooden coffee table and four hard-backed chairs. All was clean and tidy. Mr. H was dressed in traditional costume and, although he had lived in Britain for twelve years, spoke little English. In 1978 he had returned to Pakistan and hoped to repeat his journey shortly. As for the school, there were few complaints, the only one having been the teacher's insistence that the daughter wear shorts for P.E. classes. The elder daughter had faced a similar demand. In the latter case, Mrs. H had gone to the school to discuss the matter with a teacher who spoke her language. The mother had been informed that she was 'behind the times'. Despite her adherence to cultural tradition, the mother did encourage her daughters to invite their white friends to the home, which they did.

By any standards all was not well at the home of Mr. and Mrs. A. The family comprised four daughters, one of whom was a four-month-old baby. One of the girls was mentally retarded and, although eight years old, had only just begun to walk. She had never been to school. A health visitor had continually made hospital appointments for the girl but they had not been kept. Finally the community worker had taken the child to the hospital. Unlike her husband, Mrs. A spoke no English. Her husband worked in a factory between 7 a.m. and 10 p.m., or at least was out of the home for that period. The living room in the three room flat was 'a mess and the smell was terrible'. The family had been offered alternative accommodation in Wildwood, a nearby 'ghetto' for 'problem' families but, fearing vandalism, they had refused to move.

The home of Mr. and Mrs. D confirmed a comment previously made to me by the community relations workers:

> If you go into the home it's a little Pakistan ...
> I can't think of any Pakistani home where
> English is spoken at home.

My own survey of ethnic minority pupils at Rockfield

showed this claim to be quite accurate since in only
12.9 percent of 'immigrant' households did children
converse with parents in English, although they did
so to each other. But in some homes, and this was
one of them, the parents insisted on the mother
tongue, here Punjabi, being spoken at all times.
Mr. D's family was strictly Moslem: the children
came home at lunchtime to specially prepared meals;
they read the Koran daily; they dressed in traditional costume. The preference was for arranged
marriages - parents who ignored this practice were
deemed to be 'uncaring'.

These traditional views were echoed by Mr. T
whose three daughters attended Rockfield. He was an
advocate of sex-segregated schools and a critic of
the school's strong preference that girls should,
'in the interests of safety', wear shorts for P.E.
Mr. T was a concerned parent who attended Parents'
Day. His one criticism of the school concerned
homework, or the lack of it. He had approached a
teacher to request that his children be given homework, only to be told that the children did all that was
required in the classroom and that this obviated the
need for it. Nonetheless, the teacher had promised
to comply with Mr. T's request but failed to keep
his word.

Finally, we turn to Mrs. D, a divorced woman of
Indian descent who had two daughters and a son at
Rockfield. Besides being a single-parent, Mrs. D
was different in many respects from the ethnic
minority parents just described. Her father had been
a pioneer immigrant some sixteen years previous. She
herself had been the only and first immigrant at her
school, a position she remembered well:

> Well I remember I couldn't speak a word of
> English and the children used to play around.
> I can remember it to this very day: I used to
> feel the cold and I used to sit beside the door
> shivering there, you know. Because at that
> time I couldn't understand a word anybody was
> saying. At that time there was hardly anybody
> there from Asia, and especially in Drummond -
> I think there was only about six families
> throughout Drummond itself.

Indeed, Mrs. D was, quite literally, in a class of
her own: she owned four flats bought with an
inheritance; she spoke excellent English and she
was union spokeswoman at the nearby factory where
she worked the night-shift. Her flat was well-

decorated and contained expensive hi-fi and video
products. On the video-recorder an imported Indian
film was being played, watched by her son. It was
she who permitted me to record our conversation.
       I had been led to believe by most of the
teachers that 'immigrant parents' had little
interest in the school. I was, therefore, somewhat
surprised at Mrs. D's forthright views on the school,
especially on the Immigrant Department. She took
the view that it should only be available:

> ... maybe for the first year or so when they
> can't speak English, but once they come to the
> stage where they've been brought up in this
> country I don't think it's really necessary. I
> don't think it's a help because they're putting
> the children back a lot. (That is, when in the
> Immigrant Department, pupils were missing what
> was happening in the classroom with the other
> children.)

In short, ethnic minority children were being exposed
too much to each other. Her own children, she
thought, were 'getting it too easy'. Unlike her
contemporaries in her own community, she took a soft
line on her daughter's wearing of shorts for P.E.:

> I'm quite against that anyway because I mean
> it's a shame on the child. Because my husband
> was against Paula (note English name) wearing
> tights and all that. Because it's fear you put
> into them when you're not allowed to do this,
> and there comes a time when the child goes away
> and does the opposite thing, you know. I mean
> if my mother and father had to do that to me I
> would have been hurt and all my pals would have
> laughed at me.

Nor did she have much to say for cultural relevance
in the curriculum:

> I think they learn enough about it at home.

Moslem Girls: A Cloistered Minority

Recent research on sex-role socialisation practices
within working class families in Nottingham (Newson
and Newson, 1976) suggests the existence of a more
clear-cut sex-role in the working class than in the
middle class. Girls in the working class tend to
remain at home with the mother, perhaps helping her

with household chores or playing with younger
siblings. Not so for the boy whose activities with
his friends take him beyond the confines of the home
and beyond the beck and call of the mother. His
prime activity is playing football, a near obsession
with many boys and a career to be aspired to. When
I asked boys what they did with their pocket money,
it was on football matches, football gear and related
football publications that much of it was spent. At
playtime, inter-class games of football were played
in a special area of the playground, access to which
was denied to the girls. After playtime, the games
were analysed in the classroom and reputations
turned on a good or bad performance. Football cards
with photographs of leading players were exchanged
surreptitiously under the nose of the teacher.
Visits to the school were made by local football
stars. Classroom projects centred on the game. One
of the female teachers was even a qualified football
referee. As for the girls, their sorties beyond the
home were more likely to lead to playing at a friend's
house, going to supervised swimming lessons or to
clubs of one form or another. Over forty-two per cent
of white girls belonged to a club, but only thirteen
per cent of ethnic minority girls did. They did not
expect to. Their place was in the home:

> They're the subdued race (sic) in their home,
> aren't they. Not looked upon as anything:
> they're to be seen and not heard.[2]

Training in the ways of the household began early:

> They're certainly not encouraged. I have a
> little girl in this class who's not yet five
> and her mummy's just had a new baby. Now it
> takes days off to help the mummy with the
> washing, and to help with the baby. This is
> very much a girl's thing - doing dishes and
> things long before we would dream of making our
> children do these duties.

In a meeting I had with Jane and Shamin, a girl of
Pakistani background, I attempted to draw out some
of the cultural differences between the lives of the
two girls:

Jane: What sort of wedding is your wedding - I
           mean is it the same as ours?

Shamin: No, it's much different, much longer.

THE PUPILS AND THEIR SOCIAL BACKGROUND

DH: How long?

Shamin: Well, it lasts about a week. You have
         special things every day. You do special
         things, and then on the last day the bride
         goes in another person's home and that's
         the wedding finished after the week.

DH: Do you have arranged marriages?

Shamin: Well, sometimes ..

Jane: They have to marry their cousins.

Shamin: Yes, we get married to cousins, not just to
         anyone: it has to be a cousin.

DH: Who are you going to marry?

Shamin: I don't know yet.

DH: Do you know anyone who had to marry a
         cousin?

Jane: Her brother got married.

DH: What would happen if you refused and said,
         'Right, I'm not getting married to him.'

Shamin: I don't know, but they would still get
         married or engaged even if they didn't want
         to.

DH: You two are friends aren't you. What sort
         of things in your lives are different?

Jane: You see she's not allowed to eat meat.
         She's not allowed to eat it. She would get
         into trouble. You see it's her God - her
         kind of God.

Shamin: We believe in God except we don't believe
         that Jesus got whipped and hanged on the
         cross and that.

DH: What do you believe happened to Him?

Shamin: I don't know. We believe Mohammed is God's
         messenger.

DH: Do you feel different having that religion?

43

THE PUPILS AND THEIR SOCIAL BACKGROUND

Shamin: Well sometimes I hate the fact that I am a
         Muslim like that; sometimes I like it.

DH: What would happen if you turned to your mum
         and said, 'Well, I want to eat meat'.

Shamin: I wouldn't be allowed to.

DH: Are you allowed to go out at night after
         school?

Shamin: Well we don't usually go out at night after
         school, but we sometimes do ...

Jane: They go to the mosque.

DH: How often do you go?

Shamin: Every single day except Friday.

DH: But I know some girls who don't go ...

Shamin: They read at home, but my mum doesn't like
         us reading at home; she likes us to go to
         the mosque.

DH: Do you enjoy the mosque?

Shamin: Yes. All you have to do is read and the
         priest tells you to come out one by one,
         and he sees them, and then he gives you a
         bit more paragraph to read, and then about
         seven o'clock you get to go home.

DH: If your brother tells you to do something,
         do you do it?

Shamin: Well if an older person tells you to do
         something you should do it.

DH: Are you allowed to wear a dress?

Shamin: No. I'm not allowed to show my legs, but
         in the school it's alright because you see
         the same people. But if somebody we knew
         saw us they would say, 'Who's that showing
         off her legs!'

If typical, this extract suggests that for the girl
of a Moslem background an ordered and restricted home
life was the case. Her discretion appears minimal,

44

her supervision by elders considerable. It would
appear that to even think of questioning those in
authority was difficult for her. This limiting
existence at home was associated with a disposition
at school which could be regarded as not merely
compliant, but too much so. Such girls were sometimes defined as 'wee mice'. They said little, and
only when asked. They would talk to other children
but showed much reserve about approaching a teacher.
They appeared caught between the demands of home and
school, especially in respect of the required dress
code for P.E. One girl told me that the first time
she wore shorts for P.E. she had asked to get changed
in a book closet, away from the gaze of her classmates. It was very clear that the staff did not
appreciate the very strong feelings which ethnic
minority parents had on this matter of their
daughters wearing dresses and shorts. It was an
affront to their religion: it was not a matter for
the teacher to decide.

Summary

This examination of the catchment area of Rockfield
school has revealed a local social structure more
differentiated than the homogeneity implied in the
deprived label. Differences not only turn on varying
degrees of material living standards, but on the
status factors of ethnicity and sex, both of which
interact with the class factor, and with each other.
No weight has yet been given to the ways in which
teachers define these pupils from different social
groups, and to how, as a consequence, they treat
them in the classroom. Whilst an analysis of this
constitutes an important strand of the study, it
cannot be embarked upon until attention has been
given to the broad policies and classroom practices
of the head teacher and his staff, and the structural
factors which might account for them. This is now
considered.

Chapter 3

ROCKFIELD SCHOOL:'THE ONLY STABLE PART OF THEIR LIVES'

Actions derive from implicity or explicity held
ideologies. This theme is neatly captured in the
now well-worn adage of W.I. Thomas, 'If men define
situations as real, they are real in their
consequences' (Thomas, 1928:372). In this respect,
ideology refers to a collection of taken-for-granted
beliefs with which individuals make sense of the
objective world. Those, like teachers in a school,
who share a common situation may, over a period of
time, construct a shared ideology. On the other hand
there is a possibility that ideological factions may
emerge within a school, suggesting that ideologies
are shared by some but not by others. The term
ideology also has a Marxist connotation, in which
case it refers to the illusory motives which
individuals assign to their actions, the 'real'
motives lying beyond their consciousness.[1] Despite
this ambiguity of the term ideology, it will be
used here to refer to the former meaning, not the
Marxist one. In some instances, however, it will
prove necessary to draw upon the Marxist interpretation of this concept, and wherever this occurs,
clarification that this alternative connotation is
being used will be made.
    The ideologies of teachers may be stable or in
flux. If the exigencies of the teacher's situation
are regarded as predictable and stable, then her
ideology will assume a degree of relative permanence.
Indeed, so obvious might the teacher's actions seem
to her that the ideology which explains them might
be difficult for her to articulate since she is not
used to doing so. If, on the other hand, a teacher's
practice fails to 'work', then she may come to
revise it, and, by so doing, she looks at her
ideology anew. Her ideology may also require to be
changed as a result of the intervention of powerful

46

others, be they peers, pupils or superiors, who can
enforce at least a public change of ideology and
action. In some such cases, however, the teacher
may be able to retain privately, within the walls of
her classroom, her old pursuits and practices. In
this and the following chapters, we focus upon the
ideological constructions of the teachers and head
teacher at Rockfield School. A central concern of
this endeavour will be to indicate the influences
which appear to play upon them and the extent to
which these ideologies are shared, rejected or
imposed. The stance is taken that an ideology is
neither a blind acceptance of structural determina-
tions, nor a purely individual construction. The
view here takes as given, though not necessarily as
preferable, such structures as the school, the state,
bureaucracy and the stratification system, and that
they exert powerful constraints on individual
consciousness. That said, the capacity of individuals to construct differing interpretations of those
structures is not denied. Nor is it denied that
holders of these different interpretations may seek
to impose them on others. Before embarking upon the
educational ideology of Mr. McLean, the head teacher,
we develop the sociological stance here with a brief
resumé of its theoretical antecedents, beginning
with the structural functionalist position.
    During the 1950s and 1960s the sociological
study of education centred upon an analysis of the
inputs and outputs of education as an institution
within a social system. The study of educational
facts rather than a search for varying interpretations of education held sway. Indeed, from this
functionalist perspective, the quest of gathering
differing interpretations of education and its
purposes would have been regarded as redundant since
the role of education had been precisely defined in
terms of Parsonian functional prerequisites, the
expressive and instrumental goals into which they
were classified, and the social roles provided to
realise them (Parsons, 1961). As for the educational
ideologies of teachers and head teachers, these were
simply inherent in the roles which they performed.
Thus the individual was viewed as an embodiment of
the structure, a passive rather than active individual, an individual devoid of intentions and motives,
determined rather than determining.
    As a reaction to this 'oversocialized' view of
man, as Wrong (1961) put it, there occurred a
paradigmatic challenge to the functionalist
orthodoxy which sought to 'bring back' the individual

into the analysis of society. If funtionalism had over-stressed the ontological status of the social, then the emerging interpretive paradigm, led by the social phenomenology of Schutz (1967), paid too great a heed to the individual. Some strands within this paradigm placed more emphasis on the individual than others. So it was with the radical microsociology of ethnomethodology (Garfinkel, 1967) whose concern was to observe the method whereby 'members' or actors accomplished meaning in the face of absurdity. From this perspective, society cohered on the basis of a continuing construction of a constellation of meanings arising from the reality-making of all individuals. These meanings were achieved without recourse to power and without a sense of constraint: reality could be 'made' within no parameters whatso- ever - the individual, as Schutz (1967:277) put it, was a 'free being'.

To deny any constraint on individual action was to deny any sense of structure in the form of patterns of social action which could be defined as habit. Even Schutz (1967) refers to our use of 'recipes' for action which have been accumulated as a consequence of our experience and socialization by others. By resorting to these recipes in commonly- met situations, individuals embark upon repetitive patterns of action which take on a structural permanence. This theme was further developed by Berger and Luckmann (1966) who, unlike Schutz, introduced the concept of power during the negotia- tion of meanings: 'He who has the bigger stick has the better chance of imposing his definition of reality' (Berger and Luckmann 1966:127). They do not, however, provide any idea of the nature of power which is brought to bear in order to facilitate the prevalence of a definition of reality. In a further analysis, Berger and Luckmann take us closer to the structural with their discussion of the objectification of the subjective: that is, they suggest that initially men subjectively construct their reality, but that, over a period of time, this initial construction takes on the appearance of an objective reality, thereby seeming to constrain the actions of those who constructed it in the first place.

All of this reality construction among indivi- duals supposes that they are able to understand each other. As for the social scientist, it assumes that he too is able to impute the subjective meanings behind the actions of those whom he observes. Thus any analysis of the social, from this perspective,

must incorporate as part of its explanation the
subjective meanings of individuals and the degree to
which they are socially shared. For Weber, this
required the use of a method called 'verstehen'
(Weber 1978:8-9), which refers to 'understanding'.
Two types of understanding comprise this method.
Firstly there is 'direct observational understanding'
which requires the observer to grasp the manifestation of the actor's subjective meaning; the second,
'explanatory understanding', requires the observer
to impute the meaning which the act had for the actor
himself. This means, therefore, that the observer
must place himself in empathy with the actor and bear
in mind the social context in which the act occurred.
    An example may illustrate the method. Suppose
you are an observer in a classroom and you see the
teacher drop his pen on to his desk. You have
reached, according to Weber, 'direct observational
understanding'. Now you must impute the meaning
which the teacher assigned to that act. A number of
possibilities might come to mind: perhaps it was a
demonstration of gravity; perhaps he accidentally
and unintentionally dropped it, in which case he
would not have assigned a meaning before doing so;
perhaps it was a signal to the class to keep quiet,
or to line up, or to commence their work. By observing the social context of the act, the classroom,
you noticed that immediately after the pen-dropping
incident the pupils began their written work.
Given this, the last of the possibilities might hold.
Furthermore, it might have been the case that you had
observed such an incident with such a consequence
before in this teacher's class so that, by placing
the event in an historical as well as a social
context, the intended meaning is closer to being
apprehended by you, the observer. It was Schutz who,
in his debate with Weber's methodology, took him to
task for not dwelling more fully upon the philosophical dimension of what he calls 'intersubjectivity'
or how individuals come to understand each other.
Replacing Weber's term 'explanatory understanding'
with his own 'motivational understanding', Schutz
suggests that the latter will vary according to the
observer's relationship to the observed in time and
space. That is, motivational understanding will be
most likely if the observer shares a common time and
space with the observed, or is a 'consociate' of the
observed. Motivational understanding will diminish
in possibility if the two merely share a common time,
but not space, and are thus 'contemporaries'. Then,
if the observed shares neither the observer's time

nor space, thereby being his 'predecessor', his
capacity for understanding diminishes even further.
    Other comments may be made about verstehen.
The first is the assumption that the observer and
the actor share a common cultural milieu. Secondly,
as Schutz (1967) suggests, explanatory or motivational understanding can never be complete, only
approximate. For it to be complete, it would require
the observer to be the observed for, although their
'streams of consciousness' may be similar, they are
never identical. Thirdly, Weber assumes that the
actor knew at the time of acting, or could recall
later, what his intentions were. If it is accepted
that in our familiar day-to-day actions we sometimes
do not consciously intend or reflect upon our actions,
then it is necessary for the observer to bring back
the event to the surface of the actor's consciousness
and to ask him to state the meaning he would have had
if he had assigned a meaning to it at the time. This
problem is partly recognised, but not adequately
dealt with by Weber, when he states that: ('in the
great majority of cases'):

> ... actual action goes on in a state of
> inarticulate half-consciousness or actual
> unconsciousness of its subjective meaning.
> (Weber, 1978:21) [2]

Finally – and linked with the previous reservation –
the meaning of an event may be refined between the
time it occurred and the time or times later when
it was reflected upon. That is to say an interim
occurrence, or set of occurrences, may have caused
the actor to re-interpret the initial event. Say,
for example, that a passenger arrives at the railway
station at 9.02 intending to catch the 9.00 train to
London. As he reaches the platform he sees the
train leaving the station. His definition of that
event is probably not repeatable. Later, however,
it transpires that the same train had been derailed,
with loss of life and limb to passengers. The
person who had missed this train revises his initial
definition.
    To summarise this preamble to Mr. McLean's
educational philosophy, it has been argued that
functionalist and interpretive sociologies respectively ignore the emphasis of the other:
functionalism leaves out the individual; the
Schutzian-based sociologies pay too little heed, or
none at all, to the influence of social structure on
the ideologies constructed by individuals. It was

Weber's insistence that sociology should not separate
social structures from the intended meanings and
actions of men within them. Weber, therefore, is
what Ritzer (1975) calls a 'paradigm bridger' in
that his approach seeks to incorporate the structural
with the individual, seeing the two not as distinct
from each other but as essential to each other.
Sociological explanations must attend to the
empirical realities of structure in the form of
patterns of individual and shared meanings which
allow for the element of power. These meanings are
not reducible to the individual psychologies of
those who hold them but are constrained and influenced by the structures which impinge upon the
individual. With this in mind we turn now to
Rockfield School's head teacher, Mr. McLean, and
the educational ideology which informed his practice.
In interpreting and explaining his ideology due
regard will be had for the structural influences
which have been brought to bear upon his views.
However, no history-of-ideas approach will be taken
to explain, at a deeper level of analysis, the social
structures which he takes for granted. This is not
to suggest his complete gullibility and passivity in
the face of an over-arching structural presence.
Rather, it is to be concerned with his interpretation of the structure and, on the basis of that,
the construction of his educational ideology. For
example, it will be seen that much of his ideology
turns on his interpretation of the consequences of
a stratification system which affords different
material and psychological stages of being to
different sections of society. No historical explanation of that hierarchy will be made since it is
only Mr. McLean's interpretation of the educational
consequences of it which is at issue.

Stabilization in a Family Atmosphere

I state in Appendix A that I wished to adopt a
position akin to an observer who was both detached
and involved; detached in the sense of contributing
nothing to the day-to-day proceedings of the school;
involved in the sense that I exchanged common
courtesies with pupils and teachers. I also took a
limited part in staffroom discourse, not only to
make myself seem approachable, but to gain explanations of events I had witnessed. I made a point of
not conversing with the same teachers all of the time
and nor did I repeat to anybody the name of someone
who had made a comment, no matter how innocuous it

might have seemed. The non-participant researcher,
like the teachers he observes, must keep his distance
but not be too distant.
     Like the non-participant researcher, the head
teacher may choose to create an aura of detachment,
of impartiality. Moreover, the head teacher
performs many of his day-to-day tasks within the
confines of his office. It is only when he leaves
it that he can be observed in his relationships with
others. To impute the ideology of Mr. McLean from
observation was not easy. Only occasionally did he
visit a classroom. What appeared to some teachers
as reticence or unsociability ('He's no conversation',
as one teacher put it) may well have been his
preference to remain detached. Whilst he had an
'open door' policy with the children, who seemed to
like his father-figure image and his sense of fair-
ness ('He heard your side of the story and that'),
his contact with the staff centred upon his presence
in the staffroom at break-time where he would
normally occupy a corner seat. He rarely circulated
within the staffroom. Thus the possibilities for the
negotiation of school policy were very limited and
were made the more so because there were no staff
meetings, aside from a beginning-of-the-year meeting
where organisational matters were attended to.
     Probably the following comment on Mr. McLean
would summarise much of staffroom opinion - it was
written by a Primary 3 girl in her 'School Book':

     Our headmaster is called Mr. McLean. Mr. McLean
     wears a white coat and white trousers.
     Mr. McLean is a very kind headmaster. He lives
     in a little room upstairs. Mr. McLean can do
     what he likes.

A former pupil at the school recalled the headmaster:

     He was nice but you never saw a lot of him
     because he was in the background.

As for the educational ideology which informed
Mr. McLean's practice, this was difficult to impute
from the fleeting glimpses to be had of him. Nor
was it reasonable to assume that teachers in their
classrooms would have implemented his wishes. It
was the very isolation of the teacher in her classroom that prevented him from closely ensuring that
his policy was being realised. Teachers are adept
at publicly assenting to the official wisdom and
privately proceeding in their own classroom in quite

divergent ways. Thus the classroom observation of
the teacher is more an indication of her own ideology
than that of the head teacher. Given the limited
visibility of Mr. McLean which reduced the opportunity to observe him, other methods were resorted to
in order to gain access to his ideology. We begin
with the most obvious, the official description of
the school and its goals:

> Rockfield is different from some Schools in the
> Region in that it has a Nursery Unit, and is a
> centre for the teaching of English to minority
> ethnic groups.
>
> At present there are 372 Primary and Nursery
> children on the roll of the School and it is
> staffed by two Assistant Head Teachers, seven-
> teen Primary Teachers, two Nursery Teachers and
> two part-time Teachers. Five Nursery Nurses
> and Auxiliaries complete the staff.
>
> The School is two stream from Primary 1 to 7.
> The infant classrooms numbering six are on the
> lower storey. Primary 1, 2 and 3, each have
> their own toilets and general purpose area.
> Also on this level are the rooms of the Deputy
> Head Teacher, the Assistant Head Teacher and
> Caretaker and an Infant Store. The upper
> primary classrooms are eight in number and are
> situated on the first storey along with an
> Audio Visual Aids Room and a General Purpose
> Room. There is also a well-appointed gymnasium.
>
> On the lower mezzanines are the rooms of the
> Headteacher and the Secretary. Included in this
> area is the staffroom and the Primary Store.
> On the upper mezzanines are the Immigrant Unit
> and the Resources Centre. The Attic storey
> contains a Medical Room and a Remedial Room.
>
> Modernisation of the school took place in 1972.
> There is carpeting throughout and coupled with
> the use of wallpaper on a high proportion of
> the internal walls an attractive environment
> has been created. A modern Kitchen provides a
> choice of meals for over 200 children of whom
> 120 are entitled to free meals. Special meals
> are provided for Immigrant children. Many
> general purpose areas have been created and are
> in special and general use by teachers, pupils
> and parents.

> The School has a mental set towards underpri-
> vileged children and the ethos of the school is
> to attempt to create in the School an environ-
> ment both physical and mental to compensate for
> the state of deprivation which exists in the
> child's own home background. To this end there
> are many extra-curricular activities, including
> sports and hobbies which the children wish to
> further in school. The School encourages visits
> to local and distant places of interest.
>
> Parents are always welcome in the School, and
> there is an area set aside for them which
> provides comfortable seating. The School also
> provides books for the parents as well as for
> the children to borrow.
>
> The School is well provided with play areas and
> there is also a school garden with shrubs and
> trees.

Mr. McLean had been much influenced by the Plowden
Report (Plowden, 1967), particularly by its references
to provision for inner-city schools in deprived areas,
and by its recommendations about the importance of
catering to each child's unique needs and stages of
development. These two central strands in the Plowden
Report are worth re-stating, for they will enable
Mr. McLean's own educational ideology to be compared
to them. As he was an avowed supporter of what the
Plowden Report advocated, it would be expected that
he would adhere to two of the most important recommendations of relevance to the inner-city primary
school: that is, paragraphs 151 and 75(e), both of
which are quoted below, in that order:

> Schools in deprived areas should be given priority
> in many respects. The first step must be to raise
> the schools with low standards to the national
> average; the second quite deliberately is to make
> them better. The justification is that the homes
> and neighbourhoods from which many of their children
> come provide little support and stimulus for
> learning. The schools must provide a compensa-
> ting environment.

The second important strand within the Plowden Report
is an assertion that the child grows, or develops,
according to the stages defined in the literature of
developmental psychology:

> Since a child grows up intellectually,
> emotionally and physically at different rates,
> his teachers need to know and take account of

> his 'developmental age' in all three respects.
> The child's physique, personality and capacity
> to learn develop as a result of continuous
> interaction between his environment and
> genetical inheritance. Unlike the genetic
> factors, the environmental factors are, or
> ought to be, largely within our control.
> (Plowden, 1967:para 75(e))

There is an implicit contradiction between these two
strands which is developed later. Suffice it here
to say that the first strand suggests the need to
keep in mind norms of achievement whereby the child
is compared to his peers and where the school's
standard is set against those of other schools. The
second strand stresses the importance of the child
as an individual who proceeds through stages of
growth associated with his own unique development.
That being so, it is suggestive of a pedagogy and
assessment procedure which is particular to that
individual, not one which is general to a group.
    Mr. McLean's purpose was to:

> ... create in the school an environment both
> physical and mental to compensate for the state
> of deprivation which exists in the child's own
> home.

Whilst there is evidence from this statement that
the school had compensated in the 'physical' sense
by a marked improvement in material and human
resources, it is less clear that he sought an
'academic' compensation in the manner envisaged by
the Plowden Committee. The only allusion to matters
academic is his referral to 'mental' compensation.
It is doubtful, however, if 'mental' here means
academic or intellectual. If indeed this was the
case, the policies which Mr. McLean laid down for
his teachers would apppear to contradict this
academic connotation. Mr. McLean's concerns were
'social' rather than 'academic'. He was much aware
that many of his pupils led unhappy home lives: 'at
least 60 percent of the children have problems';
'We compensate 95 per cent for the home'; the
school for many children was 'the only stable part
of their lives'; his door was 'always open to the
children'; the 'child comes first'; the desired
environment in the school was a 'family atmosphere'.
    A number of practices were instigated in the
school to further this caring and stabilizing ethos
at the expense of a more competitive academic one.

In the assessment of the children the teachers were
to avoid the use of norm-referenced tests. Their
assessment was to be in the form of a record of work
and behaviour for each individual child. These were
collectively submitted by each teacher to Mr. McLean
four times a year, not only to provide him with an
idea of the pupil's progress, but of the teacher's
own work. These records of work were, in the
teachers' eyes, time-consuming and unhelpful:

> He wants an essay on each pupil.

> Our records of work are not referred to - not
> even initialled by McLean. No-one knows why
> they're done. The teachers resent it.

Norm-referenced tests, therefore, would have pitted
pupils against each other and defined some as
failures. What these children needed was a stable,
happy school life undisturbed by the worry of the
prospect of academic failure. Mental compensation
meant providing a 'stable' environment in a 'cosy'
and 'family atmosphere'.

Other organisational practices support this
view. In Primary 1 the children finished the school
day at three o'clock, half an hour before other city
schools, so that they might be eased in more gently
to the school regime. A further practice was that
of having teachers retain the same class for two or
even three years, again so that emotional disruption
allegedly caused by the change of a teacher could be
kept to a minimum. In the mornings the children
could enter the school when they arrived rather than
wait outside until they were summoned. After school
there were 'clubs' in which pupils, teachers and
head teacher participated. A stock of clothes was
available to parents in need of them for their
children. (Occasionally parents used the 'school
store' in somewhat amusing and innovative ways. One
mother was given a pair of shoes for her son whose
feet proved too large for them. Not to be deterred,
she pawned the pair of school shoes for some of the
correct size. Another mother implored Mr. McLean
for a pair of shoes for her child who was to
accompany the mother to the bingo hall where she
was concerned that, if her child had no proper
shoes, she would be accused of 'child neglect'.)
Finally, there were school outings to the countryside
and other towns, as well as residential weekends at
the rural base.

Perhaps the most curious policy, as seen by the

staff, concerned the provision of remedial education.
In Primary 1 to 3 there was none. Nor was there any
in Primary 6 and 7. This late provision was
regarded by some teachers as 'too little, too late'.
The lack of provision for the infants was explained
by Mr. McLean as being the compliance on his part
with an 'order' from the inspectorate that no
remedial reading provision be made until Primary 4.
The staff were incredulous of this 'order' ever
having been given. In any event, the lack of
remedial provision accords well with Mr. McLean's
lack of emphasis on the academic and his stress on
the need to stabilise the children. To give
remedial instruction might have been to 'push' the
children who displayed little ability or motivation.
As long as these pupils did not become disruptive
they were best left alone and kept 'busy', 'busy
books' being provided by the teachers in their classrooms. Such children were labelled by Mr. McLean as
'dead horses':

> I was going to put up a sign: 'DON'T FLOG
> DEAD HORSES'.

Whilst this policy might appear to be uncaring, it
can be explained in terms of a policy of 'stabilization'; that is, it kept a pupil going at his own
pace and did not require the disruption of his being
taken out of the classroom, thereby being labelled
before his peers as 'remedial'.
    A further perspective upon Mr. McLean's ideology
may be obtained from teachers new to the school,
particularly those who had taught elsewhere. Unlike
incumbent teachers, the newcomers bring to the school
an anthropologically strange way of seeing: what to
the incumbent is obvious and unworthy of comment is
different and remarkable for the new arrival, and it
is to the first impressions held by the latter of
Mr. McLean, and of the school in general, that we
now turn. Mr. Lane, who began his teaching career
at Rockfield, was asked to recall what Mr. McLean
had declared his ethos to be:

> I think it was basically, as it should be, that
> the kid comes first; to be perhaps more under-
> standing and be tolerant than you would in
> another school.

A more seasoned teacher, Mr. Alexander, was 'shocked'
at what he found at Rockfield. It was not 'efficient';
there were no timetables or tests, and there was 'an

air of freedom which was incredible', an atmosphere 'too relaxing'. He noted, for example, that in his previous school the teachers:

> ... were in the classroom waiting for the children after playtime - here the children are in first. After the playtime bell here some of them (teachers) sit for five or six minutes in the staffroom.

Mrs. Mack, an 'immigrant teacher', recalled the early days of the school:

DH: Were you expected to treat the children in any special way?

> No, I don't think in any special way except give them more help, you know. Knowing the background we were a little more lenient, you know - at their own stride, their own pace.

Mrs. Poyner recalled her initial impression:

> Well, could I say ... I came last year and I thought it was lacking discipline because I came from a much better area - still a working class area but much better, and I thought things were very free and easy here, but I think it is a most unusual atmosphere, a family atmosphere if anything.

However, it was Mrs. Watt who provided perhaps the most detached interpretation of Mr. McLean's 'ethos'. She had been a teacher at Rockfield who had left to become head of another school, but had returned to succeed Mr. McLean when he retired at the end of the first year of the study. Her reflections upon the similarities and differences in their respective ideologies are very instructive:

> There are similarities on what he used to call the 'ethos' of the school: that the school should be happy; that the children shouldn't be hassled, especially if there was a good reason for not being hassled. The children that come in late for instance: there are times when mother was in bed with a man and the kid would come in very late, eyes stuck together. I used to have one that came in regularly about quarter to eleven because there had just been an all-night party every night. In lots of

schools these kids would have been torn to
shreds. We're different in deciding how much a
child should learn. I believe that most
children can learn more than some of them
pretend they can. Most of them would sit there
doing nothing if left and I believe the background of the child doesn't really count while
in school. He just thought that from certain
backgrounds that most of the children weren't
going to succeed and it was a shame to push
them into doing something they wouldn't really
need in the end. He thought (by not testing)
you saved the children from seeing they had
failed. He wouldn't allow the top children to
go ahead.

The analysis by Mrs. Watt serves to underline a
theme of the present study: that educational slogans
such as 'compensation' are interpreted differently,
even within a school, not only between head teacher
and teachers, but among the teachers themselves.
These interpretations themselves appear to rest upon
previous definitions of the social characteristics
and presumed abilities and needs of the children.
Mr. McLean and Mrs. Watt, for example, both wished
'success' for their pupils. But success for
Mrs. Watt was academic success against others in a
competitive setting. Not so for Mr. McLean who
regarded success as adapting to an existing state of
affairs. If, for Mr. McLean, the individual had a
'need' for emotional security and stability, for
Mrs. Watt the individual pupil had a 'need' to make
his own way in a presumed meritocratic order:

If children are going to succeed and survive
when they get outside school, they have to
survive with what is there, not what is going
to be laid out for them. And who am I to say
that these children's backgrounds are going to
stay the same - that they're not going to get
the urge to change what's happening to them so
they've got to be prepared for what's coming,
not sitting there taking it lying down saying,
'Oh dear me, my background says I'm hopeless
and I can't get out of this rut so I'm going
to have to do the same work as everybody else.'
Teachers will have to get rid of the hang-up
that Rockfield children won't succeed.

Mrs. Watt, therefore, argued that although the local
catchment area might not change, the pupil could

leave it through marketing hard-won academic credentials. Mr. McLean would agree that material
circumstances might not be ameliorated but that the
effort implied in Mrs. Watt's strategy was so
fraught with the danger of emotional risk, in the
form of academic failure, that the endeavour was not
worth it. Indeed, this stress on individual needs
in the Plowden Report, based as it is on developmental psychology, appears, as stated earlier, to
contradict another emphasis in the Plowden Report,
namely the need to raise schools such as Rockfield
to the national average and, linked with this, to
use objective tests for comparative purposes. In
other words, the needs of the individual suggest
individual assessment where the point of reference
is that individual's own perceived abilities, but
the need to compare schools and children suggests
norm-referenced assessment procedures. In his
educational ideology, Mr. McLean had adopted the
former goal, not the latter, perhaps because he saw
the incompatibility of the two purposes. Mr. McLean
was a 'stabiliser' in a turbulent environment, a
friend to his pupils in their times of need. His
educational philosophy was a caring one, a philosophy
which, he stated, had its roots formed when, as a
young man, he had travelled in Africa where he
had witnessed levels of civilian 'degradation' the
likes of which he did not want to witness in his own
country. Like many educators in the late 1960s he
appeared to have been attracted to the capacity of
education to effect a 'just' society and the Plowden
Report provided a ready guide and fund-raiser for
his purposes.[3]

All of the foregoing aspects of Mr. McLean's
educational ideology may, for analytical purposes,
be set against an ideal typical construct which is
a logical extension of his ideology into a 'pure
form'. It should be stressed, however, that such an
'ideal type' is not, in the Weberian connotation, a
description of reality - indeed Weber (1949:10)
explicitly warned against this - and nor is it to be
thought of as ideal in the sense of being desirable.
An accentuation of Mr. McLean's ideology would
produce an ideal type of educational philosophy that
could be termed as one of 'stabilisation'. What the
'stabiliser' represents is a sense of caring for the
individual by catering to his physical and emotional
'needs'. It is an emphasis upon toleration and

encouragement of the individual's discretion to further his own interests, at a rate conducive to himself. It is a desire to shield the child from inimical social pressures. It is to allow for 'soft' rather than repressive social control. It is to lessen the social distance between teacher and taught. It is to eschew academic competition and, following from this, norm-referenced testing. It is to 'loosen' the bureaucratic structure of the school so as to minimise the impersonality of social roles and to maximise the child's individual uniqueness. If, in some schools, teachers feel themselves at cross purposes when wishing to balance the academic and the social, or the instrumental and the expressive, then, for those who come close to the philosophy of 'stabilization', the dilemma dissipates, for it will always be the expressive and the social which take precedence.

Mr. McLean's analysis and his purpose may attract the comment that it is naive. His was a view which treated the symptoms of deprivation, not the causes. It might be regarded as a view which was the result of an all-too-ready acceptance of hegemonic forces which purport to render a class-based society as natural, thereby legitimating prosperity for some at the expense of deprivation for others. By seeking to stabilize the children within their deprived environment he may be said to be giving implicit recognition of its inevitability. Mr. McLean's quest, therefore, will be destined, so this criticism goes, to contribute to the maintenance of an inequitable social order by accommodating his pupils within it rather than by making them critical of it. And it would be the very unthreatening ambience within which his 'well-intentioned' purposes were to be realised that would more effectively ensure the 'real' purpose of the school, namely to instil a commonsense which regarded the status quo as being not only natural but desirable.[4] But this supposes that his teachers and his pupils will acquiesce in and realise his educational designs, and it denies the possibility that some of them might indeed resist them. The approach adopted here is to defer any analysis of the outcomes of Mr. McLean's intentions until that outcome has been presented.

Chapter 4

ROCKFIELD SCHOOL: 'YOU'RE HERE TO WORK'

Professions tend to portray to the public a unity of purpose and practice which may mask ideological conflicts within them (Bucher and Strauss, 1961). Whilst it has been argued that those who find themselves in a common situation will construct a shared definition of it, this consensus should not be assumed (Becker, 1961). So it was in Sharp and Green's (1975) study of three teachers in a 'progressive' primary school who professed somewhat different ideologies, which in some cases were at odds with that of the headteacher. Ideologies may differ more when the treatment of the 'raw material' is open to political or philosophical debate. Thus it is within the so-called people-processing organisations, such as schools, that the members are more likely to differ over their ideology. Case studies have revealed these ideological differences within both medical settings (Elliott, 1975; Strauss et al, 1963) and in social work institutions (Street, Vinter and Perrow, 1966). Ideologies, therefore, may be imposed on others who, in response, may produce and seek to sustain defensive ideologies to resist those who would want to challenge their own.

As in medicine and social work, the institution of education is not bereft of ideological differences. These ideologies of education refer to both national systems of education and to particular organisations within them. Of the former, the typologies of Turner (1960), Hopper (1971) and Vaughan and Archer (1971) are examples. At the school level of analysis, there is a wide offering of ideological views, presented as ideal-typical categories, perhaps the most common of which is the 'traditional/progressive' dichotomy. But categorization, whether dichotomous or otherwise, does not of itself explain anything: it only classifies in a descriptive sense. Moreover,

62

the categorization of ideologies might assume that
those who profess an ideology will hold a common
reason for so doing. They may not. Finally,
professed ideologies may not be the ideologies which
individuals or groups privately adhere to – they may
give the researcher what they think he wants to hear
(Goffmann, 1971).
        For these reasons, the mere dichotomization of
teachers' ideologies at Rockfield was avoided, as
was the unquestioned reliance upon the professed
ideologies of teachers. Thus teachers were observed
in the classroom and in unguarded moments in the
staffroom, and the recollections of their pupils
were also sought. By collating these different
perspectives on their ideologies, a more sensitive
typification of them was generated. These typifications of the teachers' philosophies were themselves
'grounded' in their first-order constructs rather
than simply classified into pre-existing categories
gleaned from the literature and presented in the form
of interviews and/or questionnaires (Glaser and
Strauss, 1967; Richer, 1975). An interpretive
approach of a Weberian kind requires that typifications of motives and actions should be constructed
as a consequence of the researcher's having observed
those phenomena (observational understanding) and
having imputed the actor's intended meaning (explanatory understanding). This method of locating
typifications within the every-day world of the
teacher avoids the pitfall of presuming that
categories derived from the observer's own perspective will have relevance for the teacher. That said,
however, there may be a methodological error in too
open-ended an approach. That is to say, the
researcher may simply ask the teacher what her
philosophy of education is. This method may produce
either confusion or embarrassment for the teacher:
confusion because she may not have thought about the
matter for a long time, and may therefore be hard
put to articulate her view, especially if, as may
happen, she is asked in the hurried moments of
break-time or at lunch-time when she may be looking
to relax or to prepare for the next class; embarrassment because she may feel that, as a trained
professional, she should know the 'answer' but
cannot muster her thoughts to give it. In such cases
the teacher may come to feel threatened and under
inspection. Perhaps, as a result, she may be less
likely to co-operate at a later date or, even worse,
more likely to persuade her colleagues from doing so.
Practising teachers tend to deal with particular

events in their own classrooms, many of which are
analysed in the 'confessional' of the staffroom, as
one teacher described it. It is these matters which
they are more amenable to discuss - educational
theory and philosophy were not among their priorities:

> I haven't read a book on educational theory
> since I started teaching (five years previous).
> I haven't <u>needed</u> to read a book on educational
> theory since I started to teach. I don't have
> the time.

If, therefore, teachers are more at ease discussing
the particular rather than the general, then it must
be from the former that their ideologies are to be
imputed, and it must be in the classroom that they
are to be observed in practice.

At Rockfield School an official ideology of
'stabilization' was professed by the head teacher,
Mr. McLean. Initially, the staff appeared to assent
to this view since they did not articulate any
criticism of it, either implicitly or openly. There
was no evidence of conflict or of negotiation. A
sense of order prevailed. It seemed that the staff
and their head teacher had long since made sense of
their common situation and that this resulting
culture had not subsequently required articulation,
development or defence. It was seen as natural.
There were no staff meetings or school-based in-
service where matters of policy and practice could
be given vent. The school appeared to be in a state
of ideological drift, even inertia.

Gradually some signs of dissent became evident,
though they were rarely discussed. It was said,
for example, that Mr. McLean had once been the
practitioner of a policy not consonant with that he
now professed:

> He was strict then - belt over the shoulder.[1]

Nor had he demonstrated to his teachers what his
ideology required in practical terms:

> He expects us to do something but he has never
> done it himself.

He was regarded as being both out of touch with the
realities of classroom life, as well as being out of
sight from the pupils for whom his door was
allegedly always open:

ROCKFIELD SCHOOL: 'YOU'RE HERE TO WORK'

(i) Mrs. Letham: God I worked hard today.

    Mr. McLean: Can I have that in writing?

    Mrs. Letham: He doesn't know the half of it.
    (out of his
    earshot)

(ii) The kids don't even know who he is.

As the fieldwork progressed it transpired that his
ideology of stabilization did not have wide currency
among the teachers, not because it was not well-
intentioned, but because it ignored the exigencies
of having to deal day after day with a large group
of pupils with many 'problems'. An elaboration of
this ideological deviation is now undertaken,
beginning with that group of teachers, mainly in the
infants' section, whose ideologies may be typified
as 'stretching', not 'stabilizing'. Three aspects
are considered in a complementary way: the description of the ideology; the classroom practice which
was its consequence, and the reactions of the pupils
who had to face it.

The Stretchers

At the beginning of the academic year I was informed
by some of the teachers on the size of their 'top'
and 'tail' relative to what they had been in previous
years. Mrs. Stewart declared to her colleagues in
the staffroom:

    I've got a great 'top' this year.

'Tails' were either 'short' or 'long' and they
comprised an assortment of 'dead horses' and 'nutters',
the former being 'mentally deficient', the latter
bordering on the 'maladjusted'. As for the 'top', it
was discussed in terms of the 'brightness' of the
'spark' which its members gave off. The 'top',
therefore, were the 'good ones'; the 'tail'
something far less so. This metaphorical stratification of the school's pupils into these categories
did not square with Mr. McLean's assertion that
pupils not be defined as failures. These categories
were not, however, voiced in the same way to the
pupils themselves; that is, they were not referred
to in the classroom as 'top', 'tail', 'nutter' and
'dead horse'. Rather, they were grouped, usually on
the basis of reading achievement, into colour-,

65

animal-, or letter-coded arrangements.

A recurrent topic of staffroom discourse was the difficulty some of the teachers had 'stretching the top' and 'bringing up the tail'. This was a problem peculiar to the 'stretchers', a group who had no truck with Mr. McLean's ideology of 'stabilization'. For them the purpose of the school was to provide an academic education, not one of 'cossetting' the children in a 'cosy' atmosphere. School meant work. Although the 'stretchers' adhered to this common purpose, they sought to realise it in two different ways. Four teachers (Mrs. Findlay, Mrs. Davie, Mrs. Letham and Mr. Alexander) employed the use of strict methods of social control but 'softened' these with a readiness to commend their pupils whenever their work or behaviour warranted it. Two other teachers, Mrs. Rogers and Mrs. Preece, whilst sharing the 'stretch' ideology, tended to be stern but not laudatory. In the ensuing discussion of the 'stretchers', therefore, these two types of practitioner are treated separately, beginning with the larger group and its professed ideology.

Mrs. Letham, Mrs. Findlay, Mrs. Davie and Mr. Alexander: The Ideology

On my first visit to Rockfield School an 'angry' voice echoed through the ground floor. It turned out to be Mrs. Findlay. She had perfected what some might call a "controlled loss of cool", and I was to learn later that her pupils found it difficult to decide when she really was annoyed. Mrs. Findlay was fervent in her conviction that inner-city children should not fall by the academic wayside, nor should they be expected to do so simply because home backgrounds were in many instances very stressful. Her approach sought to counter what Mrs. Watt, Mr. McLean's successor, later defined as the 'Rockfield Syndrome'. This condition was an amalgamation of two perspectives, one held by some pupils, the other by some teachers. The pupils to whom this applied were said to be members of the 'I-can't-do-it-Miss-brigade', a group which was allegedly devoid of motivation towards matter academic. As for the teachers, they had fallen victim to the Sociological Myth (Hargreaves, 1972): that is, they had been informed of the underachievement of working class pupils and as a result had come not to expect much of that group's academic performance, an expectation which could then be realised. Mrs. Findlay, however, would have little sympathy with such pupils and teachers. Her pupils

were not allowed to 'get away with not doing
anything'.   They were cajoled into action:

> When the tears start to well, I stop - I know
> I've got through to them.

And so it was.   A pupil in Mrs. Findlay's Primary 2
class was Boris, a recent immigrant from South
America.   Boris suffered from a respiratory complaint
but one day had ventured out into the playground
without his jacket.   It had been snowing.   When I
saw him in the corridor he was cowering before
Mrs. Findlay who was admonishing him in a very loud
voice.   She reminded him of his ailment and of the
inclement weather; she praised his work in class
and she stressed her surprise at his conduct.   Boris
began to cry.   Mrs. Findlay stopped.   Mrs. Findlay
was loud and strict and she knew it.   She admitted
that she 'sounded like Mrs. Thatcher', but, she
emphasised, 'most of the time I'm a mother figure'.
The children, she said,'know where they stand'.
    Mrs. Findlay had no doubts about her ideology
and her practice. Like Mrs. Rogers she would have
nothing to do with 'educational theory' and with
fashionable trends in pedagogy and curriculum,
particularly the 'aims' and 'objectives' movement
associated with Bloom's noted (1956) taxonomy of
objectives in the cognitive domain.   All that was
mere rhetoric:

> The college of education tutor asked me ·to
> write down my aims and objectives for the
> Vikings (project).   I did.   He asked if I'd
> noted the aims <u>before</u> writing the essay.   I
> said 'no'.   He looked dismayed.

Indeed, the 'experts' from the local college of
education came in for some acidic comment:

> A lot of fancy theories ... We <u>love</u> our
> children.   These college of education people
> don't <u>know</u>.   If they loved children, they'd
> still <u>be</u> in there teaching, wouldn't they?
> My student (from the college) thinks I'm too
> formal.   I believe in good, basic teaching -
> no frills.

'Interference' from the college was as unwelcome as
it was from parents who claimed to know her job
better than she:

> They think we don't know our jobs - I wouldn't
> go and tell them what to do.

Mrs. Findlay's confidence in her own ability to
assess quickly and accurately a child in need of
remedial help was reminiscent of the ready categorization by the teacher in Rist's (1970) study in an
American ghetto school. Mrs. Findlay, however,
arraigned a more 'objective' set of criteria to
define a 'remedial' child 'after two weeks in
Primary 1': a 'lack of interest, even in play';
the child has 'difficulty holding a pencil'; or the
child 'can't draw', or 'cannot remember the sound
and formation of a letter', thereby revealing 'no
flow from eye to brain'.

If Mrs. Findlay was not one to share Mr. McLean's
ideology, nor was Mr. Alexander. He arrived as the
new deputy head teacher shortly before Mr. McLean's
retirement. It has already been stated that
Mr. Alexander found little to approve of at
Rockfield. He was critical of its relaxing and
inefficient atmosphere and he wanted to change it.
At Rockfield he found little punctuality from
teachers and pupils. There was no timetable and
there were too many interruptions during class time,
many of which were 'unnecessary':

> If a teacher knew she was going to need match-
> boxes for a lesson, why didn't she get her own
> (instead of interrupting his class to ask for
> them)?

He asked me what I was doing at Rockfield. I told
him that I wanted to study a good school:

> Who told you this was a good school?

Mr. Alexander was committed to an academic education
for his pupils:

> I want to do my best for them.

He disagreed with the no-testing movement at
Rockfield:

> I test them after every piece of work.

Mr. Alexander's missionary zeal to effect change was
viewed by some teachers with not a little amusement:

> He'll fit in.

The prophecy was realised. When I asked
Mr. Alexander six months after he had arrived how
things were going, he replied:

> I've mellowed; I've had it.

Although he found relations with other staff 'friendly
on the surface', he seemed at cross purposes with some
of them. He had been brought in with 'new ideas' to
implement. If these were not to take hold he could
see himself 'moving in two years or so'. Two other
'stretchers', Mrs. Letham and Mrs. Davie, both left
the school during the latter stages of the research
and I was unable to have discussions with them of
any length. Their ideologies, however, appear to be
close to those of Mrs. Findlay and Mr. Alexander on
the basis of my classroom observations of them. It
is to the realisation of the 'stretcher's' ideology
in the classroom that we now turn.

<u>Mrs. Findlay, Mrs. Letham, Mrs. Davie and
Mr. Alexander: The 'Stretchers' Observed</u>

Whereas Mr. McLean defined a 'successful pupil' as
one who would be well-adjusted to his life in school
and to his destiny in the working class beyond it,
the 'stretchers' took a more meritocratic and academic view of the school. Success could be earned and
this process of reward for meritorious behaviour and
work began in the classroom. The basis of this
competitive work in school was good discipline, a
discipline stern but tempered with rewards from the
teacher commensurate with the efforts of the pupil.
Pupils were grouped, exposed to public failure before
their classmates, tested and given firm direction by
the teacher about what was to be done, when it was
to be done and in what order. The pupils knew what
was expected and what the rules were. Even in
Primary 1 the pattern was established as they were
'broken in' to the regime of the classroom:

Mrs. Letham: Why are we here?

Pupils in unison: TO WORK!

The basis of good discipline was firmly laid down by
the 'stretchers' and a wide range of methods of
social control employed.[2] The (implied) threat was
a popular (for the teachers) ploy:

Mrs. Findlay: VERYLL! No work, no playtime.

	No nail biting and feet down please.
Mrs. Findlay:	Aileen. That news better be written up.
Mrs. Findlay:	Sheila, I'll be calling you out in a minute to look at the story jotters.
Mrs. Letham:	If I have to talk to you again, you'll spend the day outside. Do you wish to take your desk outside?
Mrs. Davie:	Mr. Khan. You and I are going to fall out shortly ...

These threats could apply to groups as well as to individuals:[3]

Mrs. Letham:	I'm going to shoot the boots off that group.
Mrs. Findlay:	I'm coming to see the books in five minutes. The others who are busy with their Busy Books get busy with their Busy Books now please. I'm coming round with my red pen now.
Mrs. Letham:	Come on. You're holding up your group ...
Mrs. Findlay:	Let me see how quickly we can get everything away. Which is the best group ..?
Mrs. Davie:	I would like to see jotters on my table, tables tidy, milk bottles away: one... two... three... FOUR... FIVE!

If the 'threat' and the public exhortation failed to achieve the desired effect, the teachers became 'angry' and feigned a controlled loss of composure:

Mrs. Findlay:	RIGHT: ALL YOU PEOPLE WHO ARE TALKING ... STAND ON YOUR FEET.
Mrs. Davie:	James ... JAMES ... JAMES!!!!

ROCKFIELD SCHOOL: 'YOU'RE HERE TO WORK'

Mrs. Findlay: That's Veryll's voice again. WE
                       HAD ENOUGH TROUBLE WITH YOU
                       YESTERDAY. DON'T START TODAY!

Sharon (in Mrs.   I've nothing to do ...
Letham's Primary 1
class):

Mrs. Letham: DON'T YOU BELIEVE IT. YOU'VE GOT
                       SOMETHING TO DO EVERY MINUTE OF
                       THE DAY!

Less frequently the teachers referred the work and
behaviour of the children to that of the opposite
sex or to younger children:

Mrs. Findlay: GIRLS STAND, girls sit. One more
                       time without any noise. And boys
                       watch the girls ... BOYS, you'll
                       have to work hard to beat that.
                       Girls watch the boys.

Mrs. Letham: Three boys first (to finish their
                       milk). Shows what kind of girls
                       we've got ...

Mrs. Davie: BOYS ... chairs in. GIRLS ...
                       chairs in.

Mrs. Letham: You're too big for me to write
                       for you, aren't you?

Mrs. Letham: In the nursery we got paper straws.
                       You're not in the nursery now ...

Even in Primary 2, however, the teacher's power had
its limits. In Mrs. Findlay's class the children
knew where they stood. The rules were clear:

    No kicking, biting, stealing or swearing (the
    last of these incurred the penalty of a smacked
    bottom). That goes for boys and girls.

One girl, however, flouted the rules and withstood
the punishment. Veryll, as Mrs. Findlay had
informed me before I observed her class, 'likes to
rule the roost'. In some respects she did. None of
the five methods of social control used on her
seemed to work if she did not choose to comply.
These were: a strong telling-off; expulsion from
the classroom; being kept in at playtime; a smacked

bottom; the belt. Veryll's resistance was simple and very difficult to deal with: if she did not want to do something, or if she wanted to taunt Mrs. Findlay, she wet herself and would be put outside the room, which was where I first saw her, an odour emanating from her wet clothes.

A further characteristic of the 'stretchers' was that they grouped their pupils on the basis of achievement, even in Primary 1 and 2. The large tables formed the locations of the different groups. Only Mrs. Davie's class had individual desks for pupils 'who worked better on their own'. In Mrs. Findlay's class 'the tail sit near me for extra help', but in Mrs. Letham's class they were sat in a far corner from the teacher. Mrs. Letham claimed, however, to be flexible in her grouping procedure, allowing for inter-group mobility:

> My class float. I move freely in and out. I use the top group more or less as a guide and slot children into that group to give them a boost. They may not necessarily be the best children in the class.

DH: But the children know that the 'monkeys' are the top group?

> They have a fair idea. I don't like to tar them.

Apart from reading, the activities of the pupils were common to all, although pupils might be doing different tasks, this being a consequence of their having completed a previous one which other pupils still worked on. For example, on the board in Mrs. Findlay's class she had written the order in which the different tasks were to be completed: 'READING, STORY, BUSY BOOKS, LIBRARY'. Occasionally, and especially in Mrs. Davie's Primary 3 class, an activity included the whole class at one time. Mrs. Letham, for example, would have 'games' on letter recognition and the application of a given letter to a word:

> Stand up if you know a word starting with 'O'.

Mrs. Davie had a similar quiz for arithmetic. The whole class would be required to stand. As a pupil correctly answered a question, he or she sat down. Those who failed to do so remained standing in public view but incurred no penalty save that of

being seen as unable to answer. Mrs. Davie also had
the children practise their handwriting as a class.
A sentence which emphasised a particular letter would
be generated through class discussion and written by
her on the blackboard. The children would then carefully copy the sentence in their best handwriting.
For example, one sentence permitted them to practise
the letter 'p':

Pretty pets put pennies on their paws.

Mrs. Letham, Mrs. Davie and Mrs. Findlay were all
teachers of infants. The other 'stretcher' under
discussion here, Mr. Alexander, was a classroom
teacher at Primary 7 level. And whereas his female
colleagues were quick to reprimand a pupil,
Mr. Alexander, on the three mornings I visited his
classroom, uttered virtually no such comment. But
the pupils were quiet and industrious. Social
control had been achieved and accepted and, during
my time in the classroom, had not required any
obvious need of maintenance. Indeed, Mr. Alexander's
quietness of voice and ease of manner somewhat
altered my expectation of him as a teacher, an
expectation based on accounts of him which I had
been told by pupils. One account is cited below:

I think the teachers are alright, except for
one, Mr. Alexander. He was at my old school.
Didn't like him. The way he shouts ... when
you're bad you get shouted at. Like
Mr. Alexander shouted at a boy for setting up
cheek to the lollipop man.

During the period of my observations of his classroom,
time was spent on a spelling test, a long set of
exercises in arithmetic, and on the reading of a
play, written by Mr. Alexander and to be performed
by his class for the infants. The nature of the
lessons, therefore,was very much teacher-directed:
the spelling test was administered orally; the
reading of the play was monitored by him closely and
the 80-item arithmetic exercise was to be done
quietly and quickly, the pupils having to note down
the length of time the set of exercises took to
complete, a time-clock being placed in public view
for this purpose.
It had been said that Mr. Alexander did not like
interruptions. His door was always shut. But there
were interruptions: Mrs. Scott came in to tell him
about Ahmed who had kicked a ball three times in the

face of one of her girls. Ahmed was duly lectured
for five minutes by both teachers. Soon after,
another pupil came in to display the medal he had
won at an athletics meeting. He was followed by one
of the teachers in the Immigrant Department and she,
in turn, was followed by the announcer of the day's
lunch menu, which was savoury mince, or boiled ham,
chips, beans and sweet. Finally, there occurred an
inquisition of a pupil who had 'lost' the money he
was to have given to the dinner lady, and a letter
had to be drafted and sent to the pupil's parents
so they could explain the 'mistake'.
      A closer scrutiny of the spelling test given
by Mr. Alexander is instructive of his ideology and
his expectation of the pupils. Indeed, the very fact
that he was testing the pupils was not official
practice. First, those parts of the test which
allude to his ideology:

> Spell 'education'. - education is what you
> come to school for.

> Spell 'pupil'. Pupil - what you are termed in
> school.

> Spell 'certificate'. Certificate - something
> we all like to possess at the end of the
> day.

> Spell 'maintain'. When you go up to the high
> school, you must maintain high standards.

> Spell 'engineer', a good occupation if you can
> get it.

This subtle combination of the formal and hidden
curricula is an implicit denial of much that
Mr. McLean stood for: occupational mobility
('engineer - a good occupation if you can get it);
credentialism ('certificate - something we all like
to possess'); standards ('you must maintain high
standards); testing (the substance of the lesson).
Secondly, there were allusions to the pupils
themselves:

> Spell 'extremely'. I hope that the group are
> extremely good at spelling today.

> Spell 'manageable'. Some might say that this
> class was manageable.

> Spell 'intelligence'. You are said to possess this; I sometimes wonder!
>
> Spell 'stupid'. No-one in my class could be termed stupid.
>
> Spell 'destroy'. Something Group C like to do all the time.

Thus, aside from his tongue-in-cheek references to the destructive propensities of Group C, and his feigned doubt about the class's intelligence, Mr. Alexander informs the class that they are 'manageable' and not 'stupid'. There was an air of optimism that some of his pupils could succeed academically and, in further contrast to Mr. McLean, that they should succeed.

To facilitate the pupil's success, he should, according to the 'stretchers', be both disciplined and praised whenever they were due. It was this willingness to praise the pupils in the class which differentiated this group of 'stretchers' from the two other 'stretchers', Mrs. Rogers and Mrs. Preece, more of whom later. This difference may be reported quantitatively: if we take the total of the 'approving' and 'disapproving' remarks made by Mrs. Letham, Mrs. Findlay and Mrs. Davie respectively we find that 63.9 percent of Mrs. Letham's remarks, 52.3 percent of Mrs. Findlay's, and 20.1 percent of Mrs. Davie's were within the 'approving' category. As for Mr. Alexander, much of his talk was substantive to the lesson and neither approving nor disapproving.

Some qualitative evidence representative of the willingness of these teachers to praise their pupils is cited below:

Mrs. Findlay: Very nice. On you go. Have a look at this, Dr. Hartley. He's only been writing for a month!

Great. Very good. I'm going to tell Mrs. Lacey as well.

I'm going to enjoy this. Very good indeed. Excellent.

Mrs. Davie: Looks like a dog's dinner. All correct though!

Very neat the jotters so far today.

Very neat.

Mrs. Letham: Well toots. Good reading!

Sajda. How lovely. All correct.
Isn't she coming on. And she's
coloured in without going over the
line!

The Pupils' View of the 'Stretchers'

The pupils' view of the school is a neglected area
of research, although some recent studies have sought
to remedy the omission (Woods, 1976; Birksted, 1976;
Blishen, 1973; School of Barbiana, 1970). These
studies are difficult to undertake for a number of
reasons. The first is an ethical one. By questioning the pupils about their teachers, or merely
listening to pupils discussing them in an unsolicited
manner, the researcher may appear to condone the
views of the pupils and, by implication, undermine
the authority of the teachers. Linked with this is
a second reason. The teacher may feel 'spied upon':
it is usual for the teacher to report on the pupil,
not for the pupil to report on the teacher. Thirdly,
there is, with very young children, the problem of
actually obtaining their views. Many may lack the
rudiments of reading and writing, therefore
obviating the use of the questionnaire. Others may
be reticent to talk to a stranger who may, because
he is an adult, be thought of as a teacher.
    Of these reasons, the first two are the most
problematic for the researcher. A teacher who is
suspicious of the researcher's motives and interests
may, despite the latter's attempts to allay the
teacher's misgivings, refuse to co-operate and may
cause some of her colleagues to do likewise. At
Rockfield, before I tape-recorded what the children
said, I gained the teacher's permission but I
refused to allow the teacher to listen to what her
pupils had said. I made it known, however, that I
had no objection to the teacher asking her pupils
about the gist of what had been discussed between
the pupils and myself. Whenever possible, I spoke
to the children in small groups of friends, friendship
choices having been obtained from sociograms. In
these conversations I did not pointedly ask a pupil,
'What do you think of Miss So-and-So?'. Rather, I
tended to allow the topic of the teacher to arise
out of discussion on another issue. Not all pupils
discussed their teachers specifically. As with some

pupils, some teachers are more discussed than others.
Of the 'stretchers', Mr. Alexander, Mrs. Findlay and
Mrs. Davie were more the focus of conversation.
Mr. Alexander attracted the most comment, perhaps
because he was new to the school and perhaps because
he was the deputy head teacher. Finally, the
conversations with the pupils occurred near the end
of the research. The reason for this was mainly
political; that is, I regarded this aspect of the
study to be the most sensitive for the teachers.
They had not been 'researched' in this way before.
Had they objected, and had this part of the study
been undertaken at the beginning, then the prospect
of continuing the study might have been lessened.
Furthermore, by leaving this aspect until near the
end, I was able to build up some trust between
myself and the teachers. It transpired, however,
that my concerns were unfounded. No teacher objected
to my talking to her pupils.

It has been suggested that the ideologies and
practice of Mrs. Findlay and Mrs. Davie were similar.
This analysis was confirmed by some of the pupils
who had been taught by Mrs. Findlay in Primary 2 and
had then progressed to Mrs. Davie's Primary 3 class:

DH:	Do you see any differences between this year and last year?
William:	Yes.
Mandy:	I think it's easy.
Paula:	No, I think it's hard work.
Mandy:	I liked Mrs. Findlay better because she's kind.
Paula:	So is Mrs. Davie. There's one thing I don't like about them both and that's they shout too much.
DH:	Do they teach differently?
William:	No, not really.
Paula:	Mrs. Davie's more fun; she gives them tea parties and that.

Classroom observation revealed that both teachers
were strict, an interpretation confirmed by their
pupils, beginning with those of Mrs. Findlay:

ROCKFIELD SCHOOL: 'YOU'RE HERE TO WORK'

DH: What do you think could be done to
           improve this school?

Dorothy: Stricter teachers.

DH: You don't think they're strict
           enough, or they're too strict?

Dorothy: It depends what teacher. Mrs. Findlay
           is really strict.

Although Mrs. Findlay was strict and said to be so,
her attempts at disciplining one girl, Veryll, have
already been seen to be wanting, as classroom
observation showed. I had not seen Veryll's strategy
for getting her way, but some of her classmates had:

Wendy: There used to be a girl in our class
           called Veryll. She used to wet
           herself. She used to pong the class-
           room out.

Even the belt had not subdued her:

           She used to bite when she got the
           belt.

Indeed, Veryll had taken the offensive and had
resorted to stealing from the teacher:

Angela: Well, Mrs. Findlay collected all the
           money and sometimes left it on her
           table and she took down all the names
           of the people who had sweeties (which
           had been handed to the teacher for
           safekeeping). Veryll sometimes got
           to stay in (at break) and so she
           stood up on Mrs. Findlay's chair and
           took some.

DH: Did Mrs. Findlay find out?

Angela: Yes.

DH: What happened?

Mark: At playtime when she was ready --
           inaudible/, she found out that some
           of it had been stolen.

DH: What did she do?

Angela:	She looked in everybody's school bag, pockets and looked in their shoes and socks.
DH:	Did she find the money?
Angela:	No. Veryll had eaten them.
DH:	The money!?
Angela:	Yes. No, the sweets!
DH:	What happened to the money?
Mark:	She got caught taking the money back where she had hidden it.

Shortly afterwards, Veryll left Rockfield School.

Mrs. Davie's reputation for stern discipline was documented in the following extracts from the 'School Book' of two of her pupils:

(i) I like Mrs. Davie and when you get your temper up I get scaird today you had your temper up and shouted at Tracey because tracey stoaul moira's apple and you put Tracey out the door and you shouted at paul because he was a lazy boy and you frew his book on the floor you had to change a table in the classroom and you will not be very happy and when people come in the classroom you shout and when Mrs. Leitch came you had to shout (Yvonne).

(ii) You have to be good in school because you get the belt you get a row from the teacher, you are supostoo atracke the teacher atension and do not desturb the teacher on the count (register) and you have to work hard and tidy everything in the classroom and you have to listen to the teacher and do your work on the blackboard and be good. (Ron).

The second of these extracts is akin to Jackson's (1968) analysis of life in classrooms from the perspective of the pupil: the hidden curriculum where the pupil must learn patience, tidiness, diligence, tact and consideration, or, as Henry (1955) puts it, 'giving teacher what she wants'. The first extract graphically presents an account of the consequences of any infringement of the rules.

ROCKFIELD SCHOOL: 'YOU'RE HERE TO WORK'

Both extracts are expressions of the teacher's
insistence that work and behaviour must meet the
teacher's standard. Nowhere is the policy of
'stabilization' being effected. That said, although
this account of Mrs. Davie's 'stretching' ideology
appears convincing, it does not enable a comparison
to be made with a similar ideology being implemented
in another school. However, one of her pupils,
Alison, had previously been to another school and
some of her recollections of it illustrate the point:

DH: How long were you there?

Alison: I was in Primary 2 when I left.

DH: Did your teachers there do things
           differently from your teacher here?

Alison: They moved you around the room after
           every month.

DH: Did they give you tests?

Alison: Yes. After you had finished one page,
           they gave you a test to do.

DH: Do you do that here?

Alison: No.

DH: What happens after you have finished
           your work here?

Alison: You just go and get a library book
           sometimes.

According to her pupils, Mrs. Davie did test her
children, though not as often as occurred in Alison's
former school:

DH: What about tests?

James: Yes, we get tests.

DH: Many?

James: About three a term.

Suffice it to say that Mrs. Davie and Mrs. Findlay,
compared to those teachers not subscribing to the
'stretch' ideology, were more likely to be higher in

their expectations of their pupils' work and
behaviour. This was also the case with Mr. Alexander,
to whom we return.
      Mr. Alexander was a deputy head teacher and a
classroom teacher. Those who were in his classroom
had a more approving verdict on him than did those
who crossed his path when he was out and about
'sweeping up'. Consider the views of him held by
some of the latter group:

(i) DH: And who's the deputy head?

     Christine: Mr. Alexander.

     DH: What does he do?

     Christine: Well he just sees if everything's
                going well and tells the teachers how
                to do things right.

     DH: Tell me about the playground. Is it
                true that certain people are only
                allowed in a certain part of the
                playground?

     Michelle: Yes. The Primary 1s are only allowed
                in that bit, and the Primary 4, 5 and
                6 are allowed in any bit ...

     Christine: Where the bars are.

     Michelle: And we stay beside the bars, and if
                you go beside the (football) pitch
                you get checked (told off).

     DH: Who by?

     Michelle: From Mr. Alexander because you're not
                allowed to ask questions; you just
                get shouted at.

     DH: What for?

     Michelle: If you go near the boys (playing
                football), or if you sing ...

     David: If you sing football songs around the
                playground, Mr. Alexander shouts at
                them.

Mr. Alexander's reputation for strong discipline was
much discussed by the children. Most of them would
already have encountered Mrs. Davie and Mrs. Findlay,
both of whom, though strict, were well liked. The
children had not, however, yet come to terms with
Mr. Alexander's more stern measures. They tended to
take his harsh admonitions at face value, simply
because they had little evidence to convince them
otherwise at that stage. For Mr. Alexander's part,
he was concerned to improve discipline as a prelude
to "stretching" and good teaching. Whereas the
children were not used to Mr. Alexander's disciplinary methods, Mr. Alexander was not used to what he
perceived as a laxity in standards of discpline.
The children compared him to their other teachers;
he compared the Rockfield children to those in his
previous school. As a result, Mr. Alexander may have
over-reacted to the perceived indiscipline, whilst
the children may have been over-sensitive to his
initial strictures. The latter is well illustrated
by the accounts given below by Heather and Karen,
both of which typify Mr. Alexander's attempts to
make his mark.

> Heather: One day I was running through the hall
>   (which was forbidden) and
>   Mr. Alexander stopped me and said,
>   'What do you think you're doing?'
>   And I just walked on, and he said,
>   'Come here a minute when I speak to
>   you.' So I looked at him and he said,
>   'This school isn't for running in:
>   it's just for walking.' And then he
>   said, 'Go back to your class.' (When
>   I got back) Mr. Lane said 'What was
>   he talking to you about?' and I said
>   'I was just running through the hall.'

> Karen: One day I was running up the stairs
>   and Mr. Alexander started running
>   after me, you know, to stop me, and
>   he said, 'What do you think you're
>   doing you silly girl - you might have
>   an accident on the stairs.' You know,
>   so I never said anything and he
>   started bawling and shouting at me
>   and, you know, I got awful upset about
>   it because, you know, when he shouts
>   he's like a thunderstorm and every-
>   thing, so it's really upsetting when
>   he starts shouting at you because the

> voice he's got just blows you up
> inside and you can hardly understand
> it because your eyes are full of
> tears - you just can't understand a
> thing.

These incidents occurred soon after Mr. Alexander
joined the staff. That he found a certain laxity
and inefficiency has already been mentioned.
Discipline too was not, in his view, what it should
have been. In his early days he commenced his mission
to change matters but realised that he could not do
so to the degree he would have wished. As a result
he had 'mellowed', a view confirmed by Gillian in
Miss Darby's Primary 4 class:

> At first he didn't have a class but now that he
> has a class he's not so strict anymore.

Mr. Alexander, therefore, is an example of a teacher
whose ideology was constrained by the seemingly
intractable situation of which he had become a part.
He had modified his public posture but had retained
his private ideology: if matters did not change he
intended to leave. He had learned that power had its
limits.

Such was the pupils' view of Mr. Alexander as
the deputy head. The view from his classroom pupils
was different and more favourable:

> I think Mr. Alexander's a great teacher. I
> thought at first he would be a horrible teacher,
> but he's really good.

> Paul: Our class is the best in the school.

> DH: Who said that?

> Stuart: Mr. Alexander.

Earlier, my account of Mr. Alexander as a classroom
teacher revealed a virtual absence of reproving
comments. There had been no need for him to press
for social control and effort on the pupils' part
because both were in evidence. The ground had already
been prepared. I had not witnessed any lapses but
they were reported and were dealt with sternly:

> Stuart: I like Mr. Alexander. He's good fun.
>   I don't like him when he gets bad
>   tempered though.

DH: He doesn't get bad tempered very often
          does he?

Stuart: Yes.

DH: Do you think it's because people in
          the class get him bad tempered?

Nancy: Yes. It's people like that who always
          carries on and that ...

Paul: It's like me with my bad writing.

Stuart: You can't help your writing. You've
          got to try.

In a brief period the professional identity of
Mr. Alexander had changed. His early fervour directed towards implementing a greater degree of structure
had been spent, having been confronted by the powerful, though different, 'structure' which beset him.
He had withdrawn to his classroom and his own pupils
to create a school within a school. His new
insularity was recognised by himself, his colleagues
and by the pupils throughout the school. As yet he
had not realised the correspondence of his own
analysis of the school with that of the other
'stretchers'. For the time being he had decided to
take stock and reassess his new role.

The 'Stretchers': A Sub-Group

There were two self-professed 'stretchers' whose
declared ideology accorded with those of
Mrs. Findlay, Mrs. Letham, Mrs. Davie and
Mr. Alexander. They were Mrs. Rogers and Mrs. Preece,
teachers of Primary 7 and 3 respectively. Both had
taught in other schools and both were the wives of
clergymen. What they also shared was a tendency to
refrain from praising their pupils in the classroom.
It was this which set them apart from the other
'stretchers'. To a lesser degree, they also
appeared to have moments of doubt that their advocacy
of 'stretching' could always be put into practice.
        At the level of professed rather than practised
ideology, Mrs. Rogers was perhaps the most outspoken
critic of the headteacher. He, in turn, regarded
her as an 'outsider'. Mrs. Rogers agreed that she
was an 'outsider', but not the only one: 'I have a
few allies'. Her disagreement centred on her refusal
to accept that materially deprived children were

necessarily unsuited to an academic regime. For her
there was too much underachievement and too much
prurient staffroom gossip about the pupils and their
families:

> There is too much harmful staffroom gossip about
> certain pupils and their parents. It's amazing
> how normal the children seem when you think of
> what they have to put up with at home.

Like Mrs. Findlay, her stress was on the academic:

> The children here are treated too well. They
> have it easy. There is not enough emphasis on
> academic matters: we don't push the children
> enough.

Nor did she have much time for the college of education 'experts' who had attempted to help teachers
with their restructuring of the syllabus for
environmental studies on the lines of sequentially-
ordered aims and objectives:

> Spending a lot of time thinking about 'aims'
> and 'objectives' of curriculum is largely a
> waste of time.

Mrs. Preece, a close working colleague of her
fellow Primary 3 teacher, Mrs. Davie ('We've been
together for six years') was of a similar view.
    In their classrooms, the pedagogy of Mrs. Rogers
and of Mrs. Preece differed from the other
'stretchers' in one important respect: they very
rarely commended their pupils. Over three mornings
during which I noted incidents of 'approval' and
'disapproval' in their respective classrooms, all of
Mrs. Rogers' comments in these categories fell
within the 'disapproving' one, as did 81 percent of
Mrs. Preece's. This is not, however, to state that
they never praised their pupils since both teachers
had systems of recording 'good work'. (Mrs. Rogers
kept a points table; Mrs. Preece kept a list of the
'happy faces', awarded for good work.) As with the
other 'stretchers', there was much urging of pupils
to work well:

> Mrs. Rogers (in comments over three days):
>
> Come on Fiona!
>
> GRANT. You're muttering.

Paul. That's enough. I don't want to hear any more football. Save if for playtime.

Colin.. You're an awful nuisance. Turn round ... Is he bothering you Ann?

Angela ... you're not working!

Kevin. Your book had better have something in it ...

Fiona. WORK!

Mandy I want a whole page completed today.

Fred. Stop doing that. You've not simmered down since yesterday.

Sam if you've not got your jotter tomorrow, you'll get another bad mark.

Mrs. Preece:

Get a dab of glue on your bottom!

Get off your bottom!

Who's that with an elephant's tongue?

Mrs. Rogers and Mrs. Preece were different from the other 'stretchers' in two other ways. Both wanted more single desks in their classrooms because they believed that 'some children work better on their own'. Mrs. Preece had managed to acquire six single desks, Mrs. Rogers three. Both appeared to waver in their resolve to stretch as many pupils as they could. (In this they were not alone among the 'stretchers' but they seemed the more pessimistic.) Mrs. Rogers, for example, did not appear to share the desire of the other stretchers to 'bring up the tail'; her concern was with 'stretching the top'. This was given organisational expression in her classroom: the 'tail' was seated furthest away from her whilst the 'top' was close to her, the opposite of the arrangement in Mrs. Findlay's class. Nonetheless, Mrs. Rogers knew she could not ignore the 'tail' or, more to the point, they would not allow her to do so:

These lads demand your attention. They need something to do. They take time away from the good ones.

Why she appeared to prefer the 'top' is perhaps
explained by her acceptance of the hopelessness of
the academic position of the pupils in the 'tail';
they were then in Primary 7 and so far behind that,
no matter what she did, they would not improve,
especially since no remedial provision for them was
made. She had decided to keep them busy with
'something to do', thereby 'freeing' her to attend to
the better pupils. It is noteworthy in passing that
Mr. Alexander, also a Primary 7 teacher, did not
accept the academic demise of the 'tail' but, in
defence of Mrs. Rogers, Mr. Alexander was new to
the school and committed to improving it academically.
He had not endured the years of frustration of having
to deal with 'problem' pupils and an unsympathetic
head teacher. And even he had 'mellowed'.
     Mrs. Preece had her moments of dismay at the
enormity of the task of stretching the pupils. More
than any other teacher in the 'stretchers' she was
more likely to express her consternation:

        The problem here is time. It's sheer slog. I
        think you can be in a school like this too long.

        You intend to do certain things but you never
        finish - maybe I'm too ambitious ...

Mrs. Preece's sense of despair is illustrated by the
following extract from an observation of one of her
lessons. The lesson in question took place on the
first spring-like day of the year. The children
were seated at Mrs. Preece's feet and were discussing
the pictures in a book called 'The Cuckoo Story'.
The cuckoo, along with Paul and Taval, was defined
as 'lazy' - the cuckoo because she would steal eggs
and not lay her own, Taval and Paul because they
were lolling about the floor 'not listening'.
Mrs. Preece then asked the children, 'What are signs
of spring?' and she told them to look through the
classroom window at the school garden. This
produced two answers:

        Mum scrubbing and polishing in springtime.

        The carnival comes in spring.

Seeming to despair that the children had not seen
the 'correct' signs of spring when they had looked
into the garden, she decided to take them outside to

look at it. After being told to 'creep' and put on
their coats and go to the door (girls first, boys
second), the children lined up and were given their
final instructions:

> Remember, it's not playtime; it's just a little
> walk. Look for signs of spring.

The children then entered the school garden and stood
in a long line, two abreast, Mrs. Preece positioned
at the front. Beyond the garden the noise of the
traffic was drowned by that from pneumatic drills
used by workmen in the tenements across the street
which were being renovated. Inaudible to most of
the children, Mrs. Preece pointed to the 'signs
of spring', the children not having been asked. She
proceeded to point to the trees, the sparrow, the
pigeon and the daffodils. The children at the back
of the line who could neither hear nor see her began
to push and to talk. Seeing this, Mrs. Preece in an
aside to me said in a despondent tone:

> These children don't know what to see ...

Mrs. Preece was not alone in her despair. Even
Mrs. Findlay expressed her doubts:

> I sometimes wonder if I'll ever get through
> to them ...

Mrs. Davie, too, had her infrequent moments of
concern:

> I used to worry about not finishing, but not
> now - there's no pressure.

> Paul's good here but what would he be like in
> another school ...?

The 'Stretchers': Explaining the Ideology and Defining its Constraints

The common purpose of the 'stretchers' was not
reducible to a common aetiology. The imputation of
the causal influences on a teacher's ideology is
difficult. It implies that the researcher has access
to the biography of the teachers and the history of
social contexts to which she has been exposed.
Usually there are no written records of these. The
majority of the teachers would have been exposed to
two perhaps contradictory strands of thought:

firstly, the commonplace that society and schooling are meritocratic was vindicated, for them, by the fact that they had achieved their position in the occupational middle class through the acquisition of credentials earned through effort and ability; secondly, all of them had been trained in the immediate post-Plowden era in training colleges which probably gave a grounding in developmental psychology and 'child-centred' education. There is, of course, the prior question of why they became primary school teachers in the first place. The possible answers to that are beyond the scope of the present study. If these two strands of thought were relevant in the teacher's construction of her ideology, why did this group of teachers, the 'stretchers', tend to reject the second in favour of the first, thereby rejecting the official 'ethos' of Mr. McLean?

There are a number of biographical details which may be relevant, but this must be more speculation than assertion. Mrs. Rogers, Mr. Alexander, Mrs. Preece and Mrs. Davie had all taught in other schools. The schools in which Mrs. Preece and Mrs. Rogers had taught had a greater stress on the academic aspect than that afforded by Mr. McLean. Mrs. Preece admitted her preference for private education for her own children. Mr. Alexander had children of his own whom he wanted to do well at school, and he wanted to ensure this outcome for his pupils. Mrs. Findlay's son had trained at university and she saw no reason why some of her own pupils should not succeed in this way. Other constraints may have been at work. The pupil is the bearer of his domestic socialization. Many pupils began their schooling not 'ready' to learn and this lack of readiness was attributed to that socialization. The teachers in the infants school had to 'break them in'. If they did not do this, it would not be done: the children were not thought to be 'naturally' motivated to learn. These infants teachers had much ground to make up and their task was not aided by the absence of remedial teachers. If they were to dwell upon the individual psychologies of their pupils; if they were to wait until the pupils displayed their readiness to learn; if they were to permit the pupils free rein in the classroom, then the conception which they and others had of their role as teachers would be seen as wanting. But not all of the 'stretchers' were infant teachers. Mr. Alexander and Mrs. Rogers taught at Primary 7 level, the year preceding the secondary school where the emphasis was decidedly academic and structured.

It was these teachers who had to prepare the
children as best they could for this transition. An
ideology of 'stretching' would best suit this task.
     A further factor has not been considered, namely
the bureaucratic authority of the head teacher. That
is to say, why were these dissenting teachers
permitted to proceed as they did? Three possibilities
arise. The first suggests that Mr. McLean did not
know what the 'stretchers' thought and did. The
second posits that he was aware of the dissenting
practices and policy but could not muster the power
to make them do otherwise. Thirdly, he was aware of
it, but, in the interests of 'stability', he chose
not to force the issue. In respect of the first
possibility, it would be unlikely that Mr. McLean,
though not a frequenter of the classroom nor a
circulator within the staffroom, would not, over
the years, have failed to become aware of what his
teachers thought and how they acted. Indeed, on
occasions he passed comments about them to me which
indicated this - the definition of Mrs. Rogers as an
'outsider', for example. If the second possibility
were to hold, then there would have been evidence of
his attempts to impose his ideology on the
'stretchers'. No such evidence was found. This
leaves the third possibility. Mr. McLean was not one
to enforce change; the teachers had to see the force
of his argument themselves. Teachers were not
overtly restricted:

> I have as much professional discretion as I
> want. (Mrs. Rogers)

If anything, Mr. McLean was thought not to give
enough guidance or encouragement. He was physically
distant from the staff; he did not comment upon the
reports they made of their pupils; he was reluctant
to deal with difficult children:

> I sometimes think that the boss does not take
> as much responsibility for very badly behaved
> children as he should.

There were no staff meetings. The school, said one
teacher, was 'drifting under its own momentum'. In
other words, it would seem that Mr. McLean preferred
not to risk the open expression of dissenting views.
He did not wish to be placed in the position where
he might have to defend his ethos. By so doing he
preserved the 'stability' within the staff as well
as that between staff and pupils. It might be

suspected that the head teacher, in the twilight of his career, sought to promote a period of organisational 'drift'.

That said, there were organisational arrangements initiated by Mr. McLean, which constrained the staff. The seating arrangement in the classrooms was one which mainly allowed for groups, not individual desks. The lack of remedial provision in Primary 1, 2 and 3 was disapproved of by the teachers, but remained. As mentioned, there were no staff meetings to discuss educational matters. There was his practice of not encouraging testing. Some of the teachers implied that he was indifferent to their work. Indeed, his approach in respect of the 'stretchers' appeared to be one of 'active indifference' to them. A more cynical appraisal might suggest that he knew that, in the face of his indifference and the unpreparedness of the pupils, the 'stretchers' would not succeed.

Summary

The central concern of this chapter has been with the professed ideologies of a group of teachers, the 'stretchers', within an urban primary school. It has also been concerned with the origins and practical consequence of those ideologies, and the extent to which they differed from the ideology of the head teacher. The latter, in the person of Mr. McLean, regarded his pupils as having problems not of their own making. They were the victims of unfortunate circumstances which neither they nor he could ameliorate or reverse. His concern was not with the causes of those circumstances, only with the educational policies and activities which were appropriate for them. In his view, the circumstances were for others to change; he merely dealt with its products in the form of his pupils. Thus, those who found themselves in such straits should be treated at school in a manner which facilitated their acceptance of their predicament. The purpose of the school was not to push the child away from his class situation, only to accommodate him within it. The turbulence of the home should be balanced by a stability in the school. Any practice which added to the psychological damage allegedly inflicted in the home should be removed. The 'child comes first'. Mr. McLean was not interested in meritocratic individualism. In his estimation, few of his pupils would succeed academically even were they to be in a structured and traditional school. The other children should therefore be spared the anguish caused by long-term exposure to the competitive and largely irrelevant regime of such a school. He was intentionally reproducing, or trying to, the class situation of his pupils and he was doing this for what he thought to be well-intentioned and caring reasons.

Some teachers were not persuaded by Mr. McLean's reasoning. It was these so-called 'stretchers' who espoused the meritocratic nature of school and society. Like him, they did not pause to ponder the causes of the class location of their pupils, but unlike him they offered a different treatment of them. These teachers were optimistic that some pupils would succeed and thereby leave behind their less academically successful peers. Education was the only way out of the working class. In their pursuit of academic standards, the 'stretchers' were constrained by the head teacher's perceived lack of concern with what they were trying to do. It was not that Mr. McLean actively sought to make them change; he simply did little to help them. Paradoxically, it was Mr. McLean's espousal of 'stabilization' which seemed to prevent him from imposing that authority and ideology on his dissenting teachers: that is, if he had done so he might have run the risk of resistance by the 'stretchers', thereby disturbing the 'tranquility' between himself and his teachers. He may have come to accept that his policy of stabilization could never be wholly realised and had resigned himself to a period of ideological and organisational 'drift' during the latter years of his headship. Despite the occasional twinges of pessimism among the 'stretchers', they appeared to be firm in their ideology and resolve. Other teachers saw the purpose of teaching at Rockfield to be otherwise, and it is to these teachers that the next chapter turns.

Chapter 5

'STABILIZERS', 'STRADDLERS' AND THE 'POOR RELATIONS'

In the earlier discussion of Schutz's (1967) concept
of 'intersubjectivity' - how we understand each
other - it was argued that he had little to say about
the element of power in social relations. For
Weber, however, the element of domination is never
far away:

> But in most of the varieties of social action
> domination plays a considerable role, even where
> it is not obvious at first sight. (Weber,
> 1978:941)

In the preceding chapter, evidence was adduced to
suggest that the cosy atmosphere which allegedly
pervaded Rockfield School masked 'undercurrents of
conflict', as Mrs. Rogers put it. This lack of
consensus is now discussed using Weber's concepts of
domination and legitimation, and will serve to
introduce the main theme of the present chapter,
namely the development of other ideological differences within the school under study.
        In Weber's definition of domination (Weber,
1978:946), those who claim obedience from others
must have their claim accepted as 'valid' by those
whom they seek to dominate. The dominated must
confer 'legitimacy' upon this claim. What Weber calls
'legitimation' is the leader's attempt to justify
his domination over others. Thus, legitimate domination has occurred when others assign validity to the
leader's claim. This may not always happen;
compliance may not follow. If this occurs, the
claimant to authority may proceed to enforce
compliance on others, but, in so doing, his domination will, in Weberian terms, now be 'illegitimate'.
When coercion begins, legitimate domination ends.
The teacher who coerces a pupil into compliance has

not legitimated his authority over the pupil - for this to happen the pupil must accept the teacher's claim to authority; the pupil must see 'reason'.

Weber offers a threefold typology of 'legitimation', or claims to authority. In modern, industrially developed societies marked by specialism and an advanced division of labour, regardless of the mode of production, the most important type of legitimation will be 'rational-legal'; that is, those who want others to obey them will cite their legal claim to do so. Those individuals who occupy bureaucratic office will expect others to comply with their directives. A second type of legitimation is 'traditional'; that is, those who seek obedience in others will invoke the tradition that they, and their ancestors, have always commanded and received loyalty and compliance. Unlike 'rational-legal' legitimation, where it is the office not the person in which authority lies, 'traditional' authority resides in the person. A third type is 'charismatic' legitimation of authority; that is, domination will be accepted as valid by others because they believe their leader possesses unusual powers which will guide them in a new way of life.

There is an important difference between charismatic authority and the other two types, a difference which is revealed when the moral compliance expected is not forthcoming. In the case of rational-legal authority, the law will enforce compliance if needs be. In the case of traditional authority, a group of armed henchmen of the 'traditional' leader will try to show the recalcitrants the error of their ways. But, in the case of 'pure' charismatic authority, no such means of coercion are available. Nor are they desired. Of course, this typology of legitimation is not a statement of reality; it merely consists of a group of ideal-typical constructs which act as heuristic devices. In the real world, some combination of these claims to legitimate authority may be seen to operate.

Take the case of schools. In a school the head teacher has rational-legal authority over his teachers and pupils. If his claim to legitimate authority is not accepted, then he may either turn a blind eye or try to enforce compliance. It is here that a problem arises. One of the teachers at Rockfield argued that she had as much professional discretion as she wanted. She was not aware of having to comply with rules backed up by rational-legal authority. Thus she may not define her actions as complying with rational-legal authority. She may

think that she is acting out of habit, in the same
way that she never drives on the wrong side of the
road. But driving on a certain side of the road and
coming to school at nine o'clock and leaving at four,
not two, have their initial basis in bureaucratic
rules, although they seem to be merely habitual acts.
If these 'habits' are changed, the rules on which
they are based will be made known and obedience to
them expected.

It may be suggested that a head teacher's
authority, in addition to being based on rational-
legal authority, is also based on traditional
authority. That is to say, teachers and pupils have
always obeyed the head teacher; that is the way it
was, is, and always will be. It is the custom. But,
in Weberian terms, this is not strictly 'traditional'
authority. The difference turns on the fact that,
in the case of rational-legal authority, it is to
the office, not the person, that the subordinate
defers; whilst, in the case of traditional authority,
the subordinate responds to and obeys the person, a
person who, unlike his bureaucratic counterpart, may
bequeath his authority to his offspring. In a
bureaucracy, when the incumbent dies, the office
'lives on' only to be filled by a qualified candidate
who is not a relative of the former official. As for
charismatic authority, there is a case to be put that
head teachers may elicit compliance on the basis of
their magnetic personality. They may be appointed
simply because they exude this or that quality which
it is thought may help get the job done. They may
become celebrities and sometimes the object of near
worship. But the charismatic head teacher who
supports her charisma with a little help from the rod
foregoes her claim to charismatic authority. Through
the use of coercion her domination becomes, in
Weber's view, 'illegitimate'.

Head teachers legitimate their authority usually
on the basis of bureaucratic and charismatic claims,
and the weight afforded to either will vary. At
Rockfield School, Mr. McLean presided over a very
'loose' bureaucratic structure (Bidwell, 1965).
Ironically, his very ideology, that of stabilization,
seemed to prevent him actually ordering his dissenting teachers, the 'stretchers', to comply with the
official ideology. Had he done so the surface
tranquility of his relations with these teachers
might have been disturbed and the desired 'family
atmosphere' darkened. It would seem that Mr. McLean
and the 'stretchers' reached a tacit agreement:
they accepted his bureaucratic authority in matters

of administration; he accepted their professional
discretion to proceed in the classroom virtually
unhindered. The teachers' compliance on matters of
administration did not appear too onerous since much
of what they were required to do in this respect was
viewed by them as 'habit' - taking the register for
example. Thus the legitimacy which the 'stretchers'
conferred on Mr. McLean's rational-legal authority
was both partial and not without hypocrisy:

> Loyalty may be hypocritically simulated by
> individuals or by whole groups on purely
> opportunistic grounds, or carried out in
> practice for reasons of material self-interest.
> (Weber, 1978:214)

Legitimate domination implies that the leader's claim
to dominate has been rendered valid by those who obey
him. They have conferred legitimacy upon the claim.
Our concern has been to apply Weber's classification
of types of domination to the social relationship
between Mr. McLean and the 'stretchers'. Mr. McLean's
claim to authority was not, in the main, accepted by
these teachers. They did not accept his 'rational
argument' (Weber, 1978:946) and nor did they receive
what Weber calls 'inspiration' from him. For his
part, Mr. McLean did not seek to dominate them through
illegitimate means, through coercion. As long as
these teachers adhered to his strictures on the
administration of the school, Mr. McLean tended to
let the matter rest. Weber's classification of
domination does not address the issue of why
legitimacy may or may not be attributed, preferring
to concentrate on how claims to dominate may be
typified. The previous chapter, however, sought to
locate the influences on the 'stretchers'' unwillingness to accept Mr. McLean's authority on matters of
classroom practice by pointing to the ideological
mismatch between Mr. McLean and the 'stretchers'.
That is, the ideology of the 'stretchers', firmly
rooted in meritocratic individualism, could not
allow them to confer legitimacy on what Mr. McLean
was trying to do. By the same token, the ideology
of 'stabilization' espoused by Mr. McLean prevented
him from coercing his teachers into compliance since
coercion was, by definition, inadmissible to his
ideology. This is not to say that he could not have
coerced them. It is to say that, if he had done so,
his 'theory' and 'practice' would not have corres-
ponded. Other headteachers may not manifest this
correspondence. Indeed, as a teacher myself in a

so-called progressive, flexible, open-plan primary
school, I can vividly recall a staff meeting where
the head teacher, an avowed disciple of 'progressi-
vism', firmly banged his fist on the table and
ordered compliance with his philosophy by shouting
'You will be flexible!'.

The 'Stabilizers': 'This School will Never be Academic

Unlike the 'stretchers', a second group of teachers
at Rockfield conferred legitimacy upon Mr. McLean's
claim to authority. In Weber's terms these teachers
complied through 'empathy' and through 'persuasion by
rational argument' (Weber, 1978:946). Defined here
as the 'stabilizers', these teachers (Miss Darby,
Primary 4; Mrs. Scott, Primary 7; Mr. Houston,
Primary 7) shared Mr. McLean's pessimistic and, for
them, realistic claim that the large majority of
pupils at Rockfield were not naturally motivated
towards matters academic. That being so, their
achievement would be negligible and the anxieties
which they would face, if 'stretched',would be to
little avail and to their psychological detriment.
The somewhat more coercive forms of social control
employed by the 'stretchers' would be tantamount to
using those very forms of control for which parents
were criticised. The 'stabilizers', therefore,
legitimated Mr. McLean's authority. They suffered
none of the anxiety which a refusal to comply with
authority sometimes brings. Instead, their anxiety
arose from their interactions with the pupils, a
theme to be developed after a discussion of their
ideology, to which we now turn.
    Both the 'stretchers' and the 'stabilizers'
accepted the assertion that the school's catchment
area was deprived. Where they differed was in their
treatment of deprived pupils. The 'stretchers' were
of the view that 'good teaching' could, with much
effort, overcome the inadequacies of the children's
upbringing. The 'stabilizers' thought this to be
neither possible nor worthwhile. The pupil needed a
level of 'enrichment' and 'compensation' beyond the
school's capacity. It was impossible to resist or
ignore the effects of the home:

    This school will never be academic. I mean
    we're just an institution. We try to fill a
    lot of rules that the kids don't have at home,
    but we are still an institution and we can only
    do a tiny percentage of what can be done in the

97

> home. I mean we can't really touch the child
> to any degree. I do prefer this type of
> teaching. The social demands here are huge and
> there (in her previous school) were minimal,
> and the academic demands there were huge and
> here not so.

This analysis of Miss Darby's was shared by
Mr. Houston:

> I think it's hard to raise them from what they
> are in this school. It's a human institution
> with human failings.

As for the accusation, voiced by the 'stretchers',
that the school cossetted the children, Mr. Houston
thought this to be no bad thing; after all, he had
assumed, with Mr. McLean, that this was what good
inner-city schools were about:

> I suppose there's a more community attitude here,
> which I suppose really does lead to some situa-
> tion where some folk say, 'That kid got away
> with something'. I don't think any environment
> will be too good; I don't see that as an
> argument personally. I don't see the point of
> saying, 'Right. Take away the wallpaper. Take
> away the carpets' - make it horrible or
> anything. I am sure people think the children
> are over-indulged but this, again of course, is
> a school in a deprived area.

Both Mrs. Scott and Miss Darby complained of
'interruptions' which diverted them from teaching.
These took the form of investigating the causes of
fights, bullying, pre-emptive and retaliatory raids
on nearby schools, toilet-flooding, stealing, and
bruises and cuts sustained by the children. Rather
than seeing these as matters for the head or his
deputy, they saw them as their own responsibility,
and so did Mr. McLean:

> Having the time to fulfill these (academic)
> expectations is difficult because we have to
> sort out all these fights because a lot of the
> children are quite aggressive. I spent two-
> thirds of an afternoon last week sorting out a
> hair-pulling, face-scratching fight. And I had
> to do it; I had to find out what had happened.
> (Miss Darby)

> I often say to myself how nice it would be to
> have children who don't have social problems, and
> ours do. I've seen me with a parent complaining
> about something and it was two o'clock when I
> got back to the classroom. And even today
> there's trouble - that's why I was late today.
> The frustration is that we are hampered by these
> interruptions. (Mrs. Scott)

The 'stabilizers' were aware that not all children
were fed a cultural diet as impoverished as this one
depicted by Miss Darby:

> All they have at home is a television set;
> they get their tea; they get a bed. On
> holiday they don't know what to do with
> themselves. And you discover that two-thirds
> of the class have been watching the box from
> morning 'til night.

In other words, there were children from 'good homes',
and more often than not they were the 'good ones',
those who 'gave something back' to the teacher.
These children posed a problem for the 'stabilizers':
were they to be 'stretched' or not?

> You don't stretch the good ones. Some will
> learn in spite of the teachers.

> The good ones will make it anyway.

These assertions will be examined in Chapter 9. They
will be seen to be not well-founded, particularly in
respect of intelligent boys. Nonetheless, this
unwillingness to 'stretch' pupils is consistent with
the ideology of Mrs. Scott, Miss Darby and
Mr. Houston; that is to say, if some pupils were to
reject the 'rational arguments' of the teacher that
they should work harder, the teacher could not,
without violating her ideology, resort to the coercive
methods such as those employed by the 'stretchers'.
This unwillingness to enforce compliance resulted in
some anxiety for those teachers, a theme now
developed.

'Someone has to Suffer Them'

Mrs. Scott and Mr. Houston were liked by their pupils.
They were 'nice' teachers because they did not shout
and they were approachable:

> I like Mr. Houston because he doesn't shout too much.

Mrs. Scott was popular because:

> ... she's nice. You see her and meet her and she talks to you.

One of the most frequently-quoted criteria against which the children, especially girls, judged teachers was according to the loudness and anger of their voices. 'Ones that don't yell' were preferred. It will be recalled that it was the loud and threatening sound of Mr. Alexander which, in his early days at the school, frightened the children and prompted their initial dislike and fear of him. The reputation of Mrs. Davie and Mrs. Findlay for yelling was also strong.

This premium which children placed on quiet teachers was plausibly explained by Diane in Mr. Houston's class. Her father was 'in the pub every night, and on Sunday afternoons'. When drunk he became 'very cross and bad-tempered - I keep out of his way. Mum goes next door to a neighbour's house with cans of beer most nights'. Diane did not mind:

> I can get a bit of peace then.

Her classmate, Fiona, also liked Mr. Houston:

> He doesn't shout at me.

There is thus the suspicion that teachers who did not shout provided some children with a day-time respite from adults at night who did. This might have been even more welcome by those children who lived at Wildwood, the renowned ghetto of 'problem' families. I asked John about life there:

> Are you in a flat or a house?

> Flat - there's no houses, just flats. There's vandals, nothin' but vandals. They smash up the windows and that. The police are round there all the time.

Mindful of these disturbances in the home, Mrs. Scott and Mr. Houston avoided repeating them in the school. Their tolerance of classroom noise and of the lack of concentration, however, had to be weighed against

the need, as they saw it, for some semblance of order
and academic pursuit. Their preferred method of
social control was the repeated appeal for calm and
concentration. Usually the girls heeded the appeal
but most boys did not for any length of time. Then
the appeal was re-stated. Whilst 'stretchers'
would doubtless have resorted to more coercive forms
of ensuring compliance, the ideology of the
'stabilizers' constrained them from doing so. Thus
there is a parallel between the ways in which
Mr. McLean sought the compliance of his teachers and
the reasoned arguments which Mrs. Scott and
Mr. Houston voiced to their own pupils. Neither
Mr. McLean nor these teachers resorted to what Weber
calls 'illegitimate domination', or the use of
coercion to enforce obedience. All three of them
sought normative compliance and moral persuasion.
Coercive methods were not resorted to since their
shared ideology of stabilization did not allow for
them. Mr. McLean seemed indifferent to the dissen-
sion of the 'stretchers'. Mrs. Scott 'suffered' her
'lulus' or 'nutters'. And Mr. Houston construed his
pupils' misdemeanours as humorous:

> I suppose all teachers say their class is
> 'entertaining'.

The classroom appeals for order made by Mrs. Scott
and Mr. Houston were similar in that they were
usually directed at boys. In Mr. Houston's class
the 'top' table comprised all girls. This group
sat nearest his desk whereas the more troublesome
boys were seated at the classroom periphery. The
girls were rarely admonished. Not so the boys:

> There we are again back to the noise again boys.
>
> Jim, Alan, Bruce ... SShhh
>
> Boys stop blethering.
>
> Back to noise again boys.
>
> Boys there we are again ...
>
> Come on boys.
>
> Boys you're scored off my football list if
> you don't get on ...
>
> You don't want to play football ...?

101

A similar pattern emerged in Mrs. Scott's class. By all accounts she had more than her fair share of 'nutters' or 'lulus' or, as Mr. Alexander labelled them, 'gangsters'. Frequent reminders to them to stop 'chattering', or that they were 'not working', or were 'unsettled', were to little avail. They were not 'out of control' but their conversation continued. All of the 'lulus' were boys. Indeed, it seemed at times to Mrs. Scott that she only had boys in her class:

> The trouble with teaching a class of boys ... (In fact, she had thirteen boys and fourteen girls.)

Her well-behaved girls reflected their perceived good home background:

> All my girls come from good homes.

Not all her boys were badly behaved:

> Perhaps I could take the girls to the pictures, but there are a few boys who are good. (The trip to the pictures being a reward for the 'good ones'.)

Where Mrs. Scott and Mr. Houston differed in their quest to elicit normative compliance was in the nature of 'the rational arguments' which they made. Mrs. Scott confined her appeals for order to terse prohibitory remarks such as 'stop chattering', or 'you're not working', or 'you are becoming unsettled'. Whilst Mr. Houston issued such cryptic commands, as mentioned in relation to the boys in his class, he was also given to more persuasion:

> Try and be reasonable. You're being trusted.

> You've got to do the things you don't like doing first.

> The swing park is not part of the school. Swinging swings around the bar is forbidden. You have to abide by normal rules.

Nevertheless, in both classrooms the respite from from 'chatter' and lack of concentration was only temporary, perhaps because the children knew that sterner measures would not be taken against them. Similarly, the 'stretchers' had carried on in their own way in the face of Mr. McLean's failure to obtain their compliance. Mr. McLean, however, could physically distance himself from those whose compliance he sought. Mrs. Scott and Mr. Houston had to face their intransigent pupils. A head teacher can ignore dissenting teachers but a teacher cannot ignore dissenting pupils. There is, therefore, a certain altruism in Mrs. Scott's and Mr. Houston's 'suffering': through their tolerance their pupils did not have to face the coercive kind of control which was thought to be used in the home. The 'stretchers', on the other hand, might have argued that this altruism was merely a short-term expediency which might lead to long-term 'suffering' endured by unemployment brought on by a lack of academic credentials.

We turn now to the academic demands made of their pupils by Mr. Houston and Mrs. Scott. Here it is only reasonable to compare them to Mr. Alexander since they all taught the same age group. On matters of assessment, Mr. Alexander tested after every piece of work. Not so Mr. Houston:

The value of tests is limited.

Nor for Mrs. Scott. A former pupil of hers told me that Mrs. Scott tested:

About once a year or something like that.

The frequency of testing is not, of itself, indicative of the effectiveness of a teacher. But the form of testing is implicit of a teacher's ideology. Mr. Alexander, for example, relied upon norm-referenced tests given to all pupils at the same time. This form of testing implies open competition and the public portrayal of success and failure. Pupils exposed to this form of assessment are socialised into an acceptance of hierarchy derived from the result of a supposedly fair contest. Pupils who are not exposed to this form of testing may be socialized into thinking that the yardstick of an individual's worth is the capability of that individual, not that of a standardised, 'average' individual. All this is not to say that children will passively accept these forms of schooling. It is merely to say that these forms are consequences of ideology which have as their intended ends this or that kind of psychology.

Finally, the nomenclature of 'stretching' and 'stabilizing' implies, in common parlance, that

children who are taught by the former group of
teachers will work harder than those taught by the
latter. At a subjective level, this would appear to
be so, simply on the basis that in Mrs. Scott's and
Mr. Houston's classes the pupils did not look as
industrious as those in Mr. Alexander's and
Mrs. Findlay's class. It might be argued that a
between-teacher comparison of the incidence, measured
quantitatively, of commands to work which teachers
made to their pupils might settle the matter. This
is to be doubted. Say two teachers during the same
time-span uttered the same number of admonitions to
the same number of children doing the same kinds of
task. Could it be inferred that both groups of
pupils were working at similar levels of industry?
For this inference to be correct, it must be assumed
that what constituted for one teacher a lack of
concentration would be so defined by another teacher.
Different teachers tend to have different definitions
of what constitutes a particular kind of behaviour.
What Mr. Alexander may define as unacceptable 'noise'
might be unremarkable for Mrs. Scott and Mr. Houston.
In an attempt to confirm my subjective view, two
comments from two children taught by Mr. Houston are
cited:

> DH: Is there anything you don't like about
>   the school?
>
> Donald: There's not enough work in school.
>
> DH: Not enough!
>
> Donald: Not enough.
>
> DH: Are you being serious? What would
>   you like to do? That means there's
>   too much play ...
>
> Donald: Yes, in Primary 7 anyway.
>
> DH: Why is there too much play?
>
> Donald: Well, we've got fifteen minutes (break)
>   in the morning, fifteen in the after-
>   noon and one and a half hours at dinner
>   time. On Fridays we get all afternoon
>   off - most of the day. And today
>   (a Thursday) we've hardly had any work
>   at all.

DH: Why not?

Donald: Mr. Houston's been out a lot.

I asked a pupil, then in high school, if she missed
her Rockfield teachers:

            Yes.

DH: Why?

            I don't know. Sometimes Mr. Houston
            would let you play all day, but here
            you've got to work all day.

This limited evidence that children in Mrs. Scott's
and Mr. Houston's classes had lower academic demands
made of them than those in the classrooms of the
'stretchers' is not to imply criticism of the former
and commendation of the latter. It is merely to
suggest that, for both types of teacher, there
appeared to be a correspondence between their
respective ideologies and classroom practice. This
correspondence should not, however, always be assumed:
a teacher may profess one 'theory' and practice
another. So it was with Miss Darby whom I typified
as a 'stabilizer' on the basis of her professed
views, but who, when observed, came far closer to
the classroom practice of the 'stretchers' than did
Mrs. Scott and Mr. Houston. That she did so does
not, however, require her being 're-typed' as a
'stretcher' for there were still important differences between her practice and that of the 'stretchers',
a theme which is now developed.

Miss Darby

Miss Darby shared the pessimistic notion that the
cultural discontinuities between home and school
prevented the school becoming academic. But her
avowal of the social pathology model did not mean
that very little academic work should be attempted.
What was required was a level of teacher expectation
which was mindful of the difficulties which the
children had. And whilst she acknowledged that
coercion was not the way, for the same reasons stated
by the other 'stabilizers', she was not above its
use if all else failed. In short, Miss Darby sought
a 'framework' for her children:

        I give them structure, ritual and routine.

This is not unlike Mrs. Findlay's statement:

> They (the pupils) know where they stand.

However, Miss Darby did not agree with 'stretching' and was not optimistic that the school could help the child to succeed academically. She did not accept the practice of 'suffering' the children who would not respond to calls to concentrate, as had Mrs. Scott. Unlike Mrs. Scott and Mr. Houston, Miss Darby had taught in a very traditional, middle-class area school before coming to Rockfield. Mrs. Scott and Mr. Houston had taught exclusively under Mr. McLean's headship. This difference may partly explain her more structured classroom practice, even though she shared the 'realistic' appraisal of Mr. McLean that Rockfield School could never be academic. This observed difference between the practice of Miss Darby, and of Mrs. Scott and Mr. Houston, is now discussed.

Miss Darby was a quiet teacher who rarely lost her composure. As with Mr. Houston, her preferred method of social control was to remind and explain to the pupil that something was amiss, as illustrated in this comment to Mandy:

> Mandy, you've had long enough. We're not having a race but I've given you plenty of time. Have you been writing very neatly in your new jotter? Oh yes. That's why she's been slow.

An interesting theory which was put to the children was that cleanliness and correctness were causally related:

> Ian. I think maybe you'd go and give your face a wash. Your answers are just wild this after-noon.

Another form of awakening the children's interest was 'stretch time':

> A good stretch ... All stand up. STRETCH ... BIG S T R E T C H. Flop down. And up again.

If a reminder, wash or stretch did not have the desired effect, then a sterner measure was effected, as in the case of Darren who had infringed the rule against tipping his chair back onto two legs. He was told not to. A few minutes later Miss Darby suspected he was actually about to stand on the chair:

> Darren. Would you sit down. Don't you dare
> stand up on the chair.

The final sanction was the belt:

> Miss Darby doesn't like giving it but when she
> gives it she gives it properly. She gives it
> to you hard so that you don't do it again.

Perhaps Miss Darby's sparing use of corporal punishment rested on her suspicion that if it did not
produce obedience, then nothing remained, as had
been the case with Veryll in Mrs. Findlay's class.
However, Miss Darby also appeared to have met her
match in Ian:

> Ian just sits and smiles and Miss Darby hates
> that. And one time she gave him the belt and
> he was sitting there smiling ...

What distinguished the classroom dialogue between
teacher and pupil in Miss Darby's class, as compared
to that in the classrooms of Mr. Houston and
Mrs. Scott, was a ready willingness and ability to
commend the pupil for good work. Miss Darby ensured
her pupils' compliance; Mrs. Scott sometimes
suffered a lack of it. Part of Miss Darby's repertoire
for doing so was to commend her pupils, thereby
involving them in work, not misbehaviour. In this
respect, Miss Darby differed also from Mr. Houston.
The framework which Miss Darby desired for her
children took the form of grouping the children for
reading, a practice found also in Mrs. Scott's and
Mr. Houston's classrooms. Some of her pupils elaborated upon the arrangement:

> DH: Do you have groups for reading?
>
> Yes.
>
> DH: You do. Tell me about them. How many
> groups are there Sharon?
>
> ERM!
>
> DH: OK. Let's take you. Which group are you
> in? Who is in your group?
>
> Susan, Karen.
>
> DH: That's one group. Tell me about another

group.

Christopher, Rachel, Sue and Ronald.

DH: Good. Tell me about another group.

Laura and Craig.

DH: So that's just a tiny group?

Yes.

And then there's Jim and Harry Bowen.

DH: They're in a small group together?

Yes.

There's Muhesh, Anwar and Narinder.

DH: Does anyone sit on their own?

Michelle.

DH: Good. The next question is, 'Which is the best group? Which one is on the top books?

We're on the highest books.

DH: Whose group comes next?

Christopher's group.

This stratification of reading groups appears to
contradict Mr. McLean's wish that pupils not be
ranked in relation to each other. Miss Darby did
not have names for these groups, referring to them
by calling out the name of someone in them. The
pupils' perception that Sharon's and Christopher's
groups were ranked in that order was confirmed by
Miss Darby. However, the grouping of children on
the basis of their reading achievement was not intended primarily to stratify them; it was done to
facilitate the teacher's hearing them read and it
gave them a sense of group belonging. The stratification was the unintended consequence.

The 'framework' which Miss Darby provided was
'looser' than the more rigid structure of the
'stretchers'. Three examples of this may be cited.
Firstly, like the 'stretchers', Miss Darby used
tests, though less frequently and in a slightly

different way. The pupils in Miss Darby's class were
tested every two weeks for spelling. Similar oral
tests were conducted by Mrs. Davie and Mrs. Letham
which publicly revealed the success and failure of a
pupil to answer. In Miss Darby's class, a pupil's
score remained private unless the pupil wished to
disclose it:

> DH: What sort of test is it?
>
> Spelling and numbers.
>
> No, we don't have the numbers now.
>
> DH: So it's just spelling. Who marks the test?
>
> Miss Darby.
>
> We never do it.
>
> DH: When Miss Darby has everybody's mark, does
>   she read them all out to the class or does
>   she just tell you privately what you've
>   got?
>
> No. She doesn't tell anybody. She shows
> us our test paper.

A second example indicated Miss Darby's more relaxed
regime. The children in her classroom did not have
to line up before leaving the room at playtime:

> DH: When the playtime bell goes do you have to
>   line up, or do you just walk out?
>
> Yes.
>
> DH: Do you ever have to line up?
>
> No.
>
> DH: Have you been in a class where you did have
>   to line up?
>
> Yes, with Mrs. Letham.

In a third example, again in comparison with
Mrs. Letham, the 'reality' of the children was
permitted some credence. It may be recalled that
Mrs. Letham would point out for correction any
mistakes in the children's art work. In this example

in Miss Darby's class, the pupil, with some hesita-
tion on the teacher's part, was permitted to preserve
his reality. The incident in question occurred
whilst the children were drawing a picture of a
hermit's hut, the hermit and his lifestyle having
been the subject of a class-based activity on
listening skills:

> Miss Darby: I don't think you should do huts
> bright red. The hermit did not
> want to be seen.
>
> Pupil: (inaudible)
>
> Miss Darby: You chose red because you've got
> new red pencils! It's not a very
> good reason ... Oh well, it's your
> picture.

The link, therefore, between the 'stretchers' and
the 'stabilizers' is Miss Darby. Her professed
ideology accorded well with that of the 'stabilizers'.
Her practice struck a balance between the tight
framework and discipline of the 'stretchers' with
the greater individualism of the 'stabilizers'. As
such, her classroom practice 'straddled' the two,
but her ideology was typical of 'stabilization'. We
turn now to two teachers whose ideology and practice
were more consistently definable as taking in aspects
of both the ideologies of 'stretching' and of
'stabilization'. To this third group of teachers,
the label 'straddlers' is assigned.

The 'Straddlers': Mrs. Stewart and Mrs. Carter

In his study of three infants' schools, King showed
that the teachers, with a few exceptions, character-
istically displayed 'professional pleasantness,
affection and equanimity' (King, 1978:70).
Mrs. Stewart, a Primary 1 teacher, and Mrs. Carter,
a Primary 5 teacher, shared with the teachers in the
schools King studied, and with Miss Darby, a
continuing display of composure before their pupils –
a caring, how-are-we-getting-along-today smile, a
gentle touch of affection, a willingness to understand
a pupil's actions as seen by the pupil. To this,
however, was added a structure for the children in
which they knew what was expected of them, but one
which did not coerce them into achievement.
    A number of examples may illustrate the more
indirect and individualised approach of Mrs. Stewart

110

and Mrs. Carter in matters of social control. In
Mrs. Stewart's class, Leslie had pulled Nichola's
hair whilst they had been in the Wendy House.
Nichola began to cry, but before admonishing Leslie,
Mrs. Stewart sat Nichola on her lap and comforted
her. Another pupil in her class seemed to have a
knack of getting into trouble, but:

> He can't stop being silly sometimes.[1]

The boy in question, Rakesh, was receiving steroid
treatment for a kidney ailment and this was thought
to be partly responsible for his behaviour.
Mrs. Stewart was reluctant to get 'angry' with him:

> If I get cross he just won't say anything, just
> clams up.

Thus her approach was more indirect:

> Mrs. Mack isn't pleased with you either and has
> put you back to group one.

If a word of encouragement could balance a word of
criticism, then it was to be preferred:

> That's nice Catherine, but doesn't your daddy
> wear trousers? (Mrs. Stewart)[2]

> Is it a bid hard? Just try your best. You'll
> manage, I'm sure. (Mrs. Carter)

> There's a chatterbox. Come on nicely then.
> (Mrs. Carter)

In Mrs. Carter's class her method of 'winning over'
the boys was decidedly different from that employed
by Mrs. Scott and Mr. Houston. Her general explanation of the difficult behaviour of boys was to say
that they were at the age when they were 'fluttering
their wings, showing their horns'. This metaphorical
summary of the psychological 'stage' of their
development was a theory at odds with that 'home
background' theory posited by Mrs. Scott, Mr. Houston
and Miss Darby. Her policy was to 'boost their
confidence'. But it was more than that. Again in
respect of the boys, she attempted to give academic
recognition to the commonsense which her boys brought
to the school.[3] Much of their commonsense centred
on football, as was the case in Mr. Houston's class.
But whereas Mr. Houston threatened to delete badly

behaved boys from his football list, or to confiscate
their football cards, Mrs. Carter incorporated
football into classroom knowledge. Children would
write up reports of international matches which they
had seen on television as contributions to 'Sports
Projects'. Even the girls took part:

> Some girls did excellent football projects.
> They collected the cards in class.

Mrs. Carter did not share the 'stabilization'
ideology. 'Stabilization', for Mrs. Carter, was not
the only purpose of the school as she saw it. Some
stress on academic standards was also in order. For
her, the 'stabilization' should be incidental and
secondary to the academic. Although Mr. McLean
declared Mrs. Carter to be 'a very intelligent woman
with a degree', she allegedly did not understand
what he was 'trying to do'. Mrs. Carter was interested in a balance between the academic and the child-
comes-first purposes of the school, the balance being
slightly weighted in favour of the former. Nowhere
was this divergence of the views of Mrs. Carter and
Mr. McLean more discernible than in the construction
of pupil identities. Staffroom banter often resorted
to discussion of the children from this or that
family. Pupil reputations were confirmed and
furthered. Take the case of Alastair who had
previously been a pupil at Rockfield and who had gone
elsewhere only to return one morning to be placed in
Mrs. Scott's room. He was made very welcome. She
took his overcoat and hung it up on the coatrack,
placing it on a coathanger before doing so. Alastair
was obviously not used to this kind of service.
Mrs. Scott explained:

> We're posh here!

At lunchtime, Mrs. Scott remarked that Alastair had
returned, feeling a little dejected:

> Mrs. Scott: He didn't want to leave Kildonan.
>
> Mrs. Leith: He had poor attendance here - a
>   pain in the neck.
>
> Miss Darby (who had taught him previously):
>   A poor wee soul - a rejectee.

The most damaging identity a pupil could acquire was
that of 'dead horse', a pupil deemed to be

intellectually incapable of keeping up with the other
pupils. Mr. McLean's policy for such pupils was
tersely summarised by his well-known declaration:

>   Don't flog 'dead horses'.

Mrs. Carter objected strongly to this early condemna-
tion of pupils. She cited the case of Roy, now in her
class:

>   Roy had shown difficulties from Primary 1 to
>   Primary 3. Mr. McLean regarded him as a
>   'vegetable' and considered that remedial help
>   would be 'wasted'. In Primary 4, Ian was put
>   for daily remedial reading and, in Primary 5,
>   maths and reading twice weekly. He is making
>   progress, can now write stories, answers well
>   in oral class work and in his reading group.

Mrs. Carter, like the 'stretchers', was optimistic
that the pupil, with encouragement, could succeed
academically. She was willing to see the pupil's
viewpoint:

>   Poor ability sometimes causes frustration.

But she was not willing to see no work being done.
A quick snap of the fingers and a quiet reminder had
the desired effect:

>   Let me see the noses to the grindstone.

Her approach was reminiscent of Waller's (1932)
description of the good teacher, one who 'lengthens
and shortens the rubber band of social distance with
consummate ease'. This view was shared by a former
colleague of Mrs. Carter:

>   She's brilliant. She's one of the few who has
>   whatever it takes. She's the most brilliant
>   teacher you could ever get your hands on. It's
>   difficult to explain. Mrs. Carter doesn't shout
>   a lot, doesn't punish a lot, but she gets the
>   most amazing work out of these kids. She's
>   fantastic. She treats children exactly the way
>   they ought to be treated - not harshly, not
>   soft; just right.

Mrs. Stewart also sought a balance. In her Primary 1
class, the children knew where things were and
returned them; they tip-toed to line-up before

playtime; after playtime they came in and sat down, arms folded, the 'best' pupils being allowed their milk first; they were rewarded with time in the Wendy House where they could draw the curtains, but only four at a time were permitted access; they were liberally praised by the teacher; they went at their own rate after some guidance from the teacher ('I usually do the first exercises with them sitting at their table'); their work was continually assessed:

> DH: How do you get to change your reading books?
>
> When you've finished your book you get another book. You take your book home and read it and then you get another book.
>
> We get a sheet.
>
> DH: Sorry, tell me about these sheets.
>
> There's lines on them and you have to write something in the sheet.
>
> DH: What do you have to write in the sheet?
>
> Like, how do animals live?
>
> DH: Oh I see. So this is like questions about the book.
>
> Yes, and there's pictures that you have to colour it.
>
> DH: And you take that to Mrs. Stewart do you?
>
> Yes.
>
> DH: What if its's wrong?
>
> You have to rub it out and do it again.

The close supervision by Mrs. Stewart did not involve her having to shout at and coerce her pupils. They happily skipped about the room in a purposeful manner. During the afternoons, 'work' was replaced by 'play', except for those children who needed 'remedial play', an attempt on Mrs. Stewart's part to cope with the lack of remedial provision until Primary 4. During 'play' the boys monopolised the trucks and 'drove' them around the carpeted floor,

mimicking with great accuracy the noises of the
engine and gearbox. Sometimes 'crashes' occurred and
tempers flared only to be extinguished by
Mrs. Stewart's prompting that they could come over to
the 'work side' if they didn't calm down. The girls
preferred the sand-tray and the Wendy House. Other
activities included roulette, Lego, bricks and
painting.

But despite the loose structure of Mrs. Stewart's
classroom, it could not contain James. Neither
persuasion nor coercion had much effect. As with
Mrs. Scott's 'lulus', James was tolerated. (His 'case'
is discussed more fully in the next chapter.) No
matter what Mrs. Stewart said or did, James went his
own way. Suffice it here to say that he had been
expelled from the Nippers Nursery for spitting at a
nursery assistant. On his first day in Primary 1
with Mrs. Stewart he had entered the Wendy House and
had refused to come out. He had sworn at the teacher.
His mischief ranged from merely wandering aimlessly
about the room to very audible belching, to flicking
paint and to requesting to go to the toilet more
than seemed necessary. He was constantly reminded
to behave but usually didn't. On the other hand he
was praised whenever he did something to
Mrs. Stewart's approval. For James, Mrs. Stewart
bent the rules in a way that Mrs. Findlay had not
done for Veryll. His bad behaviour allegedly began
immediately after the divorce of his parents. Whilst
he was not entirely innocent he was culpable with
extenuating circumstances. Mrs. Stewart 'couldn't
help liking him - he can be so nice sometimes'.

In summary, what typified the ideology of the
'straddlers' was a willingness to take from the
'stabilizers' a concern for the child as an individual
in difficult home circumstances, and from the
'stretchers' an optimism that the children at Rockfield could succeed academically. At the level of
classroom practice, the 'straddlers', like the
'stabilizers', were able to empathise with their
pupils and to make exceptions for lower standards of
work and behaviour if there were good reasons beyond
the pupil's control to explain them. The pupils
were seen to be partly innocent of their misdemeanours. They were regarded as responding better to a
kind word of encouragement than to loudly-expressed
admonition. The 'straddlers' were also similar to
the 'stretchers' in that they provided a structure
in which the children knew what was expected of
them.

The 'Poor Relations'

The analysis of teachers' ideologies at Rockfield
School has purported to show that, although different
groups of teachers did not always share each other's
views, there was little surface antagonism among
them. Whilst some teachers stated their goals to be
at odds with those of Mr. McLean, I did not overhear
any criticism of one teacher by another amongst the
three groups of teachers so far discussed. There
remains a fourth group of teachers - the members of
the Immigrant Department. Amongst the 'stretchers',
'stabilizers' and 'straddlers' there was the
occasional whiff of resentment towards the 'immigrant
teachers', as they were called. This elicited a
defensive posture from the latter to justify their
status. The criticism to which the 'immigrant
teachers' responded was twofold: firstly, it was
said that, as a special unit, they were superfluous;
secondly, that as teachers they had a less onerous
time than the classroom teachers. These are now
considered.
    There was a view amongst some teachers,
especially the 'stretchers', that the 'immigrant
teachers' could be better used if they were re-defined
and re-used as remedial teachers, not teachers of a
second language. This view was taken partly because
there was no remedial provision, except in Primary 4
and 5, for white pupils with learning difficulties.
Matters were not helped either by Mr. McLean's vague
policy on which children should receive more individual help in the Immigrant Department; that is,
should all ethnic minority children, regardless of
their spoken and written English, go to the Immigrant
Department, or should only those who lacked the
rudiments of the language be sent? It was said that
Mr. McLean was sometimes, not always, of the view
that the Immigrant Department provided not only
worthwhile linguistic instruction, but cultural as
well. In general, his policy was seen as ambivalent:

> Mr. McLean blows hot and cold about whether to
> send all the 'immigrants' to the Immigrant
> Department.

What appeared to be the prevalent practice, however,
was for the classroom teacher to negotiate on behalf
of an ethnic minority pupil whom she thought would
benefit from a period in the Immigrant Department.
This negotiation was normally with the teacher in
charge of the Immigrant Department, not with

'STABILIZERS', 'STRADDLERS' AND THE 'POOR RELATIONS'

Mr. McLean. And by the same token, when it was
thought by the teachers in the Immigrant Department
that a particular ethnic minority pupil was 'ready
to go back to the classroom', they would negotiate
with the classroom teacher whether or not the pupil
should be returned to the classroom.

Some of the classroom teachers took the view
that some ethnic minority pupils were better provided
for than their white counterparts. The point was
made that some white pupils 'spoke another language',
but were not given the remedial and individual help
that would improve their English usage:

> I think the white children are discriminated
> against.
>
> The provision for the 'immigrants' is better
> than for those who have learning difficulties.
> One of them (i.e. a teacher in the Immigrant
> Department) should be remedial.

The three teachers in the Immigrant Department, only
one of whom was of ethnic minority status,
rejected the remedial teacher status which some
teachers wanted for them:

> You know, people often say that teaching
> 'immigrants' is remedial, but they're not
> remedial children - it's not because they
> haven't the ability to learn. We are not
> qualified to be remedial.

In response to this view, it was pointed out, though
not by a teacher in the school, that although two of
the teachers spoke the language of the ethnic
minority children, none of the teachers in the
Immigrant Department had been formally trained in
the teaching of English as a foreign language. As
if to allay any fears that they were the professional
inferiors of their classroom colleagues, the point
was made, with some force, that:

> Not only are we trained teachers, two (out of
> three) of us are graduates (as opposed to only
> three of the thirteen classroom teachers).

A second source of contention was the widely-held
opinion that being a teacher in the Immigrant Department was something of a soft option: 'They have less
hassle', as Mrs. Carter put it. For example, there
were said to be fewer administrative tasks for the

teachers in the Immigrant Department to attend to.
Their classes were far smaller. Furthermore, the
unit was at the top of the school, away from the
corridors and the noise, as well as away from the
inquisitive gaze of others. Thus, when the declared
success of the 'immigrant teachers' fell on other
ears it met with some derision:

> The 'immigrant teachers' say that so-and-so
> has really come along. So could ours if we
> gave them that much attention.

It was also indicated that one of the teachers in the
Immigrant Department was appointed to work beside a
classroom teacher. This had not been done. The
teacher in question argued that this would have
produced problems over areas of responsibility in
the classroom. The teacher from the Immigrant
Department felt that she was the 'visitor invading
the teacher's territory'. By implication, her status
as a teacher might have been perceived as simply that
of 'teacher aide'.

The 'less hassle' observation brought its own
defence. Mrs. Poyner, a teacher in the Immigrant
Department, inverted the argument:

> Mind you, to compare what the children are
> doing down in the classroom from 9 a.m. to
> 1.30 ... you know, they'll maybe have an R.E.
> story, maybe do some hymn practice and then
> they'll maybe have a little language, arts and
> a little written work, and then they'll do their
> reading. Ours work from 9 a.m. 'til 10.30 with
> their heads down the whole time. I think they work
> harder than they do in the classroom.

To the accusation that they had more free time ('You
go up there and they're standing around chatting'),
the argument was again reversed:

> Teachers have free time when the class has
> music, and art and needlework. We have no free
> time.

The position of the teachers in the Immigrant Department was not without its irony. Although they were
a separate department, they insisted on their being
part of the school, not outsiders:

> We're not a separate group - we're part of the
> school. And if there's a teacher off we go

and take classes.

Thus it was the very department in the school which
had been established to better integrate the ethnic
minority pupils into the school which was itself
having difficulties being integrated. And, in a
manner not dissimilar to that in which ethnic
minorities in society at large are viewed, these
'immigrant teachers' were in something of a double
bind: if they entered the classroom they would be
seen as 'invading' the teacher's territory; if they
withdrew to their department to do the job, they were
open to accusations of being distant and isolated.
A second irony is that much of the criticism levied
against them came from that very group, the
'stretchers', with whom their ideology was most at
one. Both were self-professed adherents to the
academic purpose of the school.
Although the teachers in the Immigrant Department were physically distant from their classroom
colleagues, as well as feeling different from them,
they could not avoid contact with them. As stated
earlier, this contact took the form of a negotiation
between 'immigrant' and classroom teachers about
whether a given ethnic minority pupil was 'ready to
go back into the classroom full-time':

DH: Who decides when the child is ready
                to go downstairs permanently?

'Immigrant'
teacher: Well, I decide - we decide (that is
                all the 'immigrant teachers') but we
                go to the teacher and give him our
                opinion about a child's ability
                compared with how the other
                children in the class perform.

DH: And what if the teacher were to
                disagree?

'Immigrant'
teacher: So far we haven't come to a point
                where we would say, 'Look he's good
                enough', and the teacher says, 'No' -
                not a single case. Well you notice
                it's the other way round. It's
                usually the teacher who says,
                'They've come on so well; I think
                they can cope'. And you feel they're
                a bit shakey and they need more

119

> perhaps, and then you tell the
> teacher, 'Right, since you think
> like that you keep them, but if you
> find you're having difficulty, just
> send them back'.

Relations between the classroom teachers and those
in the Immigrant Department were not always cordial,
as this comment by a classroom teacher suggests:

> They think they know what the child needs. I'm
> not speaking to them at the moment.

What complicated matters was the fact that the ethnic
minority children were released for part of the day
to the Immigrant Department. Only rarely would a
pupil spend all day 'upstairs'. It was admitted by
teachers in the Immigrant Department that the pupils
who went there became emotionally attached to it.
These teachers understood the classroom teacher's
feeling that she 'might lose her children'. But
this was a concern with little foundation, as
Mrs. Poyner admitted:

> They're not our children.

These views of 'immigrant' and classroom teachers
support the interpretation that primary school
teachers, whose occupationally-defined class position
is the same, reveal differences which undermine the
notion that their perceived status is also shared.
Beneath the public rhetoric of shared professionality
are claims to professionalism (Hoyle, 1974) which
are various and in conflict. Indeed, when the
teachers as a whole at Rockfield labelled their
school as 'Skid Row' and the 'End of the Line' they
were saying things about their own status as teachers
as well as the status of their school compared
to normal schools. These status differences can be
attacked using carefully prepared appeals to 'reason',
as was the case with the teachers in the Immigrant
Department. Nevertheless, the status which others
assign may, in unguarded moments, be admitted:

> I think the teachers think we're the poor
> relations ... (Teacher: Immigrant Department)

Summary

It has been a continuing theme of the previous two
chapters to question the functionalist assertion that

the ideologies of teachers are reducible to the
official ideology of the school. The teacher is
supposed to undertake her duties in the manner
prescribed. A consensus of purpose between teachers
and head teacher is assumed. A school observed,
however, may reveal no such agreement. A Weberian
action approach provides a methodology of understanding the meanings which individuals assign to the
roles, the organisational structure, in which they
find themselves. These meanings and interpretations
of the structure will sometimes differ, as will the
ideologies which underpin them. Part of the
observer's task is to understand these individual
ideologies and to typify them on the basis of their
shared properties into second order constructs, or
'ideal-types'. The validity of these typifications
may then be tested using a variety of complementary
sources. Thus at Rockfield School the typifications
of teachers' ideologies were set against evidence
from pupils, colleagues, documents and first-hand
observation. In some instances the typification
failed the test, so to say. That is, the professed
ideology of the teacher was not an adequate account
of her pedagogical practice as seen by others. Thus
it was in the case of Miss Darby whose professed
ideology of stabilization was associated with a
classroom performance more akin to that of
Mrs. Carter and Mrs. Stewart, the 'straddlers'. In
other cases the practised ideology among those whose
professed ideology was shared was sometimes at
variance. For example among the 'stretchers', it
was found that Mrs. Letham, Mrs. Findlay, Mrs. Davie
and Mr. Alexander commended their pupils whilst
Mrs. Rogers and Mrs. Preece tended not to.
     In Weber's sociology, social relations reveal
conflict among different groups who seek to maximise
their power and status at the expense of others.
This conflict may not be explicit. So it was at
Rockfield. Mr. McLean did not seek to dominate his
teachers other than by legitimate means. If the
teachers did not understand and accept what he was
trying to do, he did not force the issue. All he
did was to preserve some minor organisational
arrangements which would facilitate the realisation
of his own ideology and of those who supported it,
and, at the same time, limit the actions of those
who did not. As for ideological conflict among the
'stretchers', 'straddlers and 'stabilizers', it
would be more accurate to define them not as open
conflicts but as rarely articulated differences in
ideology. For the most part, the 'conflict' was

latent rather than manifest. This was mainly because
the day-to-day activities of the teachers did not
require their having to consult and to negotiate
with each other. Classroom doors were kept closed.
Teachers could be oblivious to each other when
teaching, save for 'interruptions'. Even the cooper-
ation among teachers which often occurs at the end
and beginning of a year on syllabus continuity and
assessment was reduced because at Rockfield teachers
would have the same class for two or three years.
The virtual absence of staff meetings further
diminished the opportunity for differences in
ideology to be aired.
     The school was not, however, devoid of explicit
conflict. Two sources for this were found. The
first involved relations between the classroom
teachers and those in the Immigrant Department.
Here was a classic instance of different groups
seeking to degrade the other's professional status.
Both groups issued reasons to support its own higher
status and indispensibility, and, at the same time,
undermine the status of the other group. Both groups
were protective of their territory and sought to
maximise control over 'our children', not 'theirs'.
A second source of conflict, one little discussed so
far, resided in the interactions between teacher and
pupil. Here the level of conflict was associated
with the ideology of the teacher and the recalci-
trance of the pupil. That is to say, the ideology
of the teacher would imply the ways in which she
would 'treat' good and poor work and behaviour. The
'stabilizers', though not Miss Darby, appeared to be
in a continual negotiation for order with different
pupils. These pupils resisted the urgings of the
teacher to work because they knew that coercion
would not ensue. Had these same pupils faced the
'stretchers', then coercion might not have been
spared. Nevertheless, virtually all teachers, even
the strictest, experienced pupil resistance which
they could not wholly resolve. Indeed, the teachers
expected this to occur occasionally since they took
in pupils who would not usually be admissible to a
'normal' school. These pupils constrained their
teachers. How and why they did so is now discussed.

Chapter 6

'NUTTERS', 'TRAGEDIES' AND 'DEAD HORSES'

The concern of the preceding chapter was to point up
the ideological differences which obtained among the
staff at Rockfield School and to suggest some of the
influences upon their construction. Among these
influences were the individual biographies of
teachers, the bureaucratic power of the head teacher
and the nature of the school's catchment area as
personified in the pupils themselves. At the level
of teacher consciousness, it was the last of these
which posed limitations on their classroom practice
and on their educational ideologies. The teachers
were aware of the inner-city label attached to their
school and the presumed deprivation of their pupils.
This deprivation they took for granted - they, as
teachers, could not remove the material deficiencies
which the families in the catchment area had to face.
Some of the teachers, in particular the 'stretchers',
were motivated to provide an academic education which
could be used as a means for the children to find
their way out of their working class environment.
For this to occur it meant that both teachers and
pupils had to surmount the 'deficiencies' which many
children brought to the school. In short, these
teachers sought to compensate for the 'background'
of their pupils. This optimistic endeavour of the
'stretchers' was not shared by the 'stabilizers'.
The latter, who included the head teacher, were
persuaded by the argument that so great were the
handicaps which many of the children possessed that
the aims of the 'stretchers' were beyond the capaci-
ties of both teachers and pupils. These handicaps
had various manifestations: a 'bad attitude'
towards school work; a home background so tragic
that the teacher often felt herself compelled to
engage in 'social work' rather than teaching; a
lack of ability on the pupils' part. Pupils who

revealed one of these handicaps in an extreme form
were categorized as follows: poor behaviour meant
being labelled a 'nutter'; very difficult home
circumstances faced by a child would qualify the
child as a 'tragedy'; poor ability attracted the
label 'dead horse'. Pupils who were defined in one
or more of these ways could limit the teacher's
ability to discharge her duties in a manner commensurate with her professed ideology. In some cases,
however, the ideology had to be changed if the
exigencies of the classroom situation meant that the
teacher realised she could never effect it. This
pragmatically-induced shift was seen as an effective
coping procedure in the face of frustration. In
what follows, a discussion on some individual
'nutters','tragedies' and 'dead horses' is undertaken
with a view to examining the ways in which individual
teachers coped with the potential limits to their
classroom practice when they were faced with pupils
who were seen to fall well beyond the definition of
the 'good pupil'. We begin with the 'nutters'.

The 'Nutters'

Rockfield School contained a number of pupils who, for
different reasons, rendered problematic the teacher's
ability to discharge her duties. In the earlier
discussion of the teachers' ideologies it was
suggested that some teachers, the 'stretchers',
sought to correct these presumed deficiences in the
knowledge and behaviour of their pupils, thereby
helping them to cope with the academic matters at
hand. Others, the 'stabilizers', took a more
passive approach and endeavoured to live with the
problem, or, as Mrs. Scott put it, 'to suffer them'.
    Some pupils were highly intransigent in their
refusal to comply with their teachers' ideal of the
good pupil. They rejected as rhetoric the teachers'
exhortations to work and behave. Their criteria for
success were their own, not the school's, and their
attitudes and actions seemed very reminiscent of the
'lads' in Willis' (1977) study, and of the
'delinquescent' pupils in Hargreaves' (1967) study of
a secondary modern boys' school. At Rockfield, the
most common label appended to these recalcitrant
pupils was 'nutters'. The label seemed to have
originated with Mrs. Scott and was used by other
teachers of all ideological views. These pupils
were the subject of constant staffroom discussion.
All but three of the fifteen or so pupils classified
in this way were boys, and all but one were white.

Willy and John in Mrs. Scott's Primary 6 class vied
for position as the most successful 'nutter'. Their
respective 'careers' had commenced whilst they had
been in Primary 3. We begin with Willy. Willy's
trouble had started in Mrs. Davie's Primary 3 class.
He had thrown a chair at her. For this and other
'offences', he had been despatched to a school for
maladjusted children, or, as Willy called it:

> The school for ma temper.

Having apparently mended his ways, he was re-admitted
to Rockfield School:

> DH: So you kept your nose clean (at the
> school for maladjusted children)?
>
> Willy: Yeah, but ma nose got dirty again
> here!

By most accounts this was so. He had rejected the
school's dress code in favour of his own: 'white
shirt, black tie, satin trousers and sand shoes'.
He had fought with teachers:

> Pupil: He (Willy) did the toilet in a can
> and made somebody drink it.
>
> DH: Who did that?
>
> Pupil: Willy Scott.
>
> DH: Who did he make drink it?
>
> Pupil 1: I don't know who it was.
> Mr. Alexander got him out the door
> and thrashed him.
>
> Pupil 2: That was like the day before Willy
> was kicking a ball with another boy
> in Mr. Houston's class and I think
> Mrs. Reid came in and Willy Scott
> started hitting Mrs. Reid and she was
> trying to get him into Mr. Alexander's
> door but after Mrs. Reid just let him go.

On one occasion Willy told me that on the previous
day he had stolen a wig and a door handle but, not
knowing what to do with the latter, he had returned
it to the shop. He confessed to not remembering the
last time he had paid a bus fare - bus fares were a

'waste of money'. It was said of him that he bullied other children, usually 'little children', or those who 'supported the wrong football team', or ethnic minority children.

His general view of school was that it was 'rubbish' but he did have some favourable words for men teachers and for women teachers who could wield the belt 'like a man'. Men teachers, he said, 'give you the belt but they let you play games'. As for women teachers, the harder they belted, the higher was the esteem in which he held them.[1] One teacher was 'brilliant at the belt', a verdict which was supported by a stand-up demonstration of her quick-fire belting action. Another teacher was commended: 'She nearly drives you into the ground!' Thus it would appear that both his peers and his teachers were evaluated according to the same machismo criteria of how physically aggressive they were.

But Willy was not without his reluctant admirers. Just as some female teachers had a rather admired style of belting, so too was Willy seen to have a rather charismatic style in the way he went about his pranks:

> The name Willy Scott means something bad in this
> school. He's a likeable boy but all the
> teachers say, 'Oh Willy Scott!'

Mrs. Watt, for example, recounted the day she had seen him on his bicycle, contentedly puffing away at a cigarette. On seeing her, he had immediately stuffed the lighted cigarette in his pocket, causing it to smoulder. He had an air of confidence about him: 'He'll always land on his feet'. Indeed, Mrs. Watt's interest in Willy was seen to have gone too far by other teachers when she had sought to have a charge against Willy and two of his friends dropped by the police who had apprehended them for threatening an elderly man with knives tied to sticks. The teachers could not understand why she had bothered. Even his classmate Susan was not one to wholly condemn him, though she might have had reason to do so. Susan was one of the 'snobs', a label assigned to her by Willy because she 'works hard, sticks her nose up and speaks well'. Susan recounted an incident involving one of Willy's altercations with Mrs. Scott, his classroom teacher:

> Mrs. Scott told the teacher that he'd (Willy)
> tried to break it (the handbag which Willy had
> grabbed whilst she had been telling him off),

which he wouldn't leave alone. He's not that
kind of boy. Sometimes he's got a temper but
deep down he isn't bad.

DH: How do you know?

Because of the way ... I mean with girls -
sometimes he's threatening the girls, but he
would never ... sometimes when Liz (another
'snob') and that muck around with the boys he
sometimes hits them, but it's not a hard hit ...
it's a joke.

Willy's classmate John was, in Mr. Houston's
estimation, 'beyond redemption'. Since arriving at
Rockfield in his Primary 3 year, his standing had
fluctuated, as these extracts from his pupil record
card suggest.

Primary 3: John needs time to adjust and settle
down in his new surroundings.

Primary 4: In trouble, disruptive and aggressive
behaviour, but in the last two
months has made some effort.

Primary 5: John's behaviour is rather better
this year. He is less moody and
aggressive in the classroom. He
takes a lively interest in his work
and can be very helpful.

Primary 6: His progress is erratic because of
poor concentration and attitude.

John's behaviour was attested to by teachers and
pupils alike:

(1) Teacher: Con man.

(2) Pupil: He's the worst temper.

(3) Teacher: He likes to watch adults lose their
temper; he encourages parental
conflict.

(4) Pupil: John is a real rough one.
Mr. Alexander took him in and John
started to kick and punch and swear
at him.

(5)   Teacher: John seems attractive initially but
                 I'd hate to be his teacher.

By Primary 6 he had become unmanageable. His 'case'
was submitted by Mr. McLean to the Child Guidance
Clinic. In his submission to the clinic Mr. McLean
refers to John's 'behaviour in the classroom':

> Disruptive, shouting out, mimics the teacher,
> when disciplined shows violent resentment.

The 'recommendation' of the school was:

> 'Action must be taken to eliminate John's anti-
> social behaviour. It is quite evident that
> should John's outbursts of violent temper
> continue he will do some serious damage or
> injury. His defiance of authority is not
> conducive to a stable teaching situation in the
> classroom. His mother (John was a fostered
> child) says that all the school patterns are
> repeated at home. One also feels that he tried
> to play one parent off against the other.'

Thus John had threatened the realization of
Mr. McLean's 'stabilization' ideology and was
referred for treatment, but he did not receive any,
finished his Primary 7 year, again with Mrs. Scott,
and went to secondary school.
     At secondary school John had continued as
before. In his first year he had kicked a woman
teacher who was trying to break up a fight. He had
been suspended. John's personal recollection of the
incident is reported below:

> DH: Somebody told me you had been in trouble
>   with the teachers - that you kicked a
>   teacher. Is that true?
>
> John: Yes.
>
> DH: How did that happen?
>
> John: I was fighting with another boy and I
>   jumped on his back. We were just
>   playing. And then he started pushing
>   and pulling my hair and got me on the
>   ground and I couldn't get back up. So
>   the teacher came in and I tried to get
>   at him.

DH: And what did the teacher do?

John: She just started pulling my hair.

DH: She did?

John: Yes.

DH: So what happened then?

John: I can't remember.

DH: It just happened once?

John: No. The second time I was fighting with
        this second year boy and the teacher got
        in the way and I kicked her by accident.

Both John and Willy had been born when their mothers
were only sixteen years of age, and both sets of
parents had subsequently separated. So it was with
a third 'nutter' in Mrs. Scott's class, Alex. He
was by far the quietest of the three, but, like his
pals, assigned very little value to doing well in
school. When I asked him to place himself in the
class according to good pupil status, he put himself
last, which surprised me, but not his teachers.
Mr. Houston, for example, did not think it remarkable:

    He would put himself at the bottom because he
    thinks that's the best place to be.

Alex began to dislike school after Primary 1, 'when
we started to work'. He had no idea what he wanted
to be and nor did it concern him. He was in school
'to be with ma pals', not to work. He never paid on
the buses and had 'almost given up smoking'. As for
school uniform, he took the view of his friend Willy
and one morning, decked out in a jacket with an
'offensive' punk slogan, was brought before
Mr. Alexander to explain his breach of the school
dress code. His parents had never been to the school
save for the occasion when his mother had come to
complain to a teacher about his having belted her son.
Alex thought the punishment meted out to be
unwarranted:

    A lassie spat at me so I pushed her.

Alex's assertion, shared by his mother, that he was
'easily led' into trouble cut little ice with

129

Mr. Lane who saw him as 'the prime mover behind trouble'. Where Alex differed from Willy and John was that he kept a lower profile. He was not regarded as unmanageable, just lazy, as his year-end reports reveal:

Primary 1:   Alex lacks confidence but I feel sure he could put more effort into his work.

Primary 2:   Extra help in reading needed (there was no remedial reading to be had).

Primary 3:   Greatly improved reading. More effort needed in number. Conduct 'C'. Has been in trouble for behaviour outside classroom.

Primary 4:   Alex does not often work to full capacity as he is rather lazy and tends to distract other children in his group – requires repeated reprimand.

Primary 5:   Alex's behaviour still shows immaturity, he still does very inane things to show off to the other boys. In the classroom he has calmed down a lot and responds to telling off.

Primary 6:   Alex lacks concentration. He works very slowly because of this but all work is progressing.

Alex, John and Willy were the most notorious 'nutters' in the school. Alex was seen as the best plotter of pranks, Willy the best fighter and John the most quick-tempered. During their last two years of school they had been in Mrs. Scott's class. She had admittedly 'suffered' them. Occasionally they had received the belt, but to little avail. Neither Willy's 'treatment' at the school for maladjusted children, nor John's referral to the Child Guidance Clinic, had had the desired long-term effect. Both Willy and John had threatened the stability of the school by their aggressive behaviour. Mrs. Scott did not favour coercion as a form of social control and nor did Mr. McLean. Perhaps in another school they would have been permanently expelled but at Rockfield they were placed with a teacher, Mrs. Scott, who had learnt to expect what they were capable of and had come to tolerate it. Her regret was that by 'suffering' their misdemeanours she had posed great

130

limitations on her ability to teach 'the good ones',
or 'the snobs' as the 'nutters' called them.
   Just as Mrs. Scott was reluctant to meet
physical aggression with physical punishment, so too
was Mr. Houston. Both teachers subscribed to the
'ideology of stabilization'. The 'problem' in
Mr. Houston's class was Tina. She was nobody's
friend. She was a very angry young girl who, by
Primary 6, had seen her parents divorced, her mother
killed in a car crash, a stay in the same school that
Willy had been referred to, and an eviction from her
previous school. She summed up her attitude:

   I don't care about anything. Right?

When asked what she would like to be as an adult, she
replied: 'In prison'. Her father, she said, drank
in the pub every night, allegedly leaving her and
her thirteen year-old sister at home. Often she was
badly bruised and claimed that she had been beaten.
Another pupil stated: 'Her dad batters her'. She
was a notoriously unpunctual pupil for the following
reasons:

   'Cos I got to bed too late (11.30 weekdays;
   12.30 weekends) but that's the way I want it.

She shared with Willy the same criterion for evalua-
ting others: how well they fought. Even ethnic
minority children were evaluated in this way:

   They're all the same, aint they - just fight
   with a different coloured skin, that's all.

The reputation of Tina was well-known to other pupils
and well documented in school records. First the
views of other children:

   (i)   Pupil: She had a stone, but dropped it and
                   began kicking and pulling my hair -
                   I was so frightened I couldn't fight
                   back.

   (ii) Pupil: Tina picks on you if you never hit
                   back. If people hit her back she
                   wouldn't be so hard and nasty.

   (iii) Pupil: She grabs you by the collar and
                   throws you about.

         DH: Why does she do that?

> Pupil: She doesn't like people.
>
> Pupil: She's not very friendly.
>
> Pupil: She even swears at the teachers.
>
> DH: Is she unhappy?
>
> Pupil: Yes. Because I think she's only
>   got a dad; she lives with her dad.
>
> (iv) Pupil: She's mad.

Her classmates' view of this irascible, 'nasty', 'cruel' girl were partly supported by her teachers:

> Former primary
> school head: Behaviour-wise there has been
>   no improvement. Parents now
>   divorced.
>
> Previous head: Tina's behaviour has deteriora-
>   ted over the time she spent here.

Tina, John and Willy posed serious problems for the realization of the 'stabilization' ideology. This ideology put the child first but, when the discretion afforded to the child undermined the stability of the school as a whole, the limits of tolerance had been breached. What Mrs. Scott, Mr. Houston and Mr. McLean did then was to widen the parameters. In Tina's case they were prompted to do so because her tragic background rather than her individual psychology was the cause attributed to explain her behaviour. But this kind of tolerant regime had been at odds with that of the 'special school' which both Tina and Willy had attended and had been released from as fit to re-enter a normal school. The report on Tina by her special school teacher is instructive:

> In general I find Tina a keen worker who reacts
> well in a structured environment. Although she
> is a girl showing willingness and determination,
> I find her a manageable child who responds well
> to firm handling (emphasis added).

After Tina had been at Rockfield for some time, Mr. McLean indicated in his report to the child psychologist:

> We thought that the atmosphere in Rockfield

would have some lasting influence on Tina, but it seems our efforts have been in vain.

Tina, therefore, had gone from the structured regime of the special school to the far more tolerant regime in Mr. Houston's class. Not only had the school's approach not been successful in respect of Tina, but it was seen as being too 'soft' with her, exonerating her and not punishing her for misdemeanours which, had they been perpetrated by Tina's classmates, would have been criticised:

(i)   Well, Mr. Houston- that's her teacher - he lets her get away with a lot of things because she kicks people, and Mr. Houston says, 'Stop being a baby', and he just forgets about it after that.

(ii) Mr. Houston lets them off with anything. Like Tina who bullies everybody ... One time she stole five pounds from Mr. Houston's wallet and Mr. Houston found out and he never said anything.

DH: What do you think the teacher should have done in that case?

I think she should have got the belt.

Her dad gives her black eyes and that.

The reluctance to punish Tina continued with Mrs. Watt, Mr. McLean's successor. Mrs. Watt had tried to 'reach' Tina by encouraging her talents in art, but other pupils had been suspicious:

She laps it up and is allowed to draw and make things while everyone else is working.

Thus it was that Mrs. Scott and Mr. Houston 'managed' their difficult pupils until they departed for secondary school. Willy and John, by the end of their second year at secondary school, were firmly located in the lower part of the lowest of three academic 'bands'; Alex had moved away from the area, and Tina's progress was outlined by Mrs. Watt:

The last we heard she was having one-to-one teaching because she disrupted classes too much. She couldn't be allowed to stay in class. She was quite a bright girl ...

It seemed that the official practice at Rockfield in respect of 'nutters' was to wait and see if they 'matured' whilst they were in the infants' section. If they failed to become less aggressive by the end of Primary 3, then they might be referred, as had occurred with Willy. Whether or not a child is referred may be influenced by the child's teacher and her analysis of whether or not the child's behaviour is tolerable within the constraints which her ideology allows for. It will be recalled that Veryll, in Mrs. Findlay's highly structured infants' class, had infringed Mrs. Findlay's code of behaviour too often. Mrs. Findlay had refused to make allowances for Veryll. Veryll left the school. In the same way Mrs. Davie, when she had had a chair thrown at her by Willy, had referred him and he subsequently went to a special school. Both Mrs. Findlay and Mrs. Davie were avowed 'stretchers' who could not tolerate the likes of Willy and Veryll if their academic aims were to be realised. There is a certain irony in all this. Mrs. Davie and Mrs. Findlay, both avowed 'stretchers', were autonomy-seeking teachers in the face of Mr. McLean and his 'stabilization' ethos. Veryll and Willy had been autonomy-seeking pupils in the face of Mrs. Findlay and Mrs. Davie respectively. Thus these two pupils were arguably 'condemned' by teachers who were doing the same thing; that is, flouting authority. These teachers had exercised their authority to remove their intransigent and disruptive pupils; Mr. McLean had tolerated his intransigent teachers because his ideology had not permitted him to bring them to book. And if his ideology had been more akin to that of the 'stretchers', he would not have had to do so anyway. The ideology of Mrs. Scott and Mr. Houston, on the other hand, allowed for higher thresholds of tolerance and lower thresholds of academic attainment and were therefore able to cope with the likes of the 'nutters'.

We turn now to James in Mrs. Stewart's Primary 3 class. He appeared to be reaching the critical third year when his 'case' might be referred. It has already been stated that James had been expelled from his nursery school. Below is his recollection of the incident which had led to his expulsion:

DH: What was it like at nursery school?

James: Horrible. This place is worse.

DH: The nursery school was better, was it?

James: Yes.

DH: What did you like about it?

James: Well I liked playing with the toys and
        the nurses.

DH: Did you ever get into trouble at
        nursery school?

James: Only once (when he spat at an assistant).

DH: What happened?

James: I can't remember.

When I first observed Mrs. Stewart's class, it was
at Primary 1 level. Mrs. Stewart then kept the same
class as it progressed to Primary 3. By the time I
began my observation of James in Primary 1 he seemed
virtually out of control. For example, if he wished
to cross to the other side of the room, he would
sometimes simply walk over the tops of any desks in
the way of his destination. When he chose to walk on
the floor he would often do so in a very attention-
seeking manner, usually by walking as though his
legs could not bend. He was permitted to go to the
toilet whenever he wanted to: 'Sometimes he wets the
bed and we don't want any accidents' (Mrs. Stewart).
He had been known to go to the toilet in unexpected
places:

    Pupil: James gets the belt ...

    DH: What for?

    Pupil: He's very naughty though - he does the
            toilet on people.

In class he was continually being reminded to behave:

    Mrs. Stewart: WHAT ARE YOU DOING NOW! We have
                    a little boy who is going to be
                    be tied to his chair one day.

    Mrs. Stewart: JAMES: I don't know. I think I
                    have to say that name about a
                    hundred times a day.

    James: Can I paint?

>
> Mrs. Stewart: If you promise to keep the paint
> on the brush and on the paper.
> (James enjoyed flicking paint
> around the room.)

Two years later James had not mended his ways:

> DH: When I was in your class two years ago
> there was a little boy called James.
> I can't remember his last name ...
>
> Pupils: JAMES McLEISH!
>
> DH: That's right. Is he still there?
>
> Pupil: Yes.
>
> DH: How is he these days?
>
> Pupil: He's quite bad. He gets the belt.
>
> DH: Does he? What did he get the belt for?
>
> Pupil: Every time Mrs. Stewart gives him a row
> he tells her to 'shut up'.

In Primary 1, Mrs. Stewart had sat James in a desk
by himself. In Primary 3 he still sat alone:

> DH: Do you and James sit at the same table
> David?
>
> David: No.
>
> DH: Does James sit on his own?
>
> David: Yes. James has got a table of his own.
>
> DH: Why's that?
>
> David: Because he's bad and he talks too much.

James had even crossed Mr. Alexander's path:

> James: I had a glass bottle and I threw it and
> it broke ...
>
> DH: Where did you throw it?
>
> James: Outside the school. It nearly hit
> somebody.

DH: Why did you do that?

James: I don't know. The teacher give me the
         belt once when I was playing in the
         school and it was time to go home and I
         never went home. And this big girl
         asked me if I'd like to play football
         and I said 'Yes'. My mum said: 'You'd
         better be home early tonight because
         we're going to see granny'. So my mum
         hit me (for being late) and the next day
         I was told the teacher was wanting to
         see me. And the girl who asked me if
         I'd like to play football ... she got
         the hardest belt but I just got a wee
         tap.

DH: Were you frightened? Are you frightened
         of getting the belt?

James: No.

Mrs. Stewart's ideology sought a balance between
'stretching' and 'stablizing'. On the one hand she
sought to negotiate with James, but on the other hand
she would be seen by the other children to punish
him if he 'went too far'. Had James been in
Mrs. Findlay's class, it is to be suspected that he
and Mrs. Findlay would have quickly reached logger-
heads, as had occurred in the case of Veryll. In
Mrs. Stewart's analysis, James was not wholly
responsible for his misdemeanours since his trouble
had started after the divorce of his parents; and
James was still an infant, unlike Willy, John, Alex
and Tina who, by their age, should have 'matured'.
Mrs. Stewart, therefore, continually reminded James
('a hundred times a day') to concentrate; she
praised him when appropriate and she punished him
when appropriate. What perhaps made Mrs. Stewart's
task easier, and Mrs. Scott's more difficult, was
that James was the only very difficult child in her
class and, to some extent, could be isolated by
being seated alone. The 'nutters' in Mrs. Scott's
class, however, were more numerous, physically larger
and vocally louder. Only John sat alone; there was
simply not enough space for Willy and Alex to be
isolated and it is doubtful if Mrs. Scott, given her
high level of tolerance, would have wished them to
have been. The observation of Mrs. Stewart's and
Mrs. Scott's classes also suggests an architectural
influence on classroom social control: that is, the

floor area and the numbers of pupils in their respective classrooms were very similar, but the age and physical size of their pupils were very different, being much greater in Mrs. Scott's classroom. In Mrs. Scott's classroom the children were of necessity more contained and could more easily distract both each other and the teacher if they wished. Even children seated far apart, as were Willy and John, could, given their good voice projection, carry on a conversation.

The 'nutters', therefore, were constraints on the classroom practice of both teachers and other pupils. I did not have the opportunity to observe the same 'nutter' being taught by different teachers who held different ideologies. At a speculative level, however, it would appear that the ideology of the teacher has consequences for the ways in which she defines and treats such children. To give partial support to this view, it is instructive to reconsider the year-end reports on John. In Primary 5, when he had been taught by Mrs. Carter, he was 'less moody and aggressive' than in the previous year she had taught him when she reported that his behaviour had been 'disruptive and aggressive'. Also in Primary 5 he is seen as taking a 'lively interest in his work and can be very helpful'. But, in Primary 6, when Mrs. Scott took over, his progress becomes 'erratic' because of 'poor concentration and attitude'. Indeed, before the end of Primary 7, also with Mrs. Scott, he had been referred to the Child Guidance Clinic, as stated earlier. John's reported, not observed, classroom behaviour began as disruptive in the beginning of Primary 4, became more appropriate towards the end of Primary 4 and throughout Primary 5, and deteriorated in his last two years at the school. Thus John was seen as largely co-operative by Mrs. Carter, but as something far less so by Mrs. Scott. This variation in John's reported behaviour may be explicable by developmental changes, by home background factors, by changes in teacher social control methods, or by a combination of these. At a more cynical level - though this is to be suspected - the changes in John's reported behaviour may simply be due to, say, Mrs. Carter painting too rosy a picture of him, and Mrs. Scott painting too dark a picture.

The 'nutters', therefore, regardless of the teacher's ideology, posed constraints on her class-room practice. In the case of the 'stretchers', the response was to coerce the pupil into compliance and, where that did not succeed, to have the pupil referred

to an educational psychologist. As for the
'stabilizers', they appeared to avoid the use of
coercion because, as they saw it, it was often
coercion in the home which produced aggression in
the school. And it is interesting that Mrs. Scott
argued that 'the nutters <u>do not allow you</u> to stretch
the good ones', the inference to be drawn suggesting
that she, as a teacher, was not being allowed to do
what she might have preferred. Thus the 'stabilizers'
view of the 'nutters' - to tolerate them as best they
could - might have come into being because, at some
stages previous, they realised that they could not
dominate these pupils, in Weber's sense of eliciting
the pupil's compliance by rational argument.

The 'Tragedies'

The dilemma for the 'stabilizers' between putting
'the child first', as Mr. McLean advocated, and
teaching the 'good ones' was very real. If they
tolerated the 'nutters', then the latter's disruptive
actions could constrain the good pupils. Furthermore,
many of the 'good ones' resented the laxity of
disciplinary measures against the 'nutters' and they
may not have realised that in some cases - for
instance, Tina's - that the teacher was making
allowances for the home background of the pupil. In
the pupils' eyes, Tina was 'getting away with it'.
Tina's case introduces a second group of pupils who
posed dilemmas for the teachers, namely the
'tragedies'. Tina herself had an allegedly difficult
life beyond the school. So too had other children.
Often these were children whose attendance was very
spasmodic, whose clothing was inadequate, whose
bodies were neglected in that they were underfed and
dirty, and whose skin and minds bore the scars of
physical and psychological damage. In a social
worker's terminology, they would probably be seen as
being 'at risk'. In Chapter 2, the label 'deprived'
was appended to about seventy-five per cent of the
children by their teachers. The 'tragedies' were
more than deprived. Usually they came to the
attention of teachers through outside agencies, in
particular the social work department. They were the
kinds of children whose life at home was regarded by
teachers as virtually intolerable. Teachers
constantly expressed amazement at how these children
coped. The teachers also expressed the fear that
there would be some children whose trials and tribu-
lations at home would never come to light unless
something ill befell them. Of the 'tragedies' whom

139

we shall discuss here, only one was of ethnic
minority status. Teachers admitted that they knew
less about the homes of the ethnic minority children,
but there was a commonly-held view that these
children were, on the whole, in more 'stable' homes
than many of their white counterparts.

As pupils, the 'tragedies' were not always
unmanageable, and nor were they bereft of intelligence and a 'normal' disposition. They seemed
unwanted by their parents. The teachers felt that
they should make life easier in school for these
children - they could not change the ways of their
parents; they could not effect structural change in
society to ameliorate their material condition; they
could not take the children away from the home. In
short, these children posed a dilemma for the teacher:
does she intervene in the home indirectly by calling
upon other agencies, especially the educational social
worker, or does she spend class time investigating
this or that bruise? To illustrate this dilemma, we
turn to the 'case' of Margo and Alice Brown. These
children were not so much disruptive in that they
were as aggressive as Tina towards teachers and
pupils, but they brought into the school 'effects'
of their home life which the teachers had to investigate. This took time. It diverted the teacher from
her normal practice in a manner which 'wasted' just
as much time as did her having to deal with the
'nutters', such as Willy.

When I visited Mrs. Letham's Primary 1 class,
Margo was not in school. In that year she had
missed at least a hundred days. When she did come to
school, 'she's like a hurricane'. Her vest, remarked
her teacher, was 'greyer than my mother's floor
cloth'. Her 'pants were soiled and caked on her
bottom'. In a very matter-of-fact way, Margo told
me that her nickname was 'smelly bum'; her sister
Alice answered to 'Smelly Brown'. Her family, said
Mrs. Reid, 'is brutal'. For example, the parents
had not sent back 'free meals' forms on three
occasions, and finally the social workers had to try
and have them returned. The teacher was angry at
this neglect:

> They deserve to have to pay: I wanted to
> finish (my letter) 'Yours spitefully'.

Aside from this, Margo and her sister were suspected
of having been subjected to continual physical abuse
and to having sustained 'non-accidental injury'. An
official enquiry involving the school and the

educational social worker had been instigated. The
matter of 'areas of responsibility' for classroom
teachers, school administrators and social work
agencies became one of negotiation rather than stated
policy. At the centre is the child, Margo.
      The brief history of the enquiry into Margo's
well-being appeared to have been that she had been
beaten by her father with a broom. A case conference
had been called by the Social Work Department. Two
teachers had been present, but not the assistant
head teacher. Two conclusions seemed to have been
drawn from the conference: to 're-educate' the
parents; to reduce the number of professionals on
the case and see what happened. Since the conference,
the Social Work Department appeared to let the case
fall within the remit of the educational social
worker, Mr. Davey. He was to monitor the parental
treatment of the child. To do so he had enlisted
the assistance of the school, in the person of the
assistant head teacher, Mrs. French, who had not been
at the conference, and who was to inform Mr. Davey
and the medical authorities of any suspected 'non-
accidental injury' to Margo. By 'informing the
medical authorities', Mrs. French took it to mean
that she should immediately take the child to
hospital to ascertain the cause of any 'injury' to
Margo. Thus the onus fell on the school to take
initial action. The onus, therefore, shifted from
the Social Work Department to the educational social
worker, to the assistant head teacher, to, by
inference, the classroom teacher, Mrs. Letham, to
define 'non-accidental' injury and take the initial
step of having it confirmed or denied by the medical
authorities. All this was to the good if, and only
if, Mrs. French's suspicions were confirmed by the
doctors, for steps could then be made to bring the
child within the protection of the Social Work
Department. But what if Mrs. French's analysis
proved to be incorrect? What if Margo returned to
her father, told him that she had had a medical
examination, at Mrs. French's behest, and that, as a
result, the 'injury' was not an injury and/or was
not 'non-accidental'? Mrs. French, by her action -
well-intentioned though it may have been - could be
said to have implied that maltreatment had occurred
merely by her having Margo examined. She obviously
did not wish to have to be placed in the position of
explaining all this to an enquiring, and doubtless
annoyed, parent.
      It was her dilemma which she was explaining to
Mr. Davey one morning in the staffroom. She was

concerned that it was very much a matter of interpretation whether or not a bruise, a burn or an
abrasion had been accidentally received. She had
been given no guidance on this matter and she wanted
some. This was, for her, the more so in that she
had not been present at the original case conference,
the consequences of which she was now the reluctant
bearer. She correctly expressed anxiety about who
would 'monitor' the child during the school holidays.
If anything serious were to happen to the child,
could she and Mr. Davey honestly say that 'they did
not know the risk' to the child. Whose head would be
on the block?

Mr. Davey said he did not know the answers to
her questions, at which point other teachers
(Mrs. Scott, Mrs. Reid, Mrs. Letham, Mrs. Findlay)
entered the conversation. Mrs. Findlay, who had
attended the case conference, noted that the emphasis
had been on the parents, not the children - a
misplaced concern in her view. Mrs. Letham, Margo's
teacher, had information about Margo's treatment at
home which Mr. Davey admitted he did not have, but
needed. Mrs. Letham then proceeded to inform
Mr. Davey that: Margo has 'marks on her nearly
every day'; that she, Mrs. Letham, had to spend an
hour in the morning trying to discover their cause;
that Margo refused to admit that her father had been
culpable (Margo: 'I can't tell you. My mum says
that if I do daddy will go to jail'); that she had
witnessed a large weal on the back of Margo's four-
year-old sister which might have been caused by a
leather-gloved hand ('I've never seen a mark like
it'); that recently Margo had said her father had
stretched her mouth open with his fingers, causing
the skin to break; that Margo had said her neigh-
bours were alcoholics and squatters; that Margo had
a burn mark on her. Mrs. French had been told by
the mother that the father now had a job. Margo had
told her teacher that he hadn't. At the end of this
Mr. Davey said, 'I'm going away to seek counsel on
this'. On his departure Mrs. Letham turned to her
colleagues:

> Sometimes I have nightmares about the newspaper
> headlines ... (implying that the demise of her
> pupils would be the subject of them).

Alice Brown, Margo's older sister, had been, in her
teacher's view, a success. Not a 'success' in any
academic way, but one where the child had partly
overcome her allegedly tragic circumstances to become

a much better pupil than her previous teachers would
have expected:

> Alice really tries in the classroom now. She
> had a very hard attendance problem of course
> way back in the infants (she was now in Primary
> 4), but since I got her a year and a half ago
> her attendance has been really good and her
> work has come on remarkably well. When I got
> her first she'd be in the bottom reading group ...
> but Alice now has moved up two groups and it's
> really - what I would say - because she's
> attending better, and she works. She always
> does the work you give her, maybe not the way
> you asked her to do it, but she'll finish it.

DH: She expresses a certain amount of individu-
ality ...?

> That's putting it kindly, yes.

However, Alice was the 'loner amongst the girls'.
But:

> She did steal from them (we always got it back)
> but you can't blame girls for having given
> someone a chance and then this is what happens -
> you can't blame them ...

Thus there was a mistrust of Alice among the children,
something endorsed by Mr. Houston: 'She's more
sneaky than Margo'. Even when Alice had been
allegedly raped ('certainly interfered with '), one
of the teachers made the aside, though very much
tongue-in-cheek, 'She probably asked for it'.
   Another incident attesting to Alice's
'sneakiness' involved an incident when she had been
caught stealing. The police had been brought in.
She lied to the police and to the educational social
worker by saying that she was only seven, not eight,
which, had she admitted, might have involved her in
a prosecution. What was the aetiology of Alice's
deviance? One teacher summed up her view, though not
without a hint of derision:

> Alice is intrinsically bad, no matter what the
> environment!

Pupils such as Margo and Alice not only pose the
teacher with the problem of if and when to intervene
and investigate assertions or indications of

maltreatment at home, they further pose the problem
of how far such pupils, if they become disruptive,
should be exonerated on the basis of their difficult
backgrounds. This dilemma had confronted Mr. Houston
in his dealings with Tina. He had tolerated her out
of sympathy with her tragic background and in
accordance with his professed ideology. But, as was
stated earlier, some pupils saw his tolerance of
Tina's misdemeanours as being unfair if they
themselves had been rebuked for similar offences.
Mr. Houston could not publicly air confidential
information about Tina to justify his seemingly
preferential treatment of her.

But tragedy in the home did not always associate
with behavioural problems in the school. In an
earlier section, the tragic domestic circumstances
of Ann in Mrs. Findlay's class, and of Parvaz in
Mrs. Carter's class, were described. It will be
recalled that Ann had 'a dreadful background' marked
by considerable absenteeism, parental unemployment,
physical neglect and whose brothers were either in
borstal or on probation. To Mrs. Findlay's amazement
she had coped:

> How she's managed to maintain this lovely way
> I don't know.

This ability to cope revealed itself in good
behaviour; her academic achievement lagged behind
because of her absenteeism and Mrs. Findlay had to
help her catch up, there being no remedial instruction available at that level. A similar case is that
of Parvaz who had been confronted with an alternative
western/Moslem culture at home in keeping with the
changing partners of his 'parents'. As stated
earlier, he had been evicted from his home at one
point and had shepherded his younger brother and
sister to a Children's Shelter. His father was in
prison and, according to Mrs. Carter:

> They are left a lot to their own devices.

Despite all this:

> Parvaz has managed to stay clear of trouble so
> far. He had been truthful and honest.

Academically, he fared reasonably well and could
read without remedial or TESL help. Parvaz and Ann
were examples of children admired by their teachers.
Indeed they often remarked how 'normal' many of their

pupils behaved even though it was known that their
lives at home were 'emotionally' and/or 'materially
deprived'. In most instances, the 'tragedies' did
not threaten the teacher's authority. Rather, they
prompted bewilderment in the teachers that young
children could be so maltreated by adults, and
frustration that they, as teachers, could not
ameliorate their pupils' lot in the home. Apart
from 'nutters' and 'tragedies', the teachers faced
the 'dead horses', or the children of imputedly very
low ability. They posed difficulties of another kind
for the teacher, and it is to these that we now turn.

The 'Dead Horses'

At Rockfield teachers were advised by Mr. McLean
not to 'flog dead horses'. A 'dead horse' was a
pupil who was defined as virtually unteachable since
he lacked the requisite ability, or was thought to
lack it. The label had originally been constructed
by Mr. McLean and it tended to be assigned to a
pupil in his early years of schooling. In most
cases the label was assigned on a purely subjective
basis. At face value it would appear that this was
at odds with Mr. McLean's professed 'child-comes-
first' ideology, a caring ideology. As with the
category of 'nutter', the tag of 'dead horse' implies
a metaphorical stratification of pupils, a stratification which does not square well with the individualism implicit in putting the child first. In their
study of a 'progressive' primary school, Sharp and
Green (1975) note the contradiction between the
professed, 'progressive' theory of teachers and their
ready willingness to defined pupils as 'dim' and
'peculiar'; that is, the individualism implicit in
their general theory was at odds with the stratification revealed in their accounts of particular pupils.
     Remedial provision at Rockfield has been said
to be very limited. Only in Primary 4 and 5 was it
available. Its lack at other levels required the
teacher and the pupils to cope as best they could.
In the teachers' view, 'dead horses' could not be
wished away; they had to be taught or kept 'busy'.
'Dead horses' might not have to be 'flogged' but
they did require directing. Mr. McLean's assertion
that teachers 'should not waste time on them' was
variously viewed as unrealistic or uncaring. During
the period of the study, I overheard about five
pupils being classified in this way, and, of these,
one was of ethnic minority parentage, a boy called
Alan, whom we shall discuss presently.

'NUTTERS', 'TRAGEDIES' AND 'DEAD HORSES'

'Dead Horses' tended to be consigned to their
educational mortality early in their school careers.
In some instances the teacher's analysis that the
pupil was 'mentally deficient' was 'verified' by an
IQ test score, as had occurred with Jamie in
Mrs. Stewart's primary 1 class. When I visited her
class, Jamie was repeating Primary 1:

> He's repeating. He's one of eleven children.
> His work is incomprehensible. You can read
> about him in the records - he's the worst I've
> had.

Jamie did not receive remedial help. He was simply
given 'busy' work to contain his increasing tendency
to distract others. After three and a half years
with Mrs. Stewart he was transferred to a special
school.
Whilst Mrs. Stewart's diagnosis of Jamie proved
to be correct, it had not for Alan. An ethnic
minority pupil, Alan was a low achiever in his third
year with Mrs. Stewart. Over the three years, she
had attributed the cause to his laziness. It
transpired, however, that he was deaf in his right
ear, the result of an illness he had contracted when
only eighteen months old. I discussed Alan's
predicament with his mother:

DH: When did this hearing problem start with Alan?

> Well he was only about eighteen months old but
> we found out about ten weeks ago. Alan is
> really far behind and Mrs. Stewart thought for
> a while that he was a lazy child, but it was
> the illness that affected his hearing, so now
> he's supposed to be getting more attention ...

Another fallible, subjective assessment had been Roy
in Mrs. Carter's Primary 5 class, who had earlier
been defined by the head teacher as a 'vegetable'
but who, on receiving remedial help in Primary 4 and
5, had much improved. So too had Angela, a dyslexic
in Primary 5, and Donald, her classmate:

DH: When do they stop going to remedial class?

> It's supposed to stop (next year in Primary 6)
> but I think Angela will get it and I wouldn't
> be surprised if Donald got it as well, once
> it's pointed out to the powers that be that
> Donald didn't really start until the end of

> Primary 3. He obviously has a little bit,
> maybe not much further because of his
> intelligence, but he might have a little
> further to go. And because Angela's problems
> have been pointed out, I think she might be
> allowed because, as I said, her problems are
> different (dyslexia) from the others, even if
> it's to keep her working rather than falling
> behind, because she comes from a nice, earnest
> home.

'Dead horses' would be attended to if, as in Angela's
case, the parents intervened, or if they became
disruptive. An example of a quiet, 'dead horse' was
Hamish in Primary 6. His IQ was 76. He had never
received remedial help, even in Primary 4 and 5. He
was well behaved:

> Behaviourally Hamish is no problem in school.
> In many ways that's his problem; He doesn't
> seem to respond. Very few stimuli make him do
> anything, if you like. He'll sit in the class
> and work away - speaks very quietly.

His out-of-school activities appeared to be more
stimulated:

> I mean out there on the football field, he'll
> go around kicking everybody. I mean he's
> totally average in that sense, but to get him
> to give you a positive response to a specific
> question, or to get him to use his own
> initiative ... he is totally lacking in any
> drive. I find that any kind of drive in the
> classroom does not exist. There's just this
> wee lump that sits there and does his work.
> Quite honestly, I don't think he needs special
> schooling. I think that's just Hamish, if you
> like. That's not a funny thing to say; he's
> just the way he is.

Hamish, being 'just the way he is', would, it may
be inferred, progress little further regardless of
his schooling. Indeed, his whole family was imputed
to be lacking in intelligence:

> And if you look at the sister coming up, she's
> exactly the same. A wee bit more spark to her
> but exactly the same, so I don't think it's
> an individual thing; I think it's the family
> thing.[2]

Implicit in this analysis is an agreement with the
'dead horse' categorization of Mr. McLean and his
'stabilization' policy; that is, it is better not
to disturb the stability of 'dead horses' unless
they themselves begin to disturb the stability of
the school:

> If that's the only fault, if you like - it's
> not a fault in that sense. You only move them
> unless the parent asks, but if they have
> behavioural problems, then perhaps they do
> (move them). So from my point of view, the
> school will push if it's a behavioural problem,
> but if it's not a behavioural problem, my
> impression is that they go through the system.

Both Mr. Lane's account of Hamish and Mr. McLean's
policy raise the question put by Mrs. Carter in
Roy's case: what if the subjective 'dead horse'
definition is objectively incorrect in the case of a
non-disruptive pupil? It would perhaps only be the
disruptive 'dead horse' of adequate ability who
might be able to prompt the school to have its
subjective assessment 'tested' objectively. A 'dead
horse' who retains his label until Primary 6 would
face a further blockage: he would be seen as too
old for remedial help to be of assistance.

> I think the attitude by the time they got to
> Primary 7 - if they were poor at that stage,
> then it was better to concentrate on younger
> kids.   I don't agree with that policy
> personally because I think in Primary 7 more
> stretch should go on. Because if you can
> boost kids at that stage before they go on to
> secondary then that's going to make a differ-
> ence - much more than say Primary 4 or 5, to my
> way of thinking.

Thus, assuming that a pupil had been correctly
identified as being in need of remedial help by the
time he was in Primary 4, he would receive, at best,
two years of extra help to make up his deficit
incurred over the first three years of schooling. If
the pupil objectively in need of remedial help had
not been identified by the end of Primary 5, he was
beyond help.

At a pragmatic level, it is arguable that a
teacher with a large class of children which contains
'dead horses' who are not disruptive could easily
ignore their need for remedial help. Pupils who

demand the teacher's time, either by asking for it
or by misbehaving, are more likely to receive the
teacher's attention than are those 'wee lumps that
sit there' like Hamish. The choice which befalls
the teacher confronted with the likes of Hamish
requires her to make the judgement on the qualitative
differences between facilitating a little progress
in Hamish and objectively more progress in 'the good
ones that spark'. The disadvantage to the 'dead
horse' is that once the label has been assigned, it
may be realised, regardless of the accuracy of the
teacher's definition. The realization may be
explained on the basis of the innate psychological
deficiency in the pupil, not on the basis of an
initially mistaken assessment of the pupil by the
teacher. Unless the pupil either literally disrupts
the teacher, or his parents intervene, he will 'go
through the system'. Furthermore, the lack of
remedial provision at Rockfield may have reduced the
classroom teacher to thinking that if the head
teacher did not wish to deal with 'dead horses' then
why should she.

Summary

The concern of this chapter has been to examine the
pupils in the school who have been categorised as
being different. 'Nutters, 'tragedies' and 'dead
horses' reveal 'problems' more for the teacher than
for the pupil: when a teacher states that a pupil
'has a problem', she is also implying that, as a
result, so does she. The children discussed in this
chapter represent a small section of the sixty percent of pupils who were said to have 'problems' in
that they did not come from 'normal' backgrounds.
How the teacher managed the problem depended on its
type, the structural arrangements within the school
as defined by the head teacher, and on the teacher's
own ideology. 'Nutters' posed the greatest threat
to the authority of the teacher. The 'stabilization'
ideology required the head teacher and the teacher
to adjust to the pupil, not the pupil to the norms
of the school. Only when the very disruptive pupil
confronted a teacher defined as a 'stretcher',
Mrs. Findlay for example, would the head teacher have
the pupil removed, and then only after he had
established a clear pattern of disruptive behaviour
which had not responded to coercion. 'Tragedies'
and 'dead horses' tended not to counter the
teacher's authority but they could lessen the amount
of time spent with other children. In the final

analysis, little could be done to remove the cause
of a pupil's tragic circumstances, and little could
be done to provide the greater attention required
by pupils in need of remedial help if it was not
forthcoming outside of the classroom. Nevertheless,
there were differences among the teachers on the
ways in which they treated 'dead horses'. The
'stretchers' sought to 'bring up the tail' of the
class, the 'tail' including the 'dead horse'. They
appeared to take the view that the 'tail' had just
as much right to the teacher's time as did the 'top'.
The 'straddlers' took a similar view but their
pedagogy differed. As for the 'stabilizers', the
'dead horse' should not be 'stretched' perhaps
because they were thought to be incapable of being
taught much more, and because much of the teacher's
time was spent negotiating the compliance of
'nutters' and those similarly inclined. 'Nutters'
not only 'took time away from the 'good ones', but
they took it away from the 'tail'. Of all these
categories of pupil, the 'nutters' invoked the most
attention from the teachers; the 'tragedies' the
most sympathy and the 'dead horses' the most
indifference.

It has been stated that Mr. McLean intentionally
sought to reproduce the objective social class
position of his pupils. His intentions were not
devious or sinister. He was only arguing that the
majority of his pupils would not 'need' an academic
education. In his analysis, most of the children
were ill-prepared by the home for it. Whatever
compensation the school made should be in the
emotional aspect, not the cognitive and academic.
Thus the formal goal of the school was that it should
'stabilise' the lives of its pupils. It should
promote harmony. From a functionalist perspective,
this goal would be adhered to and realised by both
teachers and pupils alike. Consensus of means and
ends would follow. It did not. What intervened
between the goals of the school, as defined by its
bureaucratic head, and their realization was the
consciousness of its teachers and pupils. In
respect of the teachers, their consciousness was
neither shared amongst themselves nor between
themselves and the head teacher. Different sets of
intentions were stated and revealed in classroom
practice. The shared educational philosophies
within the 'stabilizers', 'stretchers' and
'straddlers' emerged from their individual biographies,and from their reactions to the constraints
imposed by the organisational arrangements in the

school and by the kinds of children who formed its pupils. Despite these differing ideologies, a facade of harmony prevailed among the teachers and between the teachers and head teacher. In the main, teachers took their ideologies into their respective classrooms. They were rarely explicitly stated in public. Teachers who dissented from Mr. McLean's ideology were able to preserve their autonomy in professional matters, though not in administrative ones. And it was the very ideology of Mr. McLean which prevented him from countering the 'resistance' of his dissenting teachers: he wanted stability and harmony, and any endeavour on his part to correct ideological deviations might have undermined that stability. As for the pupils, they worked for different masters, so to say, as they progressed up the school. As with some of their teachers, they did not easily forgo their autonomy, and their ability to do so varied according to the ideologies of the teachers whom they confronted. The 'nutters' appeared to know where their real interests lay, and they did not reside in the needs of society. The 'nutters', however, were very young and they had confronted a school whose coercive back-up to the failure of manipulative ideology was minimal. It was rare for the 'nutters' to be absent from school. They did not need to be since they could do most of the things inside the school which they might have wished to do outside of it. The 'dead horses' and 'tragedies' did, however, conform to the school's goal of effecting 'stabilization'. That is to say, the 'dead horses' received little in the way of academic revitali ation, and the 'tragedies' were unlikely to face the emotional and physical neglect which beset them at home. So, from the ideological viewpoint of teachers subscribing to 'stabilization', the 'tragedies' and the 'dead horses' were 'good pupils'. But if these same pupils met the scrutiny of the 'stretchers', then the school had failed since it had permitted academic expectations to be lowered in favour of emotional stability.

Chapter 7

STATUS DIFFERENTIATION: ETHNICITY AND GENDER

Functionalist theory argues that society coheres on
the basis of consensus and an obedience to authority.
This consensus is achieved despite the fact that
there are different levels in society, each of which
attracts an amount of remuneration and authority
which is different from other levels. Yet those who
occupy the lower levels do not engage in attempts to
topple those above them. This is because they accept
as legitimate society's decision that they do not
deserve more. They do not deserve more because they
lack the qualifications required for entry into the
higher levels. Put another way, they accept their
lower position as fair and just because they, like
everyone else, had their chance to succeed academically and failed to do so. Others did better and so
deserve their due reward. All accept their respective positions in the social hierarchy as being the
result of differing levels of merit, as defined by
the education system (Davis and Moore, 1945).
    From a Marxist perspective, not only is there
social differentiation and stratification, but there
is also conflict and control, not harmony and order.
Whereas for functionalism society holds together
through consensus, for Marxism it coheres because
one group is able to control another, through
methods both persuasive and repressive. And whereas
for functionalism the number of levels is many, for
Marxism social differentiation and conflict occur
ultimately on the basis of class. Although functionalism also uses the term social class, it does so
differently from Marxism. Before proceeding,
therefore, it is important to distinguish between
these two usages of the term. The functionalist
sees social class as little more than an occupational
category, a mere grading of occupations. For Marxism
it is more than this. That is to say, Marxism sees

class as representing different and opposing
positions in relation to the ownership of the means
of production. For example, take the occupation of
bus driver. From the functionalist standpoint, it
is sufficient to define all bus drivers as having
the same class position within the working class.
From a Marxist standpoint, the occupation of bus
driver tells us nothing about the social class of
the bus driver. We need to know if the bus driver
owns buses, or the means of production; and if he
employs others, on his terms. The bus driver who
meets these conditions is a capitalist. The bus
driver who is merely an employee working for a wage
is a member of the proletariat because he does not
own the means of production.[1] So Marxism requires
us to see classes as groups in relation to the
ownership of the means of production and not, as
with functionalism, as occupations which are merely
classified discretely. Furthermore, Marxism states
that those who share a common relationship to the
means of production will construct a common world-
view, a shared consciousness which is at odds with
that of the opposing social class.

This homogeneous class consciousness within the
proletariat is necessarily at odds with that within
the capitalist class for a number of reasons. In
the functionalist concept of social class, there is
a presumed consensus of interest - the needs of
society - among the various occupational strata. In
the Marxist formulation of class, this consensus,
though apparent, will eventually be eroded by an
ever-increasing realisation among the proletariat of
their having been exploited and alienated by capitalism. That there appears to be little such awareness
among the proletariat is explained by the role of
'ideology' which permeates the minds of capital and
labour alike in a manner that renders the existing
capitalist order as being natural and in everyone's
interests (Harris, 1979:87). There is, therefore,
a certain pessimism in this: if capitalist ideology
is so successful in securing the commitment of all
to capitalism, how will a 'counter-hegemony'
(Gramsci, 1971) emerge? This matter of the emergence
of a pre-revolutionary proletarian consciousness was
one which concerned Weber. He was doubtful that it
would develop as Marx had predicted.

Like Marx, Weber also defines social class as a
basis for social differentiation and conflict. His
interpretation of class is not, however, at one with
Marxism, although it is related to an economic
consideration:

> 'Property' and 'lack of property' are, therefore,
> the basic categories of all class situations.
> (Weber, 1978:827)

Weber, however, was sceptical of the Marxist view
that, as capitalism developed, the homogeneity of
consciousness within the proletariat would develop
apace.   Weber sees no such homogeneity:

> Within these categories, however, class
> situations are further differentiated: on the
> one hand, according to the kind of property
> that is usable for returns: and, on the other
> hand, according to the kind of services that can
> be offered in the market. (Weber, 1978:928)

Thus, elaborating upon this, there is within
'property' a differentiation between <u>rentiers</u> and
<u>entrepreneurs</u>;   that is, between the former who loan
capital or lease real assets, and the latter who may
borrow from the former to finance their ventures in
the productive sector. Furthermore, market differentiation occurs within the class which 'lacks
property'. This manifests itself as a contest among
workers who seek to market their skills on the best
possible terms. In their quest to do so, workers
may institutionalise their market position by
adopting 'monopolistic tactics' to exclude other
workers and therefore to protect their own
'privileges'. Examples of such exclusionary tactics
would be institutions such as the Stock Exchange
which excludes traders who are not members. The
'closed shop' is a similar device. Thus, for Marx,
social classes arise out of their relationship to
the means of <u>production</u>. For Weber, social classes
arise out of their relationship to the 'market'.
     Social differentation and conflict not only
occur between classes, they occur between 'status
groups'. The difference between 'class' and 'status
group' is as follows. A 'status group' is one which
has a shared sense of social honour, and this is
expressed by a 'specific style of life' common to
the group (Weber, 1978:932). Moreover, such groups
seek to better their social honour at the expense of
other groups. 'Class', on the other hand, derives
from economic interest and activity within the market
system. This is not to say, however, that those
whose class position is the same will necessarily
share a subjectively-felt identity, as do status
groups. That is, they may be objectively at one, but
subjectively at odds. Class and status groups <u>may</u>

overlap, or, in Weber's terms, status groups may
'knit to a class situation' (Weber, 1978:932).   Thus
in Weber's usage, class and status groups are not
discrete, but may be interrelated.   Further, the
economic basis of class would suggest that classes
seek material gains.   Similarly the social basis of
status groups would suggest that they seek only
social gains.   Status groups, however, may pursue
material aims by using their cultural solidarity as
a means of doing so.   For example, status groups
which owe their solidarity to either a common gender
or ethnicity seek economic improvement (Collins, 1976).
      Status groups may emerge from within social
classes, or even within general occupational
categories.   Take teaching, for example.   Primary
school teachers seek greater professional status by
pointing out their pedagogical expertise, as opposed
to secondary school teachers who claim a higher
status based on their perceived higher academic
qualifications.   However, in an attempt to increase
and to legitimate their claims to parity with
secondary teachers, primary teachers have called for,
and obtained, an all-graduate profession (in England
and Wales).   This is an example of what Collins (1979)
regards as an up-grading of academic qualifications
for entry into an occupation mainly for status, not
technical reasons.   That is, it is arguable than an
academic degree may not <u>necessarily</u> make its holder
a better teacher than his nongraduate colleague, but
it will confer greater status upon him as a teacher.
An earlier discussion of the so-called 'immigrant'
and classroom teachers at Rockfield was an example
of two groups of teachers who both sought to assert
their status over the other.
      We have just argued, with Weber, that some
status groups owe their shared subjectivity to an
economic consideration;   that is, one based on their
occupation.   In addition to economic considerations,
others come into play which appear to have less of
an economic basis.   These are based upon a shared
ethnicity, gender and religion.   Our concern here is
more with the first two of these.   Within the working
class there are ethnic groups, some of which differ
on the basis of a minor physical characteristic like
skin colour.   And, again within the working class,
there are gender-groups where the biological differences are far more pronounced.   If two ethnic groups -
take Black Britons and White Britons for example -
happen to differ in some small physiological way, it
is incorrect to attribute whatever socio-cultural
differences there are between them to these biological

differences.   That is, cultural differences are not
reducible to racial/biological ones.[2]   The shared
subjectivity among Black Britons is more accurately
explained historically.   The development of mercan-
tile capitalism initially led to their being
colonised and, later, to being used as migrant
workers within Britain.   As one placard put it: 'We
are here because you were there'.   Put another way,
the social solidarity of ethnic groups is to be
explained as a result of their socio-historical
conditions - if these groups happen to differ
physiologically in some small way, that difference
merely serves to accentuate the cultural differences
in so far as it may enable one group to recognise
its own members.   Weber is helpful here:

> We shall use the expression 'ethnic' group to
> describe human groups (other than kinship
> groups) which cherish a belief in the common
> origins of such a kind that it provides a basis
> for the creation of a community.   This belief
> may be based on similarities of external custom
> or practice or both, or on memories of colonisa-
> tion or migration.   <u>The question whether they
> are to be called an 'ethnic' group is indepen-
> dent of the question whether they are
> objectively of common stock</u>.   (Weber, 1978:387)
> (emphasis added)

A second status group which does not wholly explain
its social solidarity on the basis of economic
criteria is that based on gender.   Recently, the
term 'sex-role' has given way to 'gender-role', in
much the same way as 'racial group' and 'immigrant
group' have been replaced by 'ethnic' group.   This
is because terms like 'sex' and 'race' strongly
imply that social action is solely attributable to
biological characteristics, which it is not.   There
is no biological inevitability about the thoughts
and actions of men and women: gender roles have
differed across time and space.   The argument is
often raised, however, that because it is only women
who can bear children, it is they who are 'naturally'
better prepared for a home-based, 'child-centred'
life.   I shall return to this argument very shortly.
What I wish to emphasise here is that status groups,
based on ethnicity and gender, will serve to fragment
the homogeneity of consciousness within the working
class.   Within the working class, there will be both
ethnic and gender stratification, and the status
groups will seek to undermine each other, thereby

156

maximising their social status. Status group
conflict, moreover, may see different elements of
power being used. Collins (1972), in an historical
analysis of sexual stratification argues that,
traditionally, women have had to rely more on their
sexuality to achieve power over men. More recently,
however, as women increasingly enter paid employment,
they need rely less on their traditional use of
sexuality because they now have more economic power.
Men, on the other hand, must seek to redress the
balance by resorting to their sexuality to compensate
for their diminishing economic power vis-a-vis women.
In Weberian terms, therefore, status groups adopt
exclusionary practices in respect of others. They
may do this, for example, by seeking to control
access to a particular residential area, access to
academic qualifications, or whatever. Given the
distribution of power, some dominant status groups
are better placed to exclude others, whilst more
assertive groups must resist being excluded. But
what is crucial in status group conflict is that each
group must preserve its solidarity, and it is here
that ethnic groups may be better placed than gender
groups. The difference turns on the consideration
that ethnic groups tend not to intermarry, but, of
course, many men and women do, thereby perhaps
weakening their internal coherence as gender status
groups.
     Status groups based on ethnicity and gender
also hold positions in relation to the means of
production. These status groups within the working
class are admitted by Marxists. Thus Castles and
Kosack (1973), for example, take a view not
dissimilar from Cromwell-Cox (1959) when they argue
that recent immigration into Western Europe has
brought about a division within the working class.
That is to say, capitalism has succeeded in convincing the white working class of its labour superio-
rity over migrant workers. The latter are seen by
the white working class as occupying a lower class
location because they undertake the most low-paid
and menial tasks. But in fact, so the argument goes,
the objective class position of both immigrant and
white workers is the same: neither controls nor
owns the means of production; neither has any say
in the distribution of products and profits. Thus
the white working class has fallen for this ideology
which indicates the differences, not the similarities
of their class location in respect of immigrant
workers. Rather than seek an alliance with immigrant
workers, white workers choose to keep them at bay,

thereby preserving their perception of themselves as
the 'labour aristocracy'. In short, these two
groups act according to the Weberian definition of
class; that is, both 'lack property', and both
compete with each other to sell their labour on the
most favourable terms they can get. Once the status-
based differentiation within the working class is
admitted, it is very difficult to sustain the argument that as capitalism develops, so too will the
homogeneity of consciousness within the proletariat.

     It is also difficult from a Marxist perspective
to explain completely social differentiation which
is based on race and ethnicity. For Marxism, the
ultimate basis for social differentiation and
conflict is class. It is difficult to see, therefore,
how Marxism can explain racial differences as being
wholly the epiphenomenon of capitalism. This
difficulty is admitted. Wright, himself a Marxist,
states:

> A common mistake made by Marxists in analysing
> racism is to assume that all forms of racial
> discrimination are unequivocally functional for
> the capitalist class. (Wright, 1979:201)[3]

Mullard (1981:134), in his neoMarxist analysis of
multicultural education in Britain, argues that
changes in material condition can only result from:

> ... process of internal struggle, resistance,
> and alliances forged between and within race,
> class and gender groups that appear to share
> socially similar if not identical experience,
> positions and conditions in society.

Whilst there is no denying exploitation of class,
gender and ethnic groups in society, the 'alliances'
that require to be forged among those groups, would
not, for Weber, have been easy. His view would not
have been to accept that exploitation, merely to
point up the difficulties of effecting social
solidarity among these status groups.

     Just as ethnic status groups are located within
the class structure, so too are gender-based groups.
From a Marxist perspective, it is in the interests
of capitalism to sustain an ideology which sees the
family as a natural institution rather than a social
construction convenient to its needs. This ideology
is easy to sustain because it is underpinned by what
are thought by functionalism to be biological
imperatives: that is, men cannot bear children and

158

must therefore undertake the 'instrumental', bread-
winner role in the family, leaving the 'expressive',
home-based role to the wife and mother (Zelditch,
1956).   The neoMarxist critique of this analysis
argued that the traditional role of the mother as
house-worker and child-rearer could be performed by
social agencies, thereby freeing the woman to take
up her place in the socialist productive process.[4]
Capitalism resists this, for a variety of reasons:
first, as Rowbotham (1973) indicates, women are the
'reproducers of the commodity producers';   that is,
they actually reproduce the labour force;   secondly,
women socialize their children in a manner that is
functional for the school and for (capitalist)
society;   thirdly, women constitute an important
market for capitalism's goods and services;
fourthly, during times of business upturn, women may
be quickly and cheaply brought into the labour force
to cope with rising demand and, by the same token,
during recession they may be jettisoned from the
workforce to take up their alleged 'rightful place
in the home' (Mitchell, 1966).   That said, however,
the lower material position of women as opposed to
men - and the sex discrimination which is associated
with it - may not wholly be explained as the result
of capitalism.   (Wright, 1979:218;   Giddens, 1981:
242-243;   Shorter, 1976)
        To summarise the introduction of this chapter,
it has been argued, following Weber, that a social
class will tend not to have a shared subjectivity,
even though, objectively, it shares the common
condition of being a group which 'lacks property'.
Within a social class, status differentation may
occur.   That differentiation may, firstly, arise out
of a common occupational situation.   Secondly, status
differentiation, as well as being linked to an
economic consideration, may also arise out of a
common ethnicity, gender or religious socio-cultural
membership.   In our discussion of ethnic and gender
status groups, we have stressed that a gender-based
status group does not owe its shared subjectivity to
its shared biological properties, or sex.   In the
same way, an ethnic group, even though it may share
some minor biological characteristic like skin
colour, does not owe its social solidarity to that
shared biological characteristic.   Ethnicity and
gender are socio-cultural categories, not biological
ones.   Whilst these biological characteristics may
enable status groups, in some cases, to identify
their own members (and, by implication, 'outsiders')
they do not, of themselves, determine the consciousness

of a status group. That said, it was then argued
that it was the very existence of these status
groups within the working class which, for Weber,
limited the possibilities for a shared, pre-revolutionary consciousness to emerge. In Weber's analysis
the tendency would be for status groups to compete
with each other so as to maximise their social esteem
and material standing to the detriment of other
groups within the working class.

Status Differentiation and Education

In an earlier chapter, it was noted that pre-1971
educational sociology tended to confine itself to
demonstrating social class differences in occupational achievement where the IQ of the social classes
was held constant (Douglas, 1964). As an explanation
of this working class underachievement, a 'deficient'
home was cited as the cause, and was then 'compensated' for in the school (Plowden, 1967). But the
inequalities persisted, and they were not wholly
explicable in terms of the lower average IQ of
working class children, allowing for the cultural
bias of IQ testing in favour of middle class pupils.
More recent explanations have focussed upon how the
management and content of classroom knowledge
appears to favour middle class pupils (Young, 1971),
and upon teachers having lower expectations of pupils
who are perceived as being of working class background (Nash, 1973). One of the most sophisticated
explanations of working class underachievement has
been developed in France by Bourdieu (1974) who
suggests that the 'cultural capital' of the middle
class pupil is academically valued in the school
and treated as though it were a natural endowment,
and not a socially conferred one. Much of this
research and analysis has tended to focus solely on
social class, as measured by father's occupation.
Rarely have there been attempts to dwell upon
differences within the working class. Put another
way, very little attention has been paid to the
effects of status group membership within the working
class on educational achievement. It is only
comparatively recently that the status 'factors' of
gender and ethnicity have been considered as worthy
of analysis. Even then there has been little attempt
to interrelate the status factors of gender and
ethnicity within a social class group.
    It is with this omission that this section and
the next are concerned. The social composition of
Rockfield School is particularly appropriate given

its coeducational and multi-ethnic intake of pupils.
Moreover, its perceived working class composition
allows us to consider the effects of pupil gender
and ethnicity <u>within</u> a working class school setting.
We begin with ethnically-based status groups among
the pupils.

Social Relations between Ethnic Minority and White Pupils

The declared ethos of Mr. McLean in respect of
ethnic minority pupils was one of assimilation. The
school should have a family atmosphere and a sense
of community. The community was to include both
white and ethnic minority pupils, boys and girls.
This assimilationist policy, however, did allow a
few organisational practices specific to ethnic
minority pupils. The 'Immigrant Department', for
example, though it segregated these children, had
the long-term goal of facilitating their adaptation
to the teachers' definition of the school.
'Immigrant meals' and the partial relaxation of the
school dress code for girls appeared to be underpinned by religious considerations. Rockfield School
was not in the business of providing ethnic studies
solely for 'ethnic minority' pupils; it was there
to 'assimilate immigrants' through a process of
acculturation. · In the pursuit of a 'family atmosphere' and 'community', neither multicultural
education nor ethnic studies had a logical part to
play.
      If Mr. McLean's policy of realising a sense of
community were to be effected, it would not be
expected that status differentiation among the pupils
themselves would be strong. Boys and girls, ethnic
minority and white pupils, would show no particular
preference for 'their own kind'; they would not
effect exclusionary practices in respect of each
other. Evidence from other studies reveals that in
multi-ethnic British primary schools, white and
ethnic minority children, even when at the age of
five years, express a high degree of ethnocentric
behaviour when nominating a preferred or actual best
friend. The evidence tends to be drawn from two
kinds of study: the large-scale survey, and the
case-study of individual schools. An example of the
former is Jelinek and Brittan's (1975) study of 1,288
pupils in the second and fourth year of junior
school, the children being taken from thirteen
schools. The authors report considerable ethnocentric behaviour when pupils stated their actual and

TABLE 3

Preferred 'best friend' choices, dichotomised by
ethnicity at the school aggregate level

NOMINATORS	NOMINEES Ethnic Minority Pupils		NOMINEES White Pupils	
	%	Ratio of observed to expected (O÷E)	%	Ratio of observed to expected (O÷E)
All ethnic minority (n=86)	39.5	1.19	60.5	.9
All white (n=172)	18.6	.56	81.4	1.22

Note: 8 percent of white pupils were 'undecided' about their best
friend choice; for ethnic minority pupils the corresponding
percentage is 7.4. The table does not include 'undecided'
nominations.

desired friends. A similar finding was made by
Davey and Mullin (1982) of 3,953 white, West Indian
and Asian children aged seven to eleven. Of
particular interest was the result that white
children, when in a majority, tend to be less ethnocentric than when in a minority. Of further interest,
relevant here, was the finding that the most ethni-
cally-divided schools were E.P.A. schools implementing
a 'formal' pedagogy, and which had a high proportion
of Asian children. As for the case-study, a similar
reluctance to opt for cross-race choices was
observed by Braha and Rutter (1980) in their study
of a Midlands primary school of predominantly
(80 percent) Asian composition. The findings were
derived from twenty children who had been selected
from each of six age-groups. These groups, however,
were statistical artefacts which had no real social
basis in the form of actual classroom groups.

At Rockfield School pupils were asked to
nominate a preferred best friend. Such choices
might indicate the degree of social exclusivity or
closure which white and ethnic minority pupils might
want in respect of each other. Given Mr. McLean's
assimilationist and school-as-family policy, the
degree of preferred, not actual, social closure
expected would be negligible. Table 3 analyses the
choices at the school aggregate level. Take the
case of ethnic minority pupils nominating: the ratio
of observed nominations to both ethnic minority and
to white children is almost as expected. If the
nominations made by white pupils are inspected, it
can be seen that ethnic minority children receive
fewer nominations than expected, and white children
more than expected.

We turn now to nominating patterns within actual
classrooms (Figures 1 and 2). Figure 1 deals with
the nominations made by white pupils. An example
from the figure may facilitate its interpretation.
Take classroom 7a. In that class, 28 per cent of the
pupils were of ethnic minority status; 72 per cent
were white. It would be expected that ethnic
minority pupils would, therefore, receive 28 per cent
of the nominations whilst the white pupils would
receive 72 per cent. In fact, the observed percentage
for ethnic minority pupils is 11 per cent, and for
white pupils it is 83 per cent. These percentages
may be expressed as a ratio of observed percentages
to expected (that is, observed divided by expected).
So, in this example, the ratio for ethnic minority
pupils is .39; for white pupils it is 1.15. Thus
ethnic minority pupils received fewer nominations

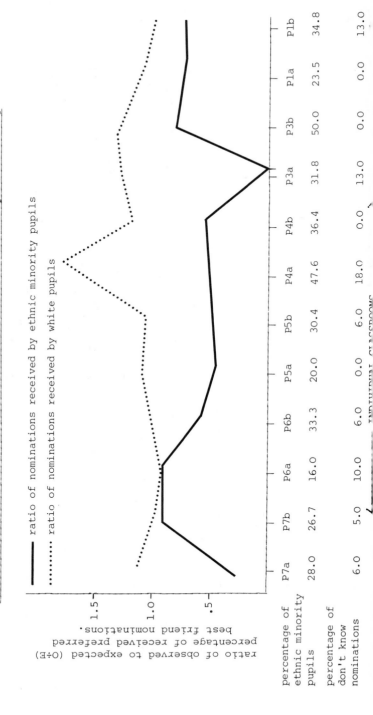

FIGURE 1

Ethnic differences in Preferred Best Friend Nominations: White Pupils Nominating

——— ratio of nominations received by ethnic minority pupils

.... ratio of nominations received by white pupils

ratio of observed to expected (O÷E)
percentage of received preferred
best friend nominations.

	P7a	P7b	P6a	P6b	P5a	P5b	P4a	P4b	P3a	P3b	P1a	P1b
percentage of ethnic minority pupils	28.0	26.7	16.0	33.3	20.0	30.4	47.6	36.4	31.8	50.0	23.5	34.8
percentage of don't know nominations	6.0	5.0	10.0	6.0	0.0	6.0	18.0	0.0	13.0	0.0	0.0	13.0

164

FIGURE 2

Ethnic differences in Preferred Best Friend Nominations: Ethnic Minority Pupils Nominating

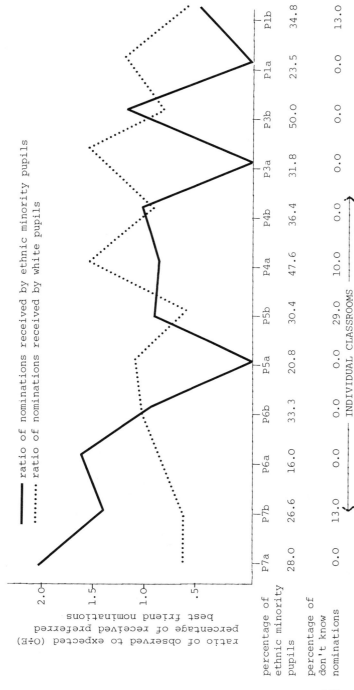

than expected, whilst white children received more
than expected. If, still with Figure 1, the ratios
for the other classrooms are inspected, in no classroom does the ratio of nominations received by ethnic
minority children exceed that received by white
children when white children are nominating. The
trend, therefore, is clear: when white pupils are
nominating, they tend to nominate white pupils more
than expected, and ethnic minority pupils less than
expected.

Consider now Figure 2, which shows the allocation of nominations made by ethnic minority children
in the different classrooms. Here the pattern is
not clear: in some classrooms the ratio for ethnic
minority children exceeds that for white, as in P7a,
P6a and P7b, although the last class has 13 per cent
'don't knows'. But in P3a and Pla, the ethnic
minority pupils nominate white pupils more than
expected. The cautious conclusion to be drawn from
both these aggregated and classroom analyses is that
there is a trend for white pupils to be more ethnocentric than expected, and for ethnic minority pupils
to be less so.

The sociometric data deal only with the preferred choice of friend - they do not deal with actual
friends, nor with hostility and aggression. And nor
can it be inferred that an unwillingness to prefer
someone as a friend means a prejudice against that
person. The appropriate methodology to investigate
the existence of social closure practices would be a
long-term or non-participant observation. Although
this method is the most appropriate, it is also the
most difficult. It is perhaps no accident that
recent ethnographic studies of the primary school
have concentrated more on teachers than on pupils
(Sharp and Green, 1975; King,1978). The problem
for the researcher in the primary school is that he
cannot easily merge into the social world of young
children when they are beyond the classroom and the
playground. Even when the children realise that the
researcher is not a teacher, they may understandably
be reluctant to recount on trust the details of
fighting and name-calling. And even if children do
offer such information, the researcher, in listening
to them, may appear to the children to have condoned
them. My information on exclusionary practices
between the ethnic groups at Rockfield is therefore
very limited, and is confined to extracts of informal
conversations I had with the children. In most cases
the reliability of this qualitative data has not been
checked, nor could it have been done so very easily

for I would have run the risk of making an 'issue'
out of something which teachers stated was 'not an
issue', namely racial discord. The incidents of
ethnic differentiation and discrimination are
reported below:

(1) Primary 3 pupil: David calls them 'Pakis' and
                         'Darkies'.

(2) Girls (white):   They're ('immigrants') always
                         quiet. And there's this girl
                         in our class ... she's always
                         crying. When people talk
                         about her she bursts out
                         crying.

     DH: In what ways do they talk
                         about her?

     Girls: They say, 'Ooo, your painting's
                         horrible' and 'I'm going to
                         batter you after school'. She
                         just starts crying.

     DH: Do you think they say that
                         because she's an 'immigrant'?

     Girls: Yes.

(3) DH: Are you ever called names?

     Ethnic minority
       boy: No.

     Girl (white):   Sometimes he's called 'pig'
                         and 'coloured'.

     Girl (white):   They sometimes call her
                         'chocolate' and everything
                         like that.

     DH: And does that upset you?

     Ethnic minority
       girl: Sometimes, but not really.

(4) Ethnic minority
       boy: I get called a 'Paki' ...

     Ethnic minority
       boy: I get called a 'Black B..'

167

DH: What do you do?

Boy: I just go and punch them or something.

DH (to other boy): And what do you do?

Boy: I just kick them in the tummy ...

(5) DH (to ethnic
       minority boy):   Is there anything in this school that annoys you a lot?

Boy: People calling me names.   That annoys me.

DH: What kind of names?

Boy: Sometimes they call us 'Pakistani' and that.

(6) Girl (white)   The coloured people get called 'Milky Bar'.

(7) Ethnic minority
       girl: I don't like being called names.

DH: And what do you do when people call you names?

Girl: I just ignore them.

Why were these derogatory labels assigned to ethnic minority children? The name-calling refers to the superficial difference in skin pigmentation between whites and the ethnic minority children. The minor physical difference is thought to be an indicator of, and the justification for, a lower social esteem. But it might have been the case that these white children saw in their ethnic minority school-mates a set of cultural characteristics which were different from, and inimical to, their own. The physical difference was then superimposed upon the cultural difference and cited as the reason for the discrimination. It is doubtful, however, if the discriminators consciously sought the explanation for their own actions. Certainly the manifestation of cultural differences in school between white and ethnic minority boys was negligible: most of the ethnic minority boys were born in Scotland and their rendering of the local patois was indistinguishable from that of the white boys. In the playground they played football together as a matter of course. The differences between white and ethnic minority girls in matters of culture were slightly more obvious: most ethnic minority girls adopted the practice of wearing trousers under their school uniform, and a few would not change into shorts for P.E. Perhaps, for most of the discriminators, the 'colour-difference' 'theory' sufficed, and is nicely put in the following extract:

DH: Why do you think Jim doesn't like them?

Girl: Because they're black.

Jim: I don't like any coloured people at all.

Some of the teachers have already been quoted as saying that the English language teaching facility for ethnic minority children, the 'Immigrant Depart-ment', was provided at the expense of remedial instruction for the white children. The presence of ethnic minority children implied an educational cost to 'our' white children. Some of the children argued that the ethnic minority pupils were given favourable treatment. A sensitive issue was the presumed higher quality of 'immigrant meals', as this extract reveals:

Girl: One day there was fish fingers for the 'immigrants', but (for us) there was horrible mince and stovies.

Boy: I know. Why don't we get fish fingers as well?

Girl: Because it's their religion ...

Girl: We asked for fish fingers and there was thousands left over and they said we couldn't have any - it was for the 'immigrants'. And we were going back and they said there was none left.

Girl: I know. And there was only about three 'immigrants' to go and get their food.

Girl: They wouldn't give us anything ...

Some children reported that teachers were 'easier' with ethnic minority pupils than with white children. Others saw no difference:

(1) White boy: The teachers take more time with learning the blacks English than with us. My mum and dad says they spend more time with the blacks than they do with us.

(2) DH: Do you think the teachers treat the 'immigrants' any differently?

Girls (3):   YES!

Girl: They're not as strict.

Girl: I think they're petted.

(3) Girl: Mrs. ----- favours 'immigrants' more than whites.

(4) Girl: I think all the teachers like them.

DH: Do they treat them in the same way as white children?

Girl: Yes.

(5) DH: Are they treated any differently by the teachers?

Boys: No, just the same way.

The sociometric data here give partial support to the notion that ethnic minority and white children at Rockfield perceive themselves as having separate identities. These data suggest that white pupils are more ethnocentric than ethnic minority children, the latter seeking to 'belong' more to the white group than vice-versa. White pupils tend more to social closure than do their ethnic minority counter-parts, at least when the data are aggregated across classrooms. Moreover, the white pupils have adopted the term 'immigrant' used by their teachers, and, in some instances, white pupils imply that ethnic minority pupils are treated differently and preferen-tially, at a cost to themselves. It may be suggested, however, that the absence of special curriculum for

ethnic minority pupils may have served to 'assimilate'
the 'immigrants', as they were termed. That is to
say, an absence of curricular division may be
associated with an absence of marked ethnocentric
behaviour. On the other hand, white pupils came to
know little of the culture of the ethnic minority
children since there was no multi-cultural curricular
provision for all of the pupils, both white and
ethnic minority. The ethnic minority pupils had to
adapt to white cultural practices, not vice-versa.
There is, however, an important proviso to be made
here: the analysis so far has not considered gender
differences in and between white and ethnic minority
pupils, in respect of their preferred social relationships. In other words, if we deal only with boys,
is there the possibility that ethnocentric behaviour
is negligible? Similarly, if we deal only with
girls, do we also find little ethnocentric behaviour
in respect of preferred best friend choices? We
shall return to this matter after we have considered
the extent to which boys and girls see themselves as
constituting distinct social groups.

Social Relations between Boys and Girls

It has been suggested that status differentiation
based on gender is less than that based on ethnicity.
We have also suggested that white ethnic groups
adopt greater exclusionary methods than do ethnic
minority groups; that is, exclusion is not
symmetrical. What evidence at Rockfield may be
adduced to suggest that teachers differentiate
according to the sex of the pupil, and what evidence
is there that boys and girls adopt exclusionary
practices in respect of each other? Firstly,
teachers do differentiate in the classroom by referring to 'boys' and 'girls'. At Rockfield,areas of
the playground were defined as accessible to one sex
only. Names on the register were divided on the
basis of gender. In some classes boys and girls
lined up separately. They had different coloured
record cards. Thus the social characteristic of
gender was given some institutional recognition.
     There is consistent evidence that boys and girls
rarely nominate a member of the opposite sex as a
'best friend' in the primary school. For example,
in the previously-mentioned study by Jelinek and
Brittan (1975), cross-sex choices were in the range
of between two and five per cent for 'desired' friends,
and only one per cent for 'actual' friends. These
results are supported here. Eighty-eight per cent of

FIGURE 3

Sex differences in Preferred Best Friend Nominations

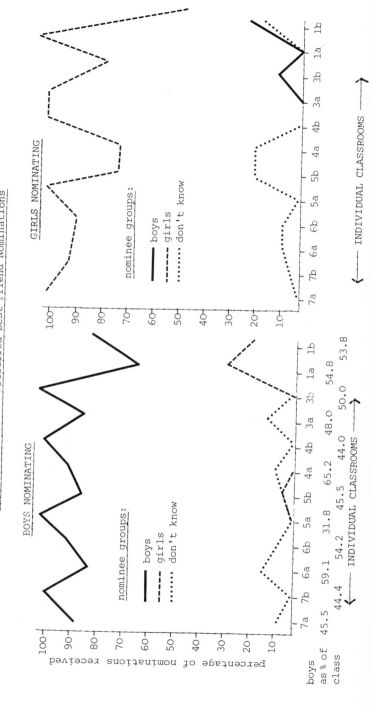

172

the pupils preferred a same-sex friend; four per cent of both boys and girls nominated a member of the opposite sex; eight per cent could not decide. These trends are strongly supported at the classroom level, as Figure 3 reveals. Using sociometric data, therefore, it would appear that there is some evidence for asserting that boys and girls as pupils perceive themselves as having separate identities. In Weberian terminology, they may constitute status groups, but they seem not to compete with each other to maximise their social honour at the other's expense. Indifference towards each other might better describe their relationship. Open hostility between boys and girls was reported to be rare:

> Ethnic minority
> boy: I used to fight a lot before Christmas.
>
> DH: Do the girls fight?
>
> Ethnic minority
> boy (2): Yes, sometimes they argue when they've been friends with other girls.
>
> DH: Do they ever fight with boys?
>
> Ethnic minority
> boy (2): No ... sometimes.

Amongst the older children, boy-girl hostility did arise and was sometimes caused by a failed 'love' affair, as with Annie and Alan:

> DH: Have any of your parents been up to the school to complain about anything?
>
> Jim: Yes, Annie Robertson's - she used to be my girlfriend.
>
> DH: Can you speak up a bit Jim.
>
> Jim: Well, we get club after school and we were playing, and I was with my friend. He bought her a flower for Christmas and she stuffed it down the drain. She got me into trouble. It was really Alan Brent and all that were hitting her. I wasn't ...

Alan: I was going to get expelled because
             of her ...

DH: Because you hit her?

Alan: Her mum said that she had bruises all
             over her back, and I never even
             touched her once. The only time I
             hit her was that time in the class.
             Remember ..? And she was calling me
             names that I don't like so I pushed
             her. She kicked me, so I kicked her,
             so she went away crying.

Jim: The only time I hit her was by
             accident.

Whereas fighting between boys and girls was rare,
fighting among boys themselves was not. The formation of gangs within the school was forbidden and
attracted corporal punishment:

DH: Do people in the school belong to
             gangs?

Boy: I don't. I used to when I lived at my
             old place at Nelson Tower, and it was
             called the 'Midget Mental Mad Squad'...

DH: Why was it called that?

Boy (1):   You get belted when you've got a gang
             in the school, isn't that right
             Leslie?

Boy (2):   Because we're all mental when we
             start fighting ...

DH: What sort of things do you do in
             gangs?

Boy (2):   Break windows.

Boy (2):   You wouldn't really call it a gang;
             you would just call it a group of
             people.

DH: So what makes a gang?

Boy (2):   People that bully you.

> Boy (1): And we had an enemy gang called the 'Big Yins' ...

The boys were at pains to indicate that there were fights and 'fights'. The following extract indicates how, firstly, a fight might arise out of an unintended conflict in the interpretation of an incident in a game of football; and secondly, how, in another event, a child's similar 'misinterpretation' of an intended playful fight led to matters turning sour.

> DH: What happened this morning?
>
> Ron: A boy came to tackle me and he kicked me in the shin by accident and I thought he meant it, and I kicked him ...
>
> DH: How do you know he didn't mean it. Who told you?
>
> Ron: The boy.
>
> DH: And he went away and told the teacher?
>
> Ron: No. Gary told the teacher.
>
> Bill: (wanting to interject) The ball came to me before it went to the other boy, so I went away and scored the goal and the ball ran to Ron and the boy thought the ball was still there ...
>
> DH: What did you have to do when Mrs. Carter came?
>
> Ron: Make an apology to him.
>
> DH: And did you?
>
> Ron: Yes.
>
> DH: In front of the whole class?
>
> Ron: Yes.

In the second incident, a 'fight' became 'for real':

> DH: Has anything else happened when you've been punished?

> Bill: We'd been fighting.
>
> DH: You were fighting. What happened?
>
> Ron: Robert battered four of them.
>
> Bill: But we were only playing with them ...
>
> Ron: He battered the whole lot of them.
>
> Bill: We were playing with Robert and then
>   Robert thought we were playing real,
>   and so he was doing karate on us and
>   then it was only Ron, Paul and Billy
>   that was playing. And then when
>   Robert was doing karate I thought he
>   was doing it for real, and it was real,
>   and so I was in the middle of it and
>   so I was telling him it was only a
>   game ...

I questioned Donald about fighting among the boys.
As a member of a boxing club, he had a discerning
eye for a fight:

> No really. It's not really fighting. It's
> just kind of fun because everybody says, 'Oh
> well, do you want to fight. I'm a better
> fighter than you. Do you want to fight with
> me?' But by the time they go home it's all
> forgotten about.

Fights among the boys were rarely planned because
too many children and teachers would get to know
about them in advance. The teachers would intervene.
Fights did occur, but usually they arose spontan-
eously out of the physical contact games in which
boys normally engaged during playtime or after
school. Fights in the classroom when the teacher
was absent, or when she was not looking, would be
defined by the boys as playful taunting at the level
of ritual.
    Occasionally the honour of the school was at
stake and it was then that the shared identity among
the boys came to the fore. Perhaps a child from
another school had hurt a Rockfield pupil or, more
seriously, children from another school had made an
aggressive 'raid' on Rockfield. When this happened
the Rockfield boys closed ranks in a common effort
to repel the invaders. I witnessed one such foray
by children from the nearby Wellington and Southbank

Schools. The general analysis was that Willy Scott, the 'best scrapper in the school', had allegedly chased some children from Southbank School. A retaliatory raid on Rockfield was made during the lunch-break. There was verbal abuse of the most vivid kind, and kicks and punches were exchanged between the children. One of the teachers apprehended a Southbank pupil who had kicked him. Boys and girls from Rockfield cheered the defenders and jeered the attackers. The police were called. In the afternoon, after tempers had cooled and culprits brought to book, the head teacher, Mrs. Watt, gave the 38 boys who had cheered the fighters a severe ticking-off. Six of the very active participants in the fight were given the belt by Mr. Lane and Mr. Alexander. Much resentment was directed at the teachers by the boys at their failure to reprimand any of the girls who had been urging on the boys during the scrap. Indeed, the reluctance of teachers to belt the girls was an important bone of contention with the boys:

> David: A good teacher is friendly, gives you good work, a lot of it, and gives all the girls the belt as well ...

> Anwarul: A good teacher is not shouting or giving the belt much; and she'll give the girls the belt as well.

> Willy: I like men better 'cos women always take pity on the girls.

Whilst girls were less likely to indulge in fighting, it was not unknown for fights between them to occur. And nor, as the boys claimed, did they escape the belt.

(1) DH: How do the girls get along? Is there much bullying amongst girls?

 Girls(3): YES!

 Wendy: Ann Foster's one of them.

 DH: That surprises me ...

 Dorothy: She fights with Angela quite a lot.

 Wendy: She shouts at you when you've got a best boy friend.

	DH:	Who has?
	Wendy:	Sometimes Ann Foster's does it, and then sometimes they go with you and she usually goes around bullying folk because they go with her lad.
	DH:	Who's her lad?
	Wendy:	Harry. And there was another one. I can't remember his name though he's from secondary school, and Ann was saying something about the games and that. And she was showing off in front of that boy and that.
(2)	Eileen:	Mandy and Louise were fighting.
	DH:	What happened?
	Eileen:	They were wanting them to fight in the Victoria Park and Mandy wouldn't do it. She said why do you not fight at my own place, but they wouldn't do it, so they fighted right in the middle of the school, and they both got the belt and they weren't allowed to play out for a long time.

This anecdotal data is a selection which is not representative of the views of all pupils. Not all pupils talked about social relations between boys and girls; it did not seem to be an 'issue' with them. Of more concern to them were social relations within their own sex, particularly the matter of fighting among the boys. The only recurring cross-sex comments were made by some boys who believed girls to be too lightly reprimanded by teachers. Thus in their preferred friendship choices, boys and girls differentiated on the basis of sex, but in their day-to-day school existence they did not appear to <u>discriminate</u> on the basis of sex. In Weberian terms, therefore, boys and girls constructed separate identities and, beyond the classroom, their social relationships tended not to include members of the opposite sex. But despite this, boys and girls as separate status groups did not appear to be openly hostile to each other, only indifferent to each other.

TABLE 4

Preferred 'best friend' choices:
gender and ethnicity interrelated at school aggregate level

NOMINEES

NOMINATORS	White Boys		Ethnic Minority Boys		White Girls		Ethnic Minority Girls	
	%	ratio of observed to expected (O÷E)	%	ratio of observed to expected (O÷E)	%	ratio of observed to expected (O÷E)	%	ratio of observed to expected (O÷E)
W Boys (n=81)	76.5	2.4	19.8	1.1	3.7	.1	0.0	
EM Boys (n=46)	50.0	1.6	43.5	2.4	6.5	.2	0.0	
W Girls (n=91)	5.5	.2	0.0		76.9	2.2	17.6	1.1
EM Girls (n=40)	0.0		0.0		65.0	1.8	35.0	2.3

179

Preferred Friendship Choice: Gender and Ethnicity Interrelated

We have so far dichotomised the sociometric data on the basis of gender and ethnicity. Pupils, however, are members of both ethnic and gender groups, and any analysis should allow for this. That is, the analysis should compare the friendship choices of the four groups (ethnic minority boys, ethnic minority girls, white boys, white girls). Table 4 presents the results of this analysis. From this, each ethnic/gender group tends to nominate itself more than expected, and more than any other group. White girls tend to nominate ethnic minority girls as expected, but ethnic minority girls tend to nominate white girls slightly more than expected. A similar pattern obtains for boys: that is, white boys nominate ethnic minority boys as expected, but the latter tend to nominate white boys slightly more than expected. Thus, within a sex, ethnic minority pupils tend to prefer an ethnic 'opposite' more than do white pupils, but neither ethnic group shows much evidence of social closure. These findings, therefore, refine those in Table 3 which merely dichotomise the sociometric choices by ethnicity and gender. The main difference is that, whereas in Table 3, white children were shown to nominate ethnic minority children less than expected, when white pupils within a sex are nominating, they do not 'under-nominate' ethnic minority children of the same sex (Table 4). We may infer, therefore, that gender differentiation within an ethnic group far exceeds ethnic differentiation within a sex.

Status Group Differences and Perceived Academic Standing

Educational research has paid considerable attention to the 'halo effect' whereby teachers are said to confuse a pupil's social attributes with his intellectual ability (Nash, 1976). Here we focus upon the pupil and his judgement of the academic standing of himself and of other pupils in his classroom. We do so by investigating how four groups of pupil, whose ethnicity and gender differ, rank the academic standing of themselves and of members of other groups. The previous analysis of the sociometric data tended to support the view that pupils prefer a same-sex best friend more than they prefer a best friend of the same ethnic group. When sex is held constant, the ethnic differences in pupil

FIGURE 4

Pupils' Classroom Rank-ordering of their Classmates:
Ethnicity and Sex

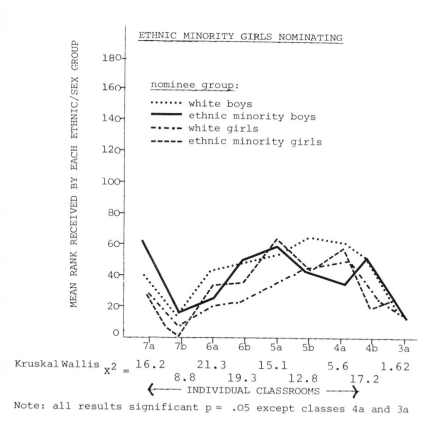

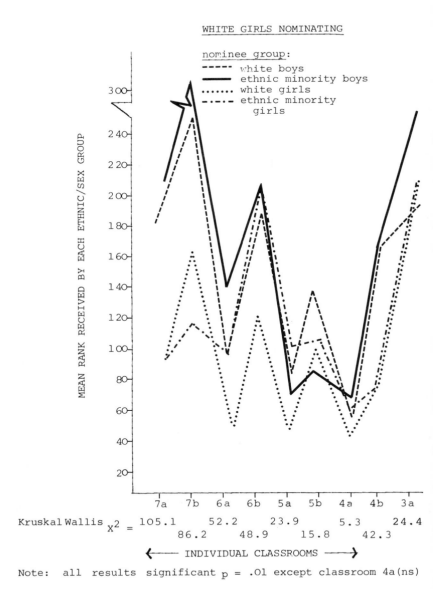

FIGURE 5

Pupils' Academic Rank-ordering of their Classmates:
Ethnicity and Sex

WHITE GIRLS NOMINATING

nominee group:
- ----- white boys
- ——— ethnic minority boys
- .... white girls
- -·-·- ethnic minority
  girls

MEAN RANK RECEIVED BY EACH ETHNIC/SEX GROUP

| | 7a | 7b | 6a | 6b | 5a | 5b | 4a | 4b | 3a |

Kruskal Wallis x^2 =

105.1   52.2   23.9   5.3   24.4
    86.2   48.9   15.8   42.3

←——— INDIVIDUAL CLASSROOMS ———→

Note: all results significant $p = .01$ except classroom 4a(ns)

FIGURE 6

Pupils' Academic Rank-ordering of their Classmates:
Ethnicity and Sex

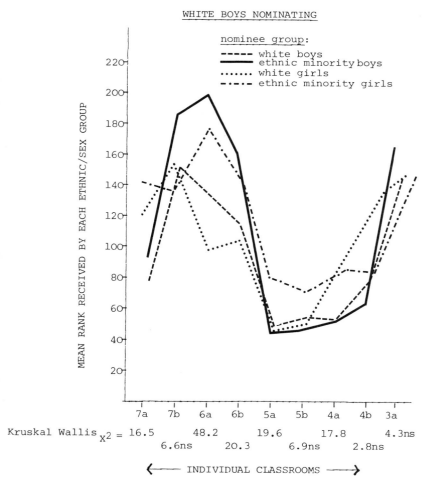

WHITE BOYS NOMINATING

nominee group:
- - - - - white boys
———— ethnic minority boys
.... white girls
-·-·- ethnic minority girls

MEAN RANK RECEIVED BY EACH ETHNIC/SEX GROUP

Kruskal Wallis X^2 = 16.5   48.2   19.6   17.8   4.3ns
                    6.6ns   20.3   6.9ns   2.8ns

←——— INDIVIDUAL CLASSROOMS ———→

Note: all results significant p = .001, except those marked ns

FIGURE 7

Pupils' Classroom Rank-ordering of their Classmates:
Ethnicity and Sex

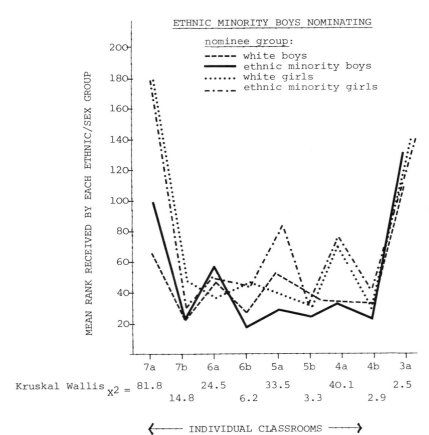

ETHNIC MINORITY BOYS NOMINATING

nominee group:
----- white boys
▬▬▬ ethnic minority boys
······· white girls
─·─·─ ethnic minority girls

MEAN RANK RECEIVED BY EACH ETHNIC/SEX GROUP

	7a	7b	6a	6b	5a	5b	4a	4b	3a
Kruskal Wallis $\chi^2 =$	81.8		24.5		33.5		40.1		2.5
		14.8		6.2		3.3		2.9	

←——— INDIVIDUAL CLASSROOMS ———→

Note: all results significant p = .01, except classes 6b, 5b, 4b

friendship choices is negligible. Our concern now,
following the halo effect, is to try to find out if
these social preferences are associated with percep-
tions of high <u>academic</u> status. That is to say, do
girls of both ethnic groups regard their own academic
status within classrooms as higher than that of boys
of both ethnic groups, and vice versa?
     The method undertaken was as follows. Each pupil
in a class was provided with a pack of cards, each
card having the name of a pupil in the class. It
was ensured that the names could be read by all of
the pupils. That done, each pupil was individually
asked to rank-order the cards on the basis of 'best-
pupil-in-the-class' status. The best pupil was to
be placed at the top of the pack with the name
showing. The pupil placed himself in the rank-order
as well. Thus, in all classrooms from Primary 3 to
Primary 7, each pupil was assigned a rank by all of
the other pupils in his class, and by himself.
     The data were then collated in the following
manner. Firstly, all of the ranks assigned by ethnic
minority girls were separated into four groups:
those ranks assigned to themselves; those to white
boys; those to white girls; those to ethnic
minority boys. A Kruskal Wallis one-way analysis of
variance was undertaken for these four independent
samples of the ranks assigned by ethnic minority
girls. Secondly, a similar data collation and
statistical analysis was made of the ranks assigned
by white girls. The ranks assigned by the remaining
two groups were analysed in the same way. For each
classroom, therefore, four Kruskal Wallis tests were
administered with a view to determining if there was
a significant difference in the ranks assigned to
each of the four samples. The results of the Kruskal
Wallis analyses are presented in Figures 4 to 7
inclusive. Figure 4 shows the nominations assigned
by ethnic minority girls; Figure 5 those assigned
by white girls; Figure 6 those assigned by white
boys; Figure 7 those nominations assigned by ethnic
minority boys. To facilitate interpretation,
consider Figure 4. In classroom 7a, it will be seen
that the mean ranks assigned by ethnic minority girls
show that ethnic minority girls were placed most
favourably (that is, had the lowest numerical mean
rank), followed by white girls, white boys and ethnic
minority boys. (Note: the Kruskal Wallis test
derives the mean rank from the total of all ranks
assigned in each of the four ethnic and sex categories; it does not present a within-sample mean rank.)
Furthermore, it will be seen that the chi-square

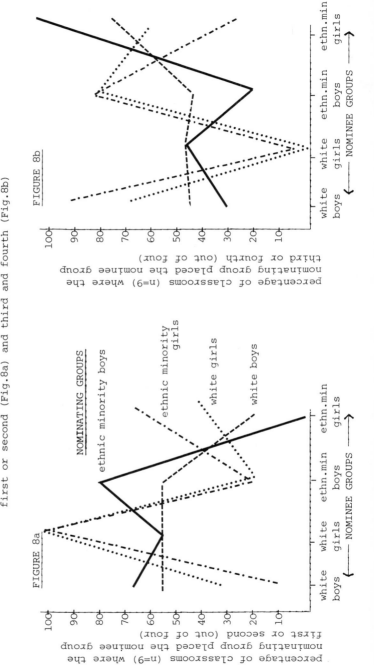

FIGURE 8

Percentage of Classrooms where the Nominating Group placed the Nominee Group first or second (Fig.8a) and third and fourth (Fig.8b)

FIGURE 8a

FIGURE 8b

NOMINATING GROUPS

ethnic minority boys

ethnic minority girls

white girls

white boys

value of 16.21 is significant at the .001 level,
thereby indicating that ethnic minority girls, when
nominating, differed significantly in the ranks
they assigned to the four groups.

It is clear from Figures 4 to 7 that nominating
groups, especially white girls, tend to differentiate
significantly when rank-ordering the four ethnic/
gender groups.   There is a slight trend for the nonsignificant results to occur in the lower age-ranges,
thereby suggesting that less differentiation occurs
among the younger children.   A number of tentative
conclusions may be drawn with the aid of Figure 8,
which offers a general summary of the findings within
Figures 4 to 7.   (Figure 8 is divided into 8a and 8b
to facilitate discussion.)

Figure 8a shows the percentage of classrooms
(n=9) where the nominating group (either white boys,
ethnic minority boys, white girls, ethnic minority
girls) placed the nominee group in either first or
second place, not third or fourth.   For example,
within a classroom where white girls had the most
favourable - that is, the numerically lowest - mean
rank, derived from the Kruskal Wallis analysis, then
they would be placed first in that classroom out of
a possible four places.   Further, in that same class,
if ethnic minority girls had received the next
favourable mean rank, then they would be placed
second, and so on.   It is important to stress that no
attention is paid to the actual degree of difference
between these mean ranks, only to the ordering of
these means.   Let us now consider Figure 8a more
carefully.   Consider the percentage of classrooms
(n=9) in which white boys, a 'nominee group', were
placed in either first or second place, not third
or fourth.   Inspecting the graph, we can see that:
only in 12 per cent of classrooms were white boys
placed first or second by ethnic minority girls;   in
only 34 per cent of classrooms were white boys placed
first or second by white girls;   but in 55 per cent
of classrooms, white boys were placed first or
second by themselves;   and in 67 per cent of classrooms they were placed first or second by ethnic
minority boys.   To further the example, consider the
next nominee group, white girls.   By inspecting
Figure 8a, we can see that the percentage of classrooms in which white girls were nominated first or
second by themselves was 100 per cent; by ethnic
minority girls, again 100 per cent; by white boys,
55 per cent; and by ethnic minority boys, 55 per cent.
The two other nominee groups, ethnic minority boys
and ethnic minority girls, may be considered in the

same way. It follows from Figure 8a that girls were
less likely to place the opposite sex higher than
were boys. Although white and ethnic minority boys
did not socially prefer white girls (on the basis of
the sociometric evidence), this did not prevent them
from ranking white girls highly on academic criteria.
Figure 8a also indicates that both white girls and
ethnic minority boys have high academic 'self-esteem',
but this seems to be confirmed by the other pupils
only in the case of white girls.

      Consider now Figure 8b. Again on the basis of
the sociometric evidence, we might expect the majority
of third and fourth place allocations to be made by
pupils of the opposite sex, regardless of ethnicity.
Figure 8b partly supports this view. It shows the
percentage of classrooms (n=9) in which each of the
four nominee groups were assigned to either third or
fourth place, not to first or second as detailed in
Figure 8a. So, let us take white boys as a nominee
group. They were placed either third or fourth by
ethnic minority boys in only 33 per cent of classrooms,
and by white boys in only 45 per cent of classrooms.
However, white boys were placed either third or
fourth in 66 per cent of classrooms by white girls,
and in 88 per cent of classrooms by ethnic minority
girls. The other nominee groups may be considered
in the same way. Thus, the results derived from
Figure 8b are the exact opposite of those which are
found in Figure 8a. That is, the percentage of
classrooms where girls placed boys third or fourth
far exceeded that where girls so placed themselves.
For girls, therefore, there does seem to be something
of a 'halo effect'; that is, they did not socially
prefer boys and they tend (perhaps as a result) to
see boys as having a relatively lower academic
standing. For boys, there appears to be a partial
'halo effect' for ethnic minority girls, but not for
white girls; that is, ethnic minority girls were
neither preferred socially, nor given high academic
rank by boys; white girls, though not preferred as
friends, were seen to have a fairly high academic
standing by boys. These patterns of academic rank-
ordering may not be the consequence of social
preference alone; they may be the consequence of the
teacher's perception of those ethnic/gender groups.
This wll be considered in the next chapter.

Summary

The purpose of this chapter has been to focus upon
status differentiation within a school whose pupils

are drawn largely from a 'deprived' working class
background. The evidence adduced on academic rank-
ordering suggests that the social structuring of
pupil identities by the pupils themselves reveals the
power of the hidden curriculum to institutionalise
the differential status of very young children in
their early years of schooling, thereby psychologi-
cally preparing them for entry into stratified
bureaucracies beyond the school. This occurs
despite the prevailing official ethos of Mr. McLean
that the 'child comes first', and that the academic
standing of a pupil should not be compared to that
of others. Even Mr. McLean, in his coining of the
'dead horse' category, contradicts his own ethos by
placing such children 'last', not 'first'. But
whilst it appears to be the case that pupil identities are hierarchically arranged by the pupils (and,
as we shall show in the next chapter, by the
teachers themselves), it is the nature of this
hierarchy which is of interest. It is of interest
because it shows that the social and economic
identities of pupils in this school are not
structured in a manner that accords with the stratification system beyond the school. The academic
standing of white girls is perceived by themselves
and by their classmates to be high. Their pupil
identity is favourable. This is unexpected, for if
schools are said to structure the social class
locations which obtain beyond them, then we would
expect the academic self-esteem of girls (and the
view which others, particularly boys, hold of them)
to be lower than boys. At Rockfield, it is only the
ethnic minority girls, not the white girls, who fit
this expectation. Moreover, it is argued that the
social class locations of ethnic minority individuals
is lower than that of white individuals. Accordingly,
if the education system is said to mediate these
locations - to reproduce them - then the school here
is an exception since there is very little difference
between white and ethnic minority boys in the ways
in which other pupils defined them as pupils.
     It has been suggested that capitalism, whilst not
creating social differentiation on the basis of
gender and ethnicity, nevertheless exploited the
differences which it met, to the detriment of ethnic
minorities and women. There is also an argument to
be made that capitalism sought to foster discord
between sexes and ethnic groups, thereby deflecting
criticism from itself. At the level of 'multi-
cultural' education policy, this may be seen as
fragmenting the curricular provision and experiences

of white and ethnic groups in those schools where
multi-cultural education takes the form of 'ethnic'
studies for ethnic minority pupils, not for all of
the pupils. Such a policy, under the guise of
curriculum'relevance', is seen as the early
institutionalisation of a divide-and-rule practice
(Mullard, 1981). Moreover, such a policy would not
serve to diminish the ethnocentric friendship choices
that prevail in some schools. In this study it was
found that white pupils were more ethnocentric than
ethnic minority pupils, but, when these choices were
analysed so that ethnicity and gender were interrelated, not separated, it was found that, within a sex,
ethnocentrism was low.

Official gender differentiation in Rockfield
School exceeded the level of official ethnic
differentiation. This organizational recognition of
gender differences appears to be the consequence of
teachers regarding gender differences as natural.
Socially, boys and girls seem to exclude each other
from their friendship choices. That exclusion,
however, does not suggest hostility between the sexes.
Rather, it seems that boys and girls are mainly
indifferent to each other. The development of gender
roles in the school is a largely unexplored area,
perhaps for the very reason that any differences
which obtain are thought to be reducible to basic,
natural differences beyond the influence of social
forces (Delamont, 1980). It has been argued that
within working class areas, sex-role differentiation
in the home is greater than within middle class
areas (Newson and Newson, 1976). Teachers in schools
like Rockfield might not have wished to contradict
the 'inevitabilities' of biology by removing
practices which divide children on the basis of sex.

By operationalising Weber's concept of status
differentiation within a predominantly working class
setting, the analysis has revealed that pupils'
definitions of the academic standing of their classmates associate with the status 'factors' of ethnicity and gender. This is not to argue that
individual pupils consciously confound the social
attributes with the academic status of other pupils.
It is only when the rank-orderings made by individuals
within a race/sex group are viewed socially that
certain social trends 'emerge' as statistical
artefacts. Thus, if the academic rank-orderings made
by the pupils reflect those made by their teachers,
then the hitherto emphasis on the social class of
the pupil as a 'predictor' of academic/occupational
success must be regarded as an oversimplification.

It may be the case that within the working class the
ethnicity and sex of the pupil may associate with
different levels of teacher expectation and academic
achievement, even when the measured ability of the
pupil is taken into account.   This is the concern of
the next chapter.

Chapter 8

TEACHERS' DEFINITIONS OF PUPILS: ETHNICITY AND SEX

It has already been stated that a central tenet of
functionalist sociology of education holds that
education and society are meritocratic. 'Talent' is
the best predictor of academic and economic success
(Davis and Moore, 1945). This relationship between
talent (as measured by IQ), educational achievement
and economic success is what Harrop (1980) calls the
'complex meritocratic' model. The model, he points
out, is widely accepted as a true representation of
reality. It is not. This is because studies have
shown that when talent is held constant, and when
social class membership differs, those born to middle
class parents will do better than their working
class counterparts (Bowles and Gintis, 1976; Floud
and Halsey, 1957). Social class is a better predictor of occupational success than IQ, which is not
what the meritocratic model advocates. Thus two
questions now arise: firstly, why do most people
believe that society is meritocratic; secondly, why
do children of working class parents leave the
education system before their capabilities are
realised? In their analysis of the French system of
education, Bourdieu and Passeron (1977) address both
of these issues. In respect of the first, they argue
that success and failure are individualised; that is,
when a pupil leaves school before being educated to
his potential, he does not blame the school for
pushing him out - he himself chooses to leave. The
school is exonerated from blame because it is able
to demonstrate convincingly that all pupils face the
same conditions in the contest for educational
credentials. As for the second question, Bourdieu
suggests that schools legitimate and reward the
'cultural capital' which is most akin to that of an
aristocratic cultural elite. The modes of speech,
dress and general demeanour and knowledge of the

192

professional and executive's child will be that much
closer to this ideal cultural capital preferred by
the school than will that of the manual worker's
child. The school proceeds to reward this 'better'
cultural capital as though it were a natural gift of
the child, not one transmitted within a privileged
social milieu. The school treats the cultural
capital of all its pupils as though it were the same,
which it is not.
There is, following Bourdieu's second point, an
assertion that teachers may prefer the cultural
attributes of some children more than others, without
being aware of doing so. They confound the intellectual attributes of the pupil with his social attributes (Rist, 1970; Keddie, 1971; Sharp and Green,
1975). A recent study, however, has claimed this not
to be the case (Croll, 1981). Strangely, however,
all of these studies omit to consider status group
differences within social class groups. They assume
an homogeneity between, say, teacher's expectations
of both working class boys and working class girls.
Such an homogeneity was lacking in the school studied
by Hartley (1978). He found significant sex differences within both manual and nonmanual samples on
indicators of classroom behaviour, as defined by the
teachers in a large infant school in England.
Similar sex differences within social class groups
were found in an analysis of the teachers' year-end
reports of the pupils: within both social classes,
girls received the more favourable reports. The
notion, therefore, that social class, as defined
occupationally, is a good predictor of academic
success may be an oversimplification. If, as Weber
argues, gender and ethnic status groups form the
basis for social differentiation within that class
which 'lacks property', then teachers in schools may
differentiate in their expections of academic success
between boys and girls, or between ethnic minority
and white pupils, within a working class school.
Accordingly, we begin this chapter with the commonsense typifications which teachers hold of boys,
girls, ethnic minority and white pupils, both in
terms of their classroom behaviour and their academic
standing. These first-order constructs will then be
used to form the basis of a quantitative analysis of
gender and ethnic differences in pupil work and
behaviour, as perceived by the teacher. We begin
with the teachers' views of the classroom behaviour
of ethnic minority and white pupils.

Classroom Behaviour: Ethnic Difference

It has been argued that most of the teachers at
Rockfield explained poor work and behaviour from
pupils on the basis of a deficient home background.
Emotional problems made manifest in the classroom had
their cause in an unstable home. A stable home,
therefore, was seen as important for the pupils. It
was further argued that ethnic minority children, in
general, came from more stable families than did
white children. Yet, despite the greater imputed
stability of the ethnic minority home, the teachers
came to define some aspects of it as at odds with the
purposes of the school. That is, ethnic minority
parents were thought to be less interested in their
children's education than were white parents. This
lack of interest was revealed, for example, in the
dearth of notes from parents to explain their
children's absenteeism, or in the low attendance
rate of ethnic minority parents at Open Day, or in
the very reluctant compliance by parents with the
school's dress code for girls. In some cases, the
perceived lack of interest in education among the
ethnic minority parents was reflected in what was
thought to be a similar uninterest among their
children.

The teachers at Rockfield School liked pupils who
'sparked'. A 'bright' pupil who sparked was thought
to be 'interested'. On this basis, ethnic minority
girls sometimes fell far short of the ideal:

(i) They tend to be quiet, shy, subdued and
submissive. You try to give them that wee
bit more confidence. You know, when they come
in and wear their shorts for gym (you praise
them). They climb up the ropes and hang from
the wall-bars and you make sure that the rest
of the class admires them for it.

(ii) They tend to take a back-seat and keep like
mice until another seems to join in.

(iii) They're certainly very quiet and they don't
offer much, but I have one in particular who is
eager to do well.

(iv) They're talkative in class in their own groups
but ask them for ideas ... they've no
imagination.

One teacher also defined ethnic minority boys to be
reticent:

194

> 'Immigrant' boys tend to be more of a mystery
> shall we say. They go home ... and they're not
> forthcoming in the sense of ... I find for
> instance they seldom come and speak to me. I
> have to specifically ask them something. The
> 'immigrant' girls ... you're troubled trying to
> get anything out of them. I mean they're just
> head-nodding.

Thus the perceived reticence of ethnic minority
children, especially of girls, was problematic for
the teachers. They could not 'bring them out'. The
pupils did not seem interested. The cause of this,
argued Mrs. Letham, was the home background:

> It's definitely background. I mean the
> 'immigrants' come from a background where there
> are no toys; there's no stimulation; there's
> no English spoken to most of them. Therefore
> they come in at a disadvantage. It's their
> parents' outlook. I mean they don't see the
> importance ... they don't have the same emphasis
> we do on education (emphasis added).

Mrs. Letham's analysis of the ethnic minority home
was not confirmed by the interviews obtained with
some of the families, as reported earlier. Indeed,
some of the 'immigrant parents' even accused the
school of not being academically demanding of their
children. Another sign of 'interest' in the school,
apart from exuding 'spark', was the degree to which
children complied with the dress code for girls.
They were at school to be assimilated:

(i)   Some of the 'immigrant' girls don't go
      swimming. Those who do have parents who are
      more enlightened or who can be brow-beaten
      (into allowing their daughters to wear a
      bathing costume) by Mrs. ... If they're
      within the culture of the school, I think
      they should follow the culture of the
      school (emphasis added).

(ii) I think they should adjust to wherever they've
      got to live. This is where we're battling
      with uniforms and so on.

This matter of compliance with dress code was, as
stated in an earlier chapter, taken very seriously
by both teachers and by parents. If the pupil did
not comply, then this was taken to mean a lack of

co-operation with the school; if the school kept
insisting that girls dress appropriately, then the
parents took this to mean that the school was
intruding on the religious practices of the family,
which, it was stated, it had no right to do. The
ideal ethnic minority pupil, therefore, was one who
met the teacher's ideal expectation of one of 'her
own' pupils:

> They came from Pakistan five or six years ago.
> They had no English, but these youngsters we
> have now have benefited from their older
> brothers and sisters. They are able to
> communicate orally as soon as they come into
> school, which is a big advantage. It's just
> like having one of our own white children in
> the class. (emphasis added)

Two further points are salient. Most of the ethnic
differentiation seemed to be from teachers of infants
who probably met the ethnically-based cultural
difference, as manifested in the pupil, in its most
obvious form. Teachers of older pupils may have
'benefited' from the efforts at assimilation made
by the likes of Mrs. Findlay and Mrs. Letham. A
second point is that infant teachers tended to define
ethnic minority children as selfish. At home they
were said to lack things to play with:

(i)   Some of the 'immigrants' have been brought up
      with no toys and they can be very very selfish
      because they haven't been used to various
      things at home. They're inclined to want it
      all for themselves more so than our own
      children. (emphasis added)

(ii) A lot of the 'immigrant' kids have tendencies
      towards grabbing things and picking things up,
      you know - an acquisitive sort of side to
      them.

All of these comments by the teachers accord with
their professed assimilationist perspective. 'Our
children' were the norm for the school against which
ethnic minority children were to be evaluated. This
unwillingness to adopt a more cultural relativist
perspective, rather than one of cultural deficiency,
was not something which the staff felt the need to
apologise for; it was what they took for granted.

Classroom Behaviour: Boys and Girls

Boys and girls bring to the school a gender role
which has been produced through primary socialisation.
In school they must make the transition from being a
boy or a girl to being a pupil.   There is evidence
that boys find the transition from home to school
more problematic than girls do (Brandis and Bernstein,
1974;   Hartley, 1980;   King, 1978).   This gender
difference also appears to obtain within both working
and middle class groups.   At Rockfield, some teachers
followed organisational practices which differentiated the sexes.   These practices were not in need of
explanation for they were presumed to be a consequence
of the 'basic' difference between the sexes.   When
teachers discussed gender differences in how children
coped with the role of being a pupil, they were
undecided whether or not boys or girls were the
better behaved.   What did emerge, however, was the
theme, previously discussed, that ethnic minority
girls were reticent and subdued;   they were too
quiet.   What follows is a collection of comments on
their views of boys and girls as pupils which is
drawn from informal conversation with teachers.   We
begin with the opinions of infant teachers:

> DH: Are boys coming into school better
>   prepared?

> (i)   Teacher: No, I don't find that at all.   I
>   find that when girls come from back-
>   grounds which are difficult, they
>   are inclined to be that wee bit more
>   aggressive than boys, and terribly
>   possessive.   I find too, very often,
>   that if a girl is again from a poor
>   background, where there is dirt and
>   filth, and nobody cares whether
>   they've been cared for, they're
>   exceptionally tidy.   Boys are not
>   concerned to keep things tidy as
>   much as girls are, but they do
>   fantasi e terribly by producing a
>   parent they haven't got.   They hear
>   the other children speaking about
>   their mums and dads, and they will
>   produce out of the air a mum or a
>   dad or a nanny.

> (ii) Teacher: At this stage you find that girls
>   will work very hard for you.   I have

two very bright boys downstairs but
they don't give me their true
potential. They don't give of their
best because there are difficulties
there at home and maybe this is something to do with it. Boys are very
much boys. I think you will get this
even in a normal school where boys
have - I wouldn't say a 'couldn't-
care-less attitude' to work - but
it's secondary to a lot of other
things they like.

DH: Does that irritate you?

Teacher: Well, I have a boy of my own. He's
twenty now and I'm quite well used
to this. I know there will come a
time when they break through ...

(iii) Teacher: You get possibly more differences
rearing their heads in Primary 3 -
more noticeably so, because you get
the horns coming out in the boys,
but on the other hand, you get the
girls sniping verbally, shall we say,
if not battering one another.

(iv) Teacher: In this class in particular, I feel
the girls are the brighter - but
that's not general.

DH: Why not?

Teacher: Just the particular children that
have come in at this stage.

These comments suggest some support for other studies
which see boys as more difficult to 'break in' to the
regime of the classroom, but the sex difference was
not often commented upon in staffroom discourse
amongst these infant teachers, perhaps because, as
stated, it was regarded as 'natural' and unremarkable.
As for the teachers of the junior children, reactions
were mixed. Mrs. Scott was decidedly of the view
that boys were the more troublesome (Willy, John and
Alex were the three 'nutters' in her class), but that
this had not been the case in previous years. This
year, however, 'all the girls are better behaved than
the boys'. Her explanation was that, 'All my girls
come from good homes'. Moreover, her boys had had

TEACHERS' DEFINITIONS OF PUPILS: ETHNICITY AND SEX

'a reputation since Primary 3'. This was not, however,
a pattern: 'Last year it was the opposite'.
Mrs. Carter agreed that there was no discernible
pattern from year to year, and so did Miss Darby:

> In my last class I would have said 'yes' (that
> boys were the more troublesome); in this class
> I would say 'no'.

Mr. Lane did discern such a pattern:

> In this class I find the girls to be more mature.
> The boys are very silly at times and I think
> that's probably been the case more than the
> other way around, although it's never been
> outstanding.

Whereas Mr. Lane saw the main sex difference as
behavioural, that of their relative maturity,
Mr. Houston saw a cognitive difference, as well as
viewing girls as the more problematic:

> DH: Do you see any differences between
>   boys and girls as pupils?
>
> Teacher: Yes, but I think that's partly because
>   of the fact that I'm a man. I think
>   mostly - I don't know whether this has
>   anything to do with this school or not -
>   I've found that in the main, girls
>   have been brighter than the boys.
>   That may be just a coincidence. On
>   the other hand, from the behaviour
>   point of view, girls are somehow more
>   of a problem as far as I'm concerned,
>   but again mainly because I'm a man.
>   Certainly , the more older girls get,
>   the more this problem arises, so I
>   suppose that's one of the differences
>   that I find, although that hasn't got
>   anything to do with their development
>   in school. Apart from that I don't
>   really see a great many differences.

Mr. Houston was at odds with his colleagues. He was
the only teacher to see an intellectual difference
between the sexes, and the only one to define girls
as normally more of a problem. Further, his comments
point to perceived conflicts between a teacher of one
sex and a pupil of another. This matter of potential
cross-sex antagonism was aired by female teachers

dealing with ethnic minority boys whose authority
in the home over the female could not be permitted in
the school:

   (i)   If a child has been in Pakistan and has been
          to school there he doesn't accept discipline -
          being disciplined by a woman they think is a
          great joke. Abdul used to think it was a
          great joke every time I checked him because he
          wasn't used to obeying a woman. They don't
          respect the teacher and it works the other way
          too. But if they have come here from the
          beginning, there's no difference. They work.
          The girls are a little shyer than the boys.

   (ii)   I think they ('immigrant' boys) look on us
          (female teachers) as different, you know. I
          don't think they would treat us the way they
          treat their own women.

Perhaps the most agreed sex difference was that
within the so-called 'immigrant' group of children.
As indicated in the previous section, girls were
viewed as very reticent compared to boys. The girl
is constrained by the father:

   (i)   Yes there is discouragement because after the
          age of fifteen they would want them to work.
          Remember that girl I had in at night and she
          wanted to go to college, but she wasn't
          allowed to?

   (ii)   They're (the 'immigrant' girls) the subdued
          race (sic) in their own home, aren't they.
          They're not looked upon as anything. They're
          to be seen and not heard. The boys have the
          voice in the 'immigrant' family.

   (iii) DH: Would you say these 'immigrant' girls
                  are discouraged from doing well at
                  school?

          Teacher: I wouldn't say discouraged but they're
                  certainly not encouraged. I have this
                  little girl in this class who's not
                  yet five and her mummy's just had a
                  new baby. Now it takes days off to
                  help her mummy with the washing, and
                  it helps with the baby - this is very
                  much a girl's thing - doing dishes and
                  things long before we would dream of

> making our children do these duties.

Mrs. Findlay saw no such problem with the ethnic minority girl:

> If they come from a 'a good background', it doesn't matter what their ethnic group is - they cope very well.

This qualitative data provides an interesting difference in the 'theories' which teachers attributed to explain perceived gender and ethnic differences. A 'nature' theory obtained for gender differences; a 'nurture' theory for ethnic differences. To elaborate, gender differences were viewed as a matter of expected differences in biological development - that is, 'boys will be boys'. Ethnic differences were regarded as less natural, as a consequence not of an objective racial difference but of a cultural difference in family socialisation practices. Gender differences, such as they were defined, were rooted in nature and were accepted as somewhat inevitable. Parents were not blamed for the behaviour of boys. Ethnic differences, however, were seen as a consequence of upbringing and, in this respect, 'immigrant parents' were thought to be doing their children a disservice by not socialising their children as white parents socialised 'our children'. Teachers took it as axiomatic that 'when in Rome, do as the Romans do'. Thus, to oversimplify, the biology of girls was thought to better prepare them for the pupil role; the family socialisation of white children better prepared them for the pupil role.

Ethnic and Gender Differences in Classroom Behaviour: A Quantitative Analysis

Sociology of education has been mainly concerned with seeking and explaining social class differences in education. Usually the term 'social class' has been operationalised on the basis of parental occupation and/or parental education. Defined in this way, the social class of the pupil is not obvious to a teacher and nor are teachers always completely accurate in their perception of the social class of their pupils (Nash, 1973). There are no such problems when the teacher wishes to decide the race or the sex of the pupil. In the case of the sex difference, the child is seen to be either a boy or a girl: in the case of the race of the child, the teacher can usually differentiate among black, brown or white pupils,

TABLE 5

Teachers' ratings of pupil behaviour:
gender and ethnic differences at Infant (P1 to P3) and Junior (P4 to P7) levels

		B	G	t	W	EM	t	WB	EMB	t	WG	EMG	t	EMB	EMG	t	WB	WG	t
Obedient/	P1-P3	3.09	2.41	2.86**	2.56	2.77	1.20	3.13	2.88	0.72	2.46	2.28	0.54	2.88	2.77	1.42	3.12	2.45	2.35*
Disobed.	P4-P7	2.91	2.31	2.83	2.75	2.63	0.49	2.76	2.85	0.63	2.44	1.88	1.31	2.85	1.88	3.13**	2.76	2.44	1.42
Forth./	P1-P3	3.20	3.27	0.25	2.96	3.56	1.99*	3.03	3.38	0.82*	2.97	3.83	2.03*	3.38	3.83	0.84	3.03	2.89	0.43
Withdwn.	P4-P7	3.06	2.98	0.41	2.69	3.78	5.01***	2.81	3.51	2.23	2.47	4.03	5.25***	3.60	4.03	1.22	2.82	2.58	1.02
Selfish/	P1-P3	4.29	4.40	0.48	4.41	4.29	0.49	4.24	4.46	0.71	4.54	4.11	1.18	4.23	4.05	0.41	4.17	4.54	1.24
Generous	P4-P7	4.84	5.21	1.98	5.11	4.85	1.31	4.98	4.60	1.56	5.22	5.23	0.00	4.68	5.06	1.02	4.89	5.24	1.51
Aggress./	P1-P3	4.54	4.84	0.99***	4.68	4.68	1.00	4.52	4.54	0.05	4.81	4.89	0.17*	4.38	4.72	0.63**	4.51	4.89	0.92***
Passive	P4-P7	4.02	5.08	5.12***	4.45	4.78	1.44	3.92	4.17	0.79	4.93	5.69	2.41	4.25	5.50	3.17	3.88	4.91	4.29
Quiet/	P1-P3	3.84	3.21	2.00*	3.63	3.34	0.92	3.93	3.63	0.60	3.37	3.00	0.84	3.61	2.88	1.36	3.96	3.40	1.45**
Noisy	P4-P7	4.38	3.73	2.84	4.17	3.77	1.58	4.57	4.05	1.46	3.82	3.53	0.80	3.94	3.57	0.81	4.55	3.79	2.80
Untidy/	P1-P3	3.49	4.01	1.61**	3.50	4.16	1.98*	3.10	3.77	1.58	3.83	4.11	0.54	4.04	4.27	0.48*	3.31	3.67	0.84**
Tidy	P4-P7	3.73	4.45	3.33	4.20	4.45	1.09	3.76	4.11	1.05	4.68	4.84	0.49	4.08	4.92	2.34	3.76	4.50	2.88
Interest./	P1-P3	3.13	3.31	0.62	3.19	3.34	0.47	3.14	3.11	0.06	3.16	3.67	1.15	3.11	3.67	1.14	3.17	3.13	0.01
Uninterest.	P4-P7	3.18	2.84	1.71	2.89	3.29	1.82	3.04	3.54	1.57	2.72	3.07	1.17	3.45	3.07	1.02	3.61	3.86	0.27

* p = .05   **p = .01   ***p = .001

NOTE: Each bipolar scale had 7 points.

although there are instances when the race of the
child is in doubt, as in the case of children of
'mixed blood'. In other words, when teachers
differentiate their pupils on the basis of race and
sex, there is usually a clear, objective indicator
on which she can rely. Similarly, when a researcher
analyses data on the basis of race and sex, it is
usually easy to dichotomise the data accurately.
But when a researcher seeks to dichotomise his data
according to 'social class', then errors are inevitable for there are no agreed-upon, objective, absolute
definitions of the term. Like the definition of what
counts as 'intelligence', what counts as 'social
class' is widely claimed to be agreed upon, but can
be shown to vary in how different researchers
operationalise the term. To return to Rockfield
School, the so-called 'immigrant' pupils were
ethnically, as well as racially, different from their
white counterparts. Thus, for teachers, an ethnic
minority pupil was physiologically different in skin
pigmentation from a white pupil; in the same way,
boys and girls differed biologically. Our concern
now is whether or not these objective differences
had consequences for the ways in which teachers
subjectively defined the classroom behaviour of boys
and girls, and of ethnic minority and white children.
      In their everyday classroom exchanges with
pupils, and in their staffroom discourse, teachers
habitually use certain descriptives of their pupils'
behaviour. Those constructs which appeared to be most
common to the staff were used as the basis for a
semantic differential-type of rating scale, comprising seven bipolar scales, against which each teacher
rated each of her pupils. The seven scales were:
obedient/disobedient; forthcoming/withdrawn;
selfish/generous; aggressive (physically)/passive;
quiet/noisy; untidy/tidy; interested/uninterested.
There is probably a certain amount of semantic
overlap between 'forthcoming' and 'interested'. That
is, some teachers saw a 'sparking' or 'forthcoming'
pupil as an 'interested' pupil.
      Table 5 analyses the results in the following
way. It dichotomises the data on the basis of sex
and on the basis of ethnicity. It interrelates the
sex and ethnic factors so that sex differences
within an ethnic group are analysed, and so that
ethnic differences within a sex are also analysed.
Each of these analyses is offered at two aggregate
levels: for pupils in Primary 1 to 3 inclusive
(the infants); for pupils in Primary 4 to 7 (the
juniors).

Consider, firstly, differences between boys and girls. Boys, at both infant and junior levels, are rated as significantly more disobedient and noisy; they are seen as more aggressive and untidy at the junior level, but not at the infant level. Secondly, the ethnic differences are fewer, the only signicant one being that white pupils are defined as more forthcoming at both age levels, a finding which supports the qualitative evidence provided earlier. Thirdly, consider gender differences within ethnic groups. There is a tendency for boys at junior level to be rated as more aggressive and untidy compared to girls, but there is a difference in forthcoming behaviour. Fourthly, ethnic differences within a sex do reveal the trend for both ethnic minority boys and girls to be rated as less forthcoming than their white counterparts. In short, as with the pupils' academic rank-ordering of other pupils, and as with their sociometric choices, it is the sex difference which exceeds the ethnic difference.

In the previous chapter it was shown that there was some association between the ways in which children saw other children as preferred friends and the ways in which they saw them as pupils. In particular, white girls saw boys of both ethnic groups as neither desirable friends nor as good pupils. To a lesser extent, this was the case with boys: they did not choose girls as preferred friends, but they did see white girls, though not ethnic minority girls, as good pupils. It was suggested that the explanation of the pupils' academic estima- tion of other pupils was not so much a consequence of social preference, or the lack of it, but more to do with their having accepted the teacher's definition of certain pupils, and then articulating that definition as though it were of their own construc- tion. Accordingly, we shall consider now whether or not there exists a relationship between how teachers defined the academic standing of these gender/ethnic groups, on the one hand, and the definitions which the pupils themselves have of the academic standing of those groups, on the other.

Teachers' Definitions of Pupils' Academic Achievement: Ethnicity and Sex

Since the publication of Pygmalion in the Classroom (Rosenthal and Jacobson, 1968), there has been continuing debate about whether or not there exists a 'teacher expectancy effect' whereby pupils allege- dly realise the expectations which teachers have of

them. The 'teacher expectancy effect', or 'self-
fulfilling prophecy', a term made popular by Merton
(1968), rests on W.I. Thomas's assertion that, 'If
men define situations as real, they are real in their
consequences' (Thomas, 1928). There is an assumed
causal link between definition and consequence.
Merton's concern was with false definitions which
are realised, and he cites, for example, the 'sociological parable' about the First National Bank in the
United States in the year 1932. The manager,
Cartwright Millingville, presides over a solvent and
successful institution. One day, however, matters
take a sudden and dramatic turn for the worst.
Depositors are queueing to withdraw their money as
never before. Anxious voices fill the bank. The
bank is thought to be on the verge of insolvency.
All the depositors withdraw their money and the bank
collapses: a false definition had been fulfilled.
    Research in education which has investigated the
'self-fulfilling prophecy' is largely of three types.
The first, such as that by Rosenthal and Jacobson
(1968), is one where the researcher, not the teacher,
provides the definition. The second, that by Palardy
(1969) for example, derives the 'prophecy' from the
teacher, not the researcher. In general, the second
type reveals the greater likelihood of a 'teacher
expectancy effect', since a teacher seems more likely
to believe her own definition than that given to her
by a researcher. She will, therefore, be more likely
to act upon it. A third type of research embodies
the teacher-derived prophecy but includes an important methodological advantage which corrects a
serious flaw in the first two types. The flaw is
that no observation is made of the process which
occurs between prophecy and outcome. If the outcome
accords with the original prophecy, then the prophecy
is assumed, of itself, to have caused the outcome.
But this conclusion may only safely be reached if the
researcher actually observes the interaction between
pupil and teacher. That is, the researcher must be
able to see if the teacher acts towards the pupil in
a manner congruent with her definition of him. And
the researcher must be able to ascertain if the pupil
acquiesces in his teacher's 'treatment' of him. A
well-known example of this third type is Rist's
(1970) study of a classroom in an American ghetto
infant school. He found that, after only eight days
of schooling in the kindergarten, the teacher
'ability'-grouped her pupils solely upon the basis
of her subjective views of their social characteristics. These groupings were preserved until the end

205

of the second year, despite the fact that there was
no significant difference in measured ability among
the groups.

Much research has considered the teacher's
confusion of occupational social class and pupil
ability. Goodacre (1968), for example, found that
teachers under-estimated the reading ability of
working class pupils, but over-estimated that of
middle class pupils. The foregoing study by Rist
(1970) is a further example. In a seminal study,
Floud and Halsey (1957) compared the proportion of
boys in different occupational groups whose IQ
qualified them to enter grammar school with those who
actually were allocated a place. They found that
51.1 per cent of 'professional' boys were qualified
(that is, scored an IQ of 114+), but 63.6 per cent of
boys from this occupational category were actually
given a grammar school place. In other words, on
the basis of measured ability, 12.5 per cent of these
boys ought not to have been in grammar schools. They
were there because, following the abolition of the
eleven-plus examination, their primary school
teachers had argued that they were grammar school
'material'. A subjective impression by the teacher
had replaced an objective measure, to the advantage
of these 'professional' boys. Similarly, Douglas
(1964) reports that pupils on the borderline of
selection for grammar school were more likely to be
given a place if they were from a middle class background. Nash (1973), however, suggests that it is
the teacher's perception of the social class of the
pupil, not the actual occupational class background,
which is crucial for the kind of ability assessment
which a teacher makes. Our concern here, however,
is with teachers' definitions of the academic
standing of pupils of different ethnicity and sex
within a working class urban primary school.

Research on teachers' definitions of ethnic
minority pupils is both sparse and inconclusive.
Much of it is of an experimental nature in university-
based research settings. Rubovitz and Maehr (1973)
conducted such a study. Sixty-six female undergradu-
ates undergoing a course of teacher-training in an
American university and 264 seventh and eigth-grade,
mixed-ability pupils, black and white, comprise the
'subjects' of the experiment. Each 'teacher' was
assigned four pupils of the same ability, but was
told that: one white pupil was 'gifted', the other
not; one black pupil was 'gifted', the other not.
The teacher was observed giving a lesson on the subject
of 'television'. The degree of encouragement,

TABLE 6

Teachers' rank-ordering of the academic standing of
pupils in their class: ethnic minority/white; boys/girls

	Ethnic Minority		White				Boys		Girls			
	$\bar{X}$	(n)	$\bar{X}$	(n)	U	P	$\bar{X}$	(n)	$\bar{X}$	(n)	U	P
P7	16.41	(11)	14.14	(18)	83.5	.481	16.44	(16)	13.23	(13)	81.0	.308
P7	15.75	(04)	14.88	(25)	47.0	.849	17.71	(14)	12.47	(15)	67.0	.097
P6	17.93	(07)	11.87	(19)	35.5	.073	15.59	(16)	10.15	(10)	46.5	.077
P6	19.07	(07)	12.23	(20)	34.5	.049	15.33	(12)	12.93	(15)	74.0	.434
P5	12.50	(10)	10.67	(12)	50.0	.509	11.41	(11)	11.59	(11)	59.5	.947
P5	11.13	(08)	12.47	(15)	53.0	.751	11.15	(10)	12.65	(13)	56.5	.598
P4	11.83	(06)	12.06	(17)	50.0	.942	13.70	(10)	10.60	(13)	48.0	.291
P4	12.09	(11)	11.92	(12)	65.0	.950	09.58	(12)	14.64	(11)	37.0	.074
P3	17.22	(09)	14.76	(21)	79.0	.483	15.35	(17)	15.69	(13)	108.0	.917

elaboration, praise and indifference which the
teacher showed with each pupil was observed.   The
results: most favourably treated in these respects,
in the following order, were: 'gifted'whites;   'nongifted' whites;   'nongifted' blacks and 'gifted'
blacks.   This unfavourable treatment of 'gifted'
blacks was not confirmed by Taylor's (1979) study of
'phantom' pupils taught by white female, trainee-
teachers in the United States.   These were not real
pupils;   the teacher had merely to imagine that she
was teaching them.   The results: teachers treated
high-ability black 'pupils' and low-ability white
'pupils' most favourably.

     This inconclusive research tells us nothing of
pupils in actual classrooms.   The omission is
addressed in a later study by Rist (1978).   In a
school in Oregon, Rist provides a perceptive, non-
participant analysis of what occurs when a group of
working class black pupils are 'bussed' into a
prosperous, white elementary school.   Despite the
professed enthusiasm of the receiving school, the
consequences for these black children were not those
intended.   These children were entering a high-
powered academic setting whose aim was to stay near
the top of the ciy's league-table of elementary
schools, as measured by scores on objective tests.
The principal was concerned that 'these new students
are going to pull us down' (p.69).   The black
children were to be in the school on the school's
terms.   Over time, the bussed pupils receded into the
academic wilderness of the classroom.   Whilst they
busied themselves with time-consuming 'projects' in
the bottom ability group, their white counterparts
were taught as before.   Although the black pupils
were physiologically visible as different and as
present, they became 'invisible' to the teacher.

     We turn now to teachers' definitions of boys and
girls as pupils.   The research literature on British
primary schools is consistent in its conclusion that
girls are thought to be the better pupils (Douglas,
1964;   Hartley, 1978;   King, 1978), although there
is no sex difference in overall measured intelligence.
This might suggest that the regime of the classroom
in the primary school is more congenial to girls.
They are seen to master the 'hidden curriculum' more
easily and willingly than boys, and are thought of
by their teachers as the better pupils as a result.

     The data in Table 6 suggest a trend in this
direction.   Particularly in the classrooms for the
older children, girls are ranked higher than boys,
though not significantly.   At the school aggregate

TABLE 7

Classroom academic standing as defined by
(i) pupils themselves (ii) teachers: ethnicity with gender

Nominators	Nominees X̄	Nominees X̄	t	p	df
	W Boys	W Girls			
Teachers	14.45	11.50	2.19	.031	158
Pupil self	10.03	8.09	1.69	.101	158
	W Boys	EM Girls			
Teachers	14.45	14.77	.00	1.000	116
Pupil self	10.03	9.57	.26	.792	116
	EM Boys	EM Girls			
Teachers	14.45	14.77	.18	.857	71
Pupil self	9.57	10.30	.40	.685	71
	W Girls	EM Girls			
Teachers	11.50	14.77	1.96	.052	113
Pupil self	8.09	10.30	1.57	.119	113

Notes: (1) white boys (n=75); white girls (n=85); em boys (n=43); em girls(n=30)

(2) The correlations between the teachers' ranks and the pupils' self ranks are (r): ethnic minority girls .283 (p = .065); white girls .349 (p = .001); white boys .610(p = .001); ethnic minority boys .528 (p = .001).

level of analysis, a similar nonsignificant trend
obtains (boys $\bar{x}$ rank = 14.43; girls $\bar{x}$ rank = 12.49,
t = 1.88, p = .061 with 231 df). Table 6 also
compares the ranks received in each classroom by
ethnic minority and white pupils. Again the trend
is for white pupils, particularly in Primary 6 and 7,
to be ranked higher than ethnic minority pupils,
though significantly in only one classroom. At the
aggregate level, this trend is confirmed (white $\bar{x}$
rank = 12.98; ethnic minority $\bar{x}$ rank = 14.49,
t = .134, p = .181, with 231 df).

Teachers' Definitions of Pupils' Academic Standing: Ethnicity and Sex Interrelated

Our earlier analysis of the pupils' sociometric
choices and of their academic rank-ordering of their
classmates revealed the importance of not merely
considering sex differences and ethnic differences
separately, but of interrelating them. Now the
teachers' rank-orders are analysed in a similar way
(Table 7). Table 7 also allows us to compare how the
pupils ranked themselves. It will be recalled that
each pupil, in each classroom, rank-ordered his
classmates according to perceived academic standing
and that he included himself in that order. It is
these ranks which each individual pupil assigned to
himself, not to others, that are analysed here and
are termed 'pupil self ranks'.

   If the teacher-nominated ranks are inspected in
Table 7, a number of trends emerge. It is clear that
white girls are the most favourably positioned,
significantly above white boys. Moreover, the very
favourable view which teachers have of white girls is
reflected in the view which white girls have of themselves. White girls rank themselves higher than any
other of the four ethnic/sex groups rank themselves.
It will be recalled, too, that white girls were the
most favoured group in respect of classroom behaviour,
as defined by their teachers. Thus, at the aggregate
level, there is an association between the teachers'
subjective view of the work and behaviour of white
girls. Secondly, consider the differences between
ethnic minority boys and girls. Here boys rank
themselves slightly higher than girls rank themselves,
but the difference is very small. Similarly,
teachers rank ethnic minority boys marginally higher
than ethnic minority girls. Furthermore, if the mean
ranks are inspected, ethnic minority girls have the
lowest position of any of the four groups: they see
themselves as having the lowest position and so do

their teachers. Furthermore, in the previous chapter
it was shown that other pupils ranked ethnic minority
girls as the least academic of the four sex/ethnic
groups. Thirdly, there is very little difference in
the ranks which boys of both ethnic groups assign to
themselves, and there is very little difference in
the ranks which teachers assign to boys of both
ethnic groups. Finally, for all of the sex/ethnic
groups, except ethnic minority girls, there is a
significant positive correlation between the ranks
assigned by the teachers and the ranks which individual pupils assigned to themselves (see Note 2,
Table 7).

To conclude this chapter, our concern has been
to consider how the classroom teachers of Primary 3
to Primary 7 defined the classroom behaviour and the
academic standing of four groups of pupil: ethnic
minority girls; ethnic minority boys; white girls;
white boys. In the previous chapter our concern had
been to investigate the preferred social relationships among these four groups, as well as how they
defined each other's academic standing. The findings
in this chapter, therefore, offer an opportunity to
weigh the views of the pupils, obtained in the
previous chapter, against the views of the teachers,
obtained in this chapter. In both chapters, both
qualitative and quantitative methods have been used
in a complementary manner and, whenever possible,
the quantitative data have been analysed at both the
aggregate level and at the individual classroom level.

The results strongly suggest that the status
group membership of the pupil within a school
officially defined as 'deprived' in a working class
area will have consequences for the ways in which
pupils see themselves and each other as desirable
friends and as pupils. Moreover, the social attributes of the pupil will also have consequences for
the ways in which teachers will define his classroom
behaviour and his academic standing. Whilst it is
difficult to summarise all of the findings in the
two chapters, a number of conclusions seem very clear.
Firstly, white girls have the highest academic self-
esteem and they are seen as the best behaved and the
most academically accomplished of the four groups.
Even boys support this view to some extent, though
they do not prefer white girls as friends. 'Immigrant'
girls, on the other hand, appear to be seen as the
poorest achievers by teachers, other pupils and by
themselves. Socially, however, they are not excluded
by white girls and there are many reciprocated
friendships between them. Ethnic minority boys and

white boys are defined in much the same way by their
teachers. Academically, they share a position
slightly above ethnic minority girls and somewhat
further below white girls. Socially, they do not
effect closed relationships towards each other, but
they do towards girls.
     The prestigious academic standing of white girls,
and the similar standing between ethnic minority and
white boys, comprises a hierarchy of pupil identities
which are somewhat at odds with previous neoMarxist
interpretations of the primary school. For example,
Sharp and Green (1975) view the micro structure of
the classroom as reflecting, and being reproduced by,
the macro structure at the societal level. This is
an oversimplified and deterministic view. It is a
view which is correct in the sense that the institutionalisation of hierarchy in the classroom accords
with the fact that society itself is hierarchical.
But it is incorrect in its implication that the nature of
the classroom hierarchy and that of the macro hierarchy is the same. That is, the social location of
working class females and males in the wider structure
is different: males are perceived as superior to
females. Further, the social location of working
class ethnic minorities is perceived as inferior to
that of working class whites. If we take an emanationist perspective, then we would expect the pupil
identities of boys to be superior to girls, and we
would expect those of white pupils to be higher than
those of ethnic minority pupils. This is not wholly
the case. At Rockfield, white girls had a higher
pupil identity than white boys, which a structuralist
view would not have predicted. Nor would it have
predicted the finding that ethnic minority and white
boys had very much a similar pupil status. The only
group whose social location at the macro level accords
with that at the classroom level is the ethnic
minority girl. It should be stressed, however, that
these comments relate to a single case study. That
said, they tentatively suggest that a more sceptical
posture towards structuralist accounts of the primary
school should be taken. The internal organisation of
the school, and the external forces which impinge
upon it, do not of themselves elicit passive responses
from teachers and pupils. Teachers and pupils interpret structure. The empirical reality of a school
has a patterned regularity, but the nature of that
regularity cannot be presumed independently of
empirical analysis. A Weberian account of the school
allows for the purposive intentions and actions of
those within it to be understood and to be compared

so that shared typifications emerge. Furthermore, by introducing Weber's concept of 'status group', it is possible to go beyond a narrow class-based analysis of social differentiation without having to forgo the very powerful insight that economic factors have a significant part to play in explaining it.

In the next chapter we focus upon two further claims made from emanationist perspectives. The first is the functionalist assertion that the school is meritocratic. On that basis, we would expect some positive correlation between measured intelligence and pupil achievement, irrespective of the social characteristics of the pupil. The second is the neo-Marxist argument that school and society are not meritocratic, and that class membership, not talent, is the better predictor of academic success (Bowles and Gintis, 1976).

Chapter 9

'THE GOOD ONES WILL MAKE IT ANYWAY'

According to the meritocratic ideology, teachers are
expected to be able to identify the level of a pupil's
ability and to convert that ability into marketable
credentials. The accuracy with which a teacher can
define the ability of the pupil may have favourable
or detrimental consequences for the pupil's actual
achievement. That is, if the teacher under-estimates
a pupil's ability and conveys her estimation to the
pupil, then the pupil may perform at a level commensurate with his imputed ability, not his actual
ability. This is because too little may be expected
of him, too little demanded and too little achieved.
The teacher's imputation of the pupil's ability is
therefore usually of crucial importance, especially
during the early years of schooling when a pupil's
identity of himself, and that held of him by his
peers, is being formed. We have so far suggested
that at Rockfield School, the early pupil identity
of white girls is particularly favourable; that of
boys of both ethnic groups somewhat less so. We have
not so far considered if these different pupil identities have any basis in fact; that is, are white
girls objectively the most able and objectively the
highest achievers? In the strict sense, the social
attributes of ethnicity and gender ought not to have
any influence upon the teacher's imputation of the
pupil's ability and achievement. In what follows,
this matter is considered more fully, both at the
school aggregate level and at the individual classroom level. Moreover, since we shall have need to
measure the actual performance of pupils, we shall
be in a position to pose the question, 'Has the
school compensated academically?'.

TABLE 8

Teachers' over(+) and under (-) estimations of pupils' IQ and reading comprehension: ethnicity and sex[2]

	INTELLIGENCE					COMPREHENSION				
	mean (1)						mean			
Group (n)	+/- est. (2)	t	p	df		(n)	+/- est.	t	p	df
Boys (60)	-1.10	2.26	.027*	122		(61)	-1.23	2.09	.039*	123
Girls (64)	2.18					(64)	1.48			
E.M. (35)	2.36	1.52	.132	122		(35)	1.28	1.10	.274	123
White (89)	-0.10					(90)	-0.32			
White Boys (39)	-2.51	2.67	.009**	87		(40)	1.53	1.33	.188	88
White Girls (50)	1.74					(50)				
E.M. Boys (21)	1.52	.71	.485	33		(21)	-0.67	2.45	.020*	33
E.M. Girls (14)	3.78					(14)	4.64			

*p = .05   **p = .01

Note: (1) Each pupil in a group is assigned a number which indicates the number of positions he has been either under- or over-estimated by the teacher.

(2) - = under-estimate (in ranks)   + = over-estimate (in ranks)

215

TABLE 9

IQ and Reading Comprehension:
actual scores by ethnicity and sex

	IQ	Difference between 'predicted' and actual reading comprehension ages in months (mean scores)	Difference between chronological age and actual reading comprehension age in months (mean scores)
White girls	92.16	-09.10	-18.65
Ethn.M. girls	87.07	-19.66	-23.00
White boys	92.03	-09.97	-18.65
Ethn.M. boys	90.80	-16.52	-24.70

Ethnicity and Sex: IQ Estimated by Teachers[1]

During the final year of the study I was able to
obtain over and under-estimations of pupil's IQ in
five classes: two Primary 7;   one Primary 6 and two
Primary 4.   The procedure was as follows.   Each
teacher was asked to rank-order her pupils according
to imputed ability.   Towards the end of the academic
year each of the pupils was tested individually for
measured intelligence using the Weschler Intelligence
Scales for Children (revised version).   Five items
were used: vocabulary, similarities, digit span,
block design and object of assembly.   The scaled
scores of these five items were summed and doubled to
provide the full IQ.   These IQ scores were then
ranked and were compared to the teacher's rank-order
previously obtained.   It was then possible to obtain
a measure, for each pupil, of 'over' or 'under-
estimation', as follows.   An over-estimation is
derived thus: take, for example, pupil X.   His
teacher estimated him to be fifth in the class;   his
actual IQ score placed him tenth in the class and
this gives him an over-estimation of five positions.
Similarly, if the pupil had been assigned a rank of,
say, ninth, but had achieved one of third, then he
would have been under-estimated by six positions. In
this way, therefore, each pupil was assigned a
measure of over or under-estimation.
    Were some pupils more likely than others to be
over or under-estimated?   Our concern to-date has
been with the status groups of ethnicity and gender
within a working class school.   It has been suggested
that to be a white girl may attract more favourable
views of pupil standing from both pupils and teachers
alike.   It has further been argued that the sex of
the pupil, not his ethnic background, may be the more
powerful differentiator.   In the analysis here it is
possible to find out if pupils are seen favourably
or not, allowing for their actual measured ability.
Table 8 confirms the previous findings that girls
are more favourably regarded by their teachers.   They
are over-estimated for intelligence whilst boys are
under-estimated, and significantly so.   As for ethnic
differences, there is a mean under-estimation of
white pupils and a mean over-estimation of ethnic
minority pupils, the result not being significant.
If the ethnic and sex factors are interrelated, then
a more refined analysis is possible.   Consider the
sex difference within the two ethnic groups: within
the ethnic minority group both boys and girls are
over-estimated, the difference not being significant;

within the white group, boys are under-estimated but
the difference is not significant. Thus if the four
ethnic/gender groups are taken in relation to each
other, then ethnic minority girls, white girls and
ethnic minority boys are over-estimated (in that
order), whilst the trend is for white boys to be
under-estimated.

Ethnicity and Sex: Reading Comprehension Estimated

As with intelligence, the over and under-estimation
of pupils' reading comprehension was derived from
two sets of ranks. The first set was generated by
each teacher who rank-ordered her pupils on the basis
of imputed reading comprehension achievement. The
second set of marks was obtained from the actual
scores which each pupil achieved on the Neale
Analysis of Reading (Form A) (Neale, 1966), a test
which is administered individually. By comparing the
two sets of ranks, a measure of over or under-
estimation for each pupil was calculated. These
measures were then dichotomised by ethnicity and sex.
Table 8 reveals, at the aggregate level, that the
overall sex difference again exceeds the ethnic
difference. That is, boys were under-estimated and
girls over-estimated, significantly. Ethnic minority
pupils were over-estimated and white pupils under-
estimated, though not significantly. As for the sex
difference within an ethnic group, boys are under-
estimated compared to girls, significantly for ethnic
minority pupils but not for white pupils. If the
ethnic difference within a sex is considered, then
ethnic minority boys are over-estimated and white
boys are under-estimated, but not significantly.
And girls of both ethnic groups are over-estimated,
ethnic minority girls the more so, but again not
significantly.
    Thus the teacher's expectations of pupils'
intelligence and reading comprehension show some
similarities. Firstly, the sex difference exceeds
the ethnic difference, with girls the more over-
estimated. Secondly, ethnic minority pupils are more
likely to be over-estimated than are white pupils.
Thirdly, the most under-estimated group is white
boys. These findings, however, hold for aggregated
data across five classrooms. They are not based on
the actual classroom situations from which the
original data were generated. In order to avoid the
possibility of perpetrating an aggregative fallacy,
we turn now to the particular classrooms themselves
and consider the extent to which the sex and ethnicity

of the pupil associates with his teacher's estimation of him. Before this, however, we shall note the actual scores for IQ and for reading comprehension, at the aggregate level, for the various ethnic/sex groups since we shall have need to refer to these in the discussion of individual classrooms.

Table 9 provides both IQ and reading comprehension scores for the four ethnic/sex groups. In respect of IQ, the mean scores for white boys and girls is virtually identical. Ethnic minority girls, however, score lower than ethnic minority boys. If the scores for comprehension are inspected, it is clear that all four groups of pupils fail to read at their chronological age. There is, within ethnic groups, virtually no sex difference in this regard, but white pupils fare better than ethnic minority pupils.

The centre column in Table 8, however, provides a useful indicator of underachievement in reading comprehension. That is, the results take into account the measured intelligence of the pupils so as to give a 'predicted' reading comprehension age using the well-validated regression equations devised by Yule (1967). Thus the middle column of Table 9 shows the difference, in months, between the predicted and the actual comprehension age for the four ethnic/sex groups. Again, white pupils reveal virtually no sex difference, but there is a much wider difference between the scores of ethnic minority and white pupils. It is noteworthy, however, that for all groups there is considerable under-achievement in reading, a matter to be returned to later when the question of 'compensation' in the school is addressed. For the moment we turn to some descriptive data of the classrooms themselves, beginning with Mr. Houston's Primary 7 class.

Mr. Houston

Mr. Houston was a 'stabilizer' and had taught exclusively at Rockfield School. He had taught his Primary 7 class for the previous two years. Figure 9 shows the seating arrangement for his pupils, their individual IQ scores and the number of months by which they were below or above their predicted reading comprehension age (see note (2) Figure 9). The 'top' table was defined by Mr. Houston as comprising Emma, Ann, Rachel, Elspeth and Nighat. The 'tail', or the end of it, was Alan, Neil, Sandra and Susi. It is of interest that the composition of the 'top' table had not changed since the beginning

FIGURE 9

MR. HOUSTON: SEATING PLAN

IQ AND READING COMPREHENSION SCORES AND ESTIMATES

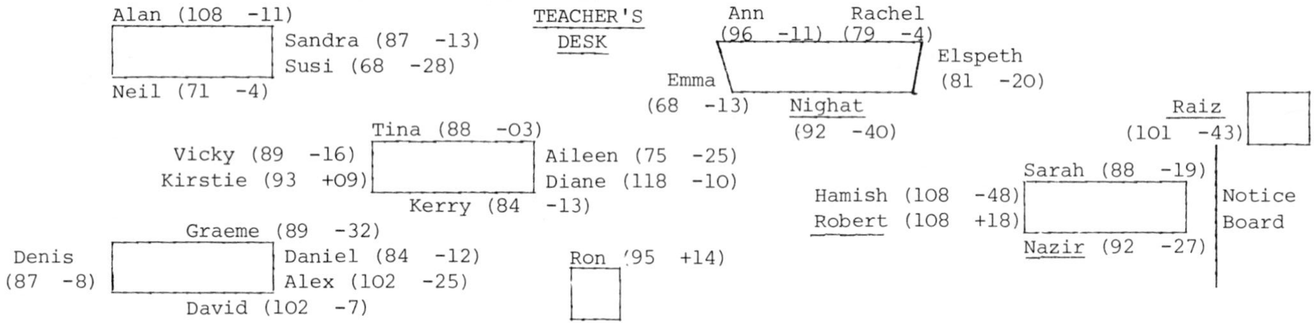

Alan (108 -11)

Sandra (87 -13)
Susi (68 -28)

Neil (71 -4)

TEACHER'S DESK

Ann (96 -11) Rachel (79 -4)

Elspeth (81 -20)

Emma (68 -13)

Nighat (92 -40)

Tina (88 -03)

Vicky (89 -16)
Kirstie (93 +09)

Aileen (75 -25)
Diane (118 -10)

Kerry (84 -13)

Graeme (89 -32)

Daniel (84 -12)
Alex (102 -25)

Ron (95 +14)

David (102 -7)

Denis (87 -8)

Raiz (101 -43)

Notice Board

Sarah (88 -19)

Hamish (108 -48)
Robert (108 +18)

Nazir (92 -27)

NOTES

(1) Pupils whose names are underlined were educated in the UK, though of ethnic minority status.

(2) The first number in the brackets is the pupil's IQ; the second number represents the number of months the pupil's reading comprehension is above (+) or below (-) his predicted reading age, not his chronological age.

(3) The mean over-estimation of girls for IQ by the teacher was 4.78; the mean under-estimation for boys was 6.50, the difference being significant (p= .012). Again for intelligence, the mean under-estimation for ethnic minority pupils was 5.75 positions, the mean over-estimation for white pupils was 0.09 positions (p= .380).

(4) The mean over-estimation of girls and boys for IQ reading comprehension were .91 and .36 positions respectively, (with p= .886). The mean over-estimation of ethnic minority and white pupils for reading comprehension was .01 and .73 positions respectively, (with p= .892).

(5) Results in notes (3) and (4) derived from Mann Whitney U test, two tailed.

220

of Primary 6, and nor had its geographical location
in the classroom next to the teacher's desk. Notes
(3) and (4) in Figure 9 indicate the extent to which
boys and girls, ethnic minority and white pupils,
were over or under-estimated for IQ and reading
comprehension. Girls were significantly over-
estimated for IQ compared to boys.

A number of well behaved girls were greatly
over-estimated and a number of less well behaved boys
were greatly underestimated. This is particularly
obvious if the girls on the 'top' table are considered.
Emma and Nighat illustrate this. Mr. Houston had
over-estimated Emma's classroom rank for IQ by 20
positions and had similarly over-estimated her
reading comprehension position. Nighat had been over-
estimated for IQ and comprehension by 9 and 11
positions respectively. Ann had been over-estimated
for IQ and comprehension by 7 and 21 positions
respectively.

Not so, however, for a number of boys. For
example, Robert, Alan and Hamish, all with a measured
intelligence of 108, which gave them joint second
place in the class, were assigned ranks for imputed
ability of 17th, 24th and 18th respectively. Indeed,
Alan was a member of the 'tail' table. He was
defined by Mr. Houston as 'slightly disturbed', a
condition which manifested itself in an 'odd writing
style'. Hamish was 'not supervised at home very
much', and his 'mother had him very late', his
mother being a single parent. He was often late for
school:

> You just saunter in. You're whole attitude
> shows as you walk in.

His 'attitude' was confirmed by himself. He was
'interested in nothing except art'. He had 'never
really liked school' and found it 'boring from the
minute I started'. Why did he come to school:

> Just come for a play ...

Sarah, who sat next to him, confirmed Hamish's view
of himself:

> He tries to get away from his work and he sits
> and giggles all the time.

His reading achievement was 48 months behind his
'predicted' level. It would appear that Hamish's
'attitude' might partly have been responsible for
Mr. Houston's low opinion of his ability. Nor could
his behaviour be corrected other than by suggestion
since Mr. Houston's philosophy did not admit coercive

forms of social control; he was not going to make
Hamish, or anyone else, work if they did not respond
to his advice.

An unfavourable teacher estimation did not
necessarily associate with under-achievement from
the pupil. Some pupils seemed able to counter their
teacher's view. For example, seated on his own was
Ron who had been under-estimated by 14 and 12
positions for IQ and reading comprehension respectively, yet he was in excess of his predicted reading
age by 14 months. Before I showed Mr. Houston Ron's
reading scores, I asked him what he thought about
Ron's reading:

> Just certain academic things were beyond him and
> his reading wasn't very good as we'll no doubt
> find when we come to his score ...

According to Mr. Houston, Ron had been 'totally
spoilt by his mother' whilst his father had been away
from home in the navy. He had been difficult and had
thrown 'tantrums'. But his parents 'expect a lot',
and this suggests itself in the fact that Ron was
the only pupil in the whole school whom I saw wearing
the school blazer, other pupils opting for a grey
pullover. Ron seemed to be unpopular with his
teacher. He seemed even less congenial to his classmates:

> He used to fight a lot - thinks he's great. He
> hits girls.
>
> Nobody likes Ron.
>
> Ron doesn't work so he distracts everyone else.

Ron sensed his unpopularity:

> They call me names ...

He sat alone but when he sought the company of others
he was told to 'mind his own business'. During my
observation of Mr. Houston's class, Ron attracted an
unusually vehement rebuke from Mr. Houston:

> Mr. Houston: It's nothing to do with you ...
>
> Ron, about to reply ...
>
> Mr. Houston: Should you be over there?
>   SHOULD YOU?

Ron: No.

Mr. Houston: Don't answer back. I said you
                   shouldn't be over there and that's
                   all there is to it ...

Ron: I was helping ...

Mr. Houston: I don't care if you were helping
                   or not.

Another boy who had been much under-estimated was
Robert, an ethnic minority pupil. He had been under-
estimated by 15 and 7 places for IQ and reading
achievement respectively. His reading comprehension
age exceeded his predicted age by 18 months.
     Not all poorly behaved boys were given low
estimations. This is especially so of Graeme's table.
When Mr. Houston called out 'BOYS!', it was usually
to this table that his gaze was directed. They were
continually reminded to do their work but they paid
little heed. Yet Denis was over-estimated for IQ and
for reading by 14 and 10 places respectively; Daniel
by 9 and 5 places respectively; and Graeme by 8 and
17 places respectively. All three boys were members
of the school football team which Mr. Houston coached.
Denis was widely regarded as its best player and it
may be speculatively suggested that Mr. Houston may
have confused his football prowess with his academic
ability.
     Mr. Houston was of the view that 'the good ones
will make it anyway', implying that they were, in the
primary school, virtually teacher-proof. This was
not so of recalcitrant boys, such as Robert and
Hamish. When they entered the local secondary school
they were placed in the remedial group. At the end
of their second year at secondary school, both were
placed in the 'C' block, which comprised the lowest
23 per cent of the age group, and which was destined
to pursue non-credential courses. Ron, on the other
hand, who had been keen to do well, despite
Mr. Houston's dim view of him, had managed to re-type
himself as a 'good pupil' at secondary school, being
placed in the top 'A' block which prepared for higher
education. Thus the 'good ones' would 'make it',
perhaps, if they wanted to; if they did not in
Mr. Houston's class, they were tolerated, but not
compelled. When I indicated the low reading comprehension levels of his pupils, Mr. Houston seemed
unperturbed; he had expected it. His concern was
a social one, not academic. If the pupil did not

FIGURE 10

MRS. SCOTT: SEATING PLAN

IQ AND READING COMPREHENSION SCORES AND ESTIMATES

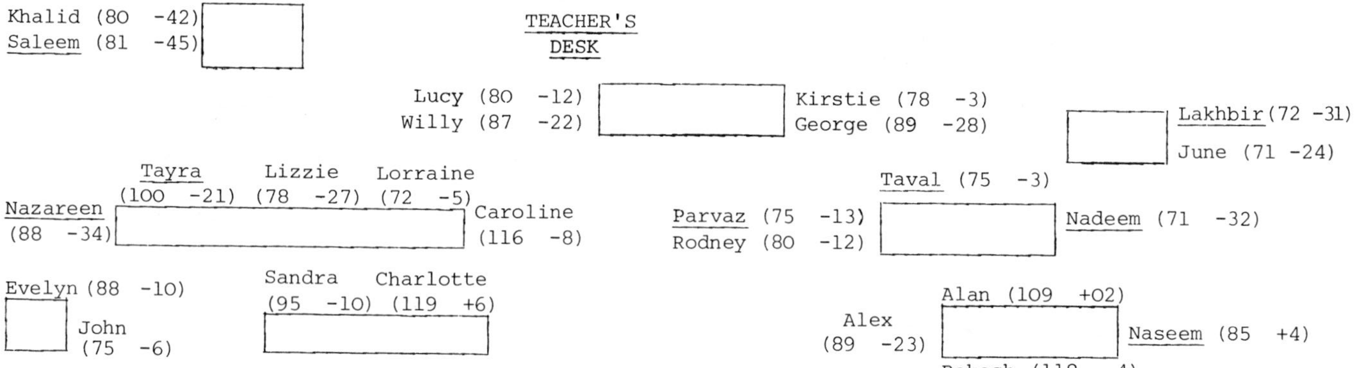

Khalid (80 -42)
Saleem (81 -45)

Lucy (80 -12)
Willy (87 -22)

TEACHER'S
DESK

Kirstie (78 -3)
George (89 -28)

Lakhbir (72 -31)
June (71 -24)

Tayra Lizzie Lorraine
(100 -21) (78 -27) (72 -5)   Caroline (116 -8)

Nazareen (88 -34)

Parvaz (75 -13)
Rodney (80 -12)

Taval (75 -3)

Nadeem (71 -32)

Evelyn (88 -10)
John (75 -6)

Sandra Charlotte
(95 -10) (119 +6)

Alex
(89 -23)

Alan (109 +02)
Naseem (85 +4)

Rakesh (118 -4)

NOTES

(1) Ethnic minority pupils are underlined. All had been completely educated in the UK.

(2) The first number in the brackets denotes the pupil's IQ; the second number represents the number of months the pupil's reading comprehension is above (+) or below (-) his predicted reading age, not his chronological age.

(3) The mean over-estimations for IQ for both boys and girls are 4.61 and 4.92 positions respectively (p= .916). The mean over-estimations for IQ for both ethnic minority and white pupils are 7.40 and 3.12 positions respectively (p=.143).

(4) The mean under-estimation for reading comprehension for boys is 0.30 positions; the mean over-estimation for girls is 1.15 positions (p= .563). The mean over-estimation for reading comprehension for ethnic minority pupils is 1.80 positions; the mean under-estimation for reading comprehension for white pupils is 0.43 positions (p= .386).

wish to show concern with matters academic, he was not
forced. Mr. Houston was not in a dilemma about this;
that is, he was not worried that the 'good ones' were
not being 'stretched' - they did not need to be for
they would, of themselves, 'make it' anyway.

Mrs. Scott

We turn now to Mrs. Scott, who, like Mr. Houston, was
a Primary 7 teacher who had taught the class for a
two-year period. She too was a 'stabilizer', though,
as we shall argue, something of a reluctant one.
Like Mr. Houston, her seating arrangements were sex-
segregated in the main but, unlike Mr. Houston, she
did not over-estimate girls relative to boys
(Figure 10, notes (3) and (4)). Unlike Mr. Houston,
she tended to over-estimate her ethnic minority
pupils more than white pupils, but not significantly.
And, as in Mr. Houston's class, there was 'under-
achievement' in reading comprehension; only three of
her pupils exceeded their predicted levels.
   Mrs. Scott's reactions to the pupils' actual
scores is instructive of her ideology. Though I have
typed her as a 'stabilizer', she seemed to harbour
conflicts about her practice which distinguishes her
slightly from·Mr. Houston. Whereas Mr. Houston was
philosophical about the low performance of his pupils
('It's a human institution with human failings'),
Mrs. Scott regretted that, for a number of reasons,
she was 'unable to push the good ones'. She perceived
three reasons for her frustration. The first was the
'nutters' (Willy, John and Alex). They shared
Hamish's view of school: it was to be enjoyed. They
too found themselves in remedial classes at secondary
school, and they also entered 'C' block at the end of
their second year there, a 'destiny' which seemed to
give some comfort to Mrs. Scott: other teachers
could not cope with them either. The second
constraint on Mrs. Scott's practice was the ethnic
minority group in her class. Some of them seemed
distant and lacked 'spark':

>   Mrs. Scott: Again the 'immigrants' are so shy
>   that you don't really get to know
>   them too well ... I can count on
>   one hand the amount of times Saleem
>   has actually spoken to me.
>
>   DH: He's really quiet isn't he ...?
>
>   Mrs. Scott: And his sister was the same ...

> Some of them - in the beginning
> especially - are always on the
> defensive; they always thought you
> were trying to catch them out and
> always seemed to have a conscience
> about something. This class has
> shown me that 31, with mixed
> 'immigrants' and behavioural
> problems - it's just no use, and
> I'm just sorry for the people who
> are at the top and who could have
> been pushed.

Mrs. Scott's concern about the 'top' was revealed in
the assertions made by others that her 'top' was not
comparable to the 'top' in another school:

> You see, to me Charlotte, Evelyn,
> Rakesh, Alan and Caroline would
> probably be just 'good average' in
> another school, you know. I've
> been here long enough to know that.
> At Moorfield I was told that
> Wellington (a nearby primary school
> in a 'better' working class district)
> Ds, even Es - I wouldn't agree there -
> maybe Ds; but they were equal to
> our Cs. Now that's a bit much, but
> I wouldn't have done anything
> differently for them, I don't think.

A third constraint was time, time to prepare for
classes. Since the 'cuts' Mrs. Scott had no preparation time at all.
     Despite Mrs. Scott's concern about the 'top',
she shared with Mr. Houston a wish to be 'nice' to
the children, and they defined her as such. She had
not used the belt for eight years. She was unable
to control the 'nutters' and 'suffered' them. Although
she might have wished to 'stretch the good ones', she
was not able to because her ideology did not allow
for coercion. But whereas Mr. Houston did not seem
concerned about the 'good ones', Mrs. Scott was.
Whereas Mr. Houston could intend the 'dilemma' away,
Mrs. Scott could not.

Mrs. Reid

During the year in which I undertook the classroom
observation, Mrs. Reid was the acting deputy head
teacher. On the arrival of Mr. Alexander she resumed

FIGURE 11

MRS. REID: SEATING PLAN

IQ AND READING COMPREHENSION SCORES AND ESTIMATES

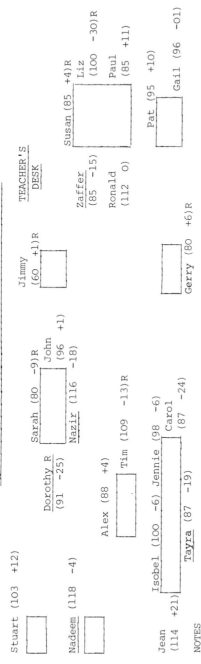

NOTES:

(1) All pupils underlined are ethnic minority pupils completely schooled in the UK.

(2) The first number in brackets denotes the pupil's IQ; the second number represents the number of months the pupil's reading comprehension is above (+) or below (-) his chronological age. An 'R' after the brackets indicates that the pupil had remedial reading instruction from a specialist teacher each day.

(3) For IQ, the teacher's mean under-estimation of boys was 4.70 positions, compared to a mean over-estimation for girls of 1.50 positions (p= .011). For IQ, the teacher under-estimated both ethnic minority and white pupils by 1.00 and 1.53 (mean scores) positions (p= .865).

(4) For reading comprehension, the teacher's mean under-estimation of boys was 2.72 positions, compared to a mean over-estimation of girls of 3.00 positions (p= .045). For reading comprehension, the teacher over-estimated both ethic minority and white pupils by 2.80 and 0.27 (mean scores) positions respectively (p= .514).

her classroom teacher status, being responsible for a Primary 4 class, previously taught by Mrs. Davie.

Mrs. Reid shared with Mr. Houston the practice of significantly over-estimating girls (Figure 11, notes (3) and (4)) for both IQ and reading comprehension. That girls were expected to perform better than boys was attributable to Mrs. Reid's interpretation of the stage of development which the sexes were at:

> Well, I've found that the girls are usually very earnest, and they'll sit and work very hard for you and that gives them their (high) performance, whereas boys - the boys usually - if they've got it all - they don't perform as well in (Primary) 4 and 5. I think you'll find that most girls work more up to their intelligence at this age than boys do.

Mrs. Reid's favourable expectations of girls in general was confirmed by her estimation of the particular girls on the 'top' table, comprising Jean, Isobel, Jennie, Carol and Tayra. Tayra, for example, was over-estimated by 11 and 13 positions for IQ and reading respectively. Although on the 'top' table, she was 19 months behind her predicted reading age. Carol, who sat beside her, was 24 months behind in reading. Both of these girls, however, had been in Mrs. Davie's 'top' group in the previous year. Tayra was not unlike Nazareen in Mrs. Scott's 'top' group, or Nighat in Mr. Houston's. All three were well-behaved and greatly over-estimated ethnic minority girls, and all three sat beside highly-thought-of white girls. Another girl on the top table, Jennie, had been over-estimated by 13 positions for reading comprehension.

A few 'difficult' boys had been considerably under-estimated by Mrs. Reid. John and Gerry had been under-estimated by 15 and 10 positions respectively for reading comprehension. These two boys, and Jimmy, had acquired a 'reputation' the previous year with Mrs. Davie:

> Stuart: Gerry's on his own ... He's silly.
>
> DH: Anybody had the belt this year?
>
> Gerry: Me.
>
> DH: How many times?

Gerry: About twice - not this year.

DH: Have you had it this year?

Stuart: No.

DH: Last year?

Stuart: Lots of times.

DH: What for?

Stuart: Fighting.

DH: In class?

Nadeem: Throwing pencils around ... running around the room.

Stuart: He got it for chattin'.

Nadeem: I wasn't chattin'.

Stuart: He was ...

DH: Have you had it John? ... What for?

John: Fighting.

DH: In class ... who were you fighting?

John: Alex ... Jimmy had it twenty-one times last year. He's always fighting.

This figure was confirmed on another occasion by Isobel:

DH: Who sits on their own?

Isobel: Alice Brown and Jimmy.

DH: Why?

Isobel: Because Jimmy has had the belt twenty-one times ... Carol keeps count!

DH: Now they're on separate tables, do they still talk?

Isobel: Yes, but Jimmy goes over to Gerry.

'THE GOOD ONES WILL MAKE IT ANYWAY'

These comments suggest that Nadeem, Gerry and John
were not well-behaved. Nor was Stuart who had to
sit on his own. Of all the boys, Jimmy had the worst
reputation with Mrs. Reid. He sat closest to her in
a single desk. Yet, in her estimation of Jimmy,
Stuart and Nadeem, Mrs. Reid proved to be very
accurate, but not so for John and Gerry. In the case
of Nadeem and Jimmy, they were, respectively, 'bright'
and 'dim', and seemed obviously so to Mrs. Reid. But
John and Gerry were more difficult to assess, being
nearer 'average', neither conspicuously bright nor dim.
Their poor behaviour may have prompted Mrs. Reid to
under-estimate them.
    Mrs. Reid's class was a Primary 4 class and
therefore was provided with remedial help. On the
basis of the objective data, a number of pupils
ought not to have received remedial help, whilst some
pupils who were not receiving it should have been.
For example, on the 'top' table were Tayra and Carol,
both of whom were 'under-achieving' in reading
comprehension, in Carol's case by two years. Yet
they received no remedial help because they were seen
not to need it; on the contrary, they were errone-
ously defined as very high achievers. On the other
hand, Jimmy, Susan and Gerry all received remedial
help, yet they were reading beyond their predicted
comprehension age, and could have been 'released' in
favour of others if Mrs. Reid's estimations had been
accurate. That Carol and Tayra were thought of as
being good readers may be true in the sense that they
were accurate readers who were fluent. Their comprehension, however, was, on the basis of the objective
test, not on a par with their accuracy and the
teacher may have confused reading accuracy with
reading comprehension.

Mr. Lane

We turn now to Mr. Lane's Primary 6 class which had
previously been with Mrs. Carter. Mr. Lane was in
his early years of teaching. He shared the concern
of the 'stabilizers' that the teachers should show
some toleration for children from deprived backgrounds, but he was also of the view that 'we should
give them some form of assessment'. His explanation
of the objective test data was very much rooted in a
social pathology model and he admitted openly that
expectations in Rockfield were low:

        Mr. Lane: I think (the low reading scores) it's
                  just a reflection of where the school

FIGURE 12

MR. LANE: SEATING PLAN

IQ AND READING COMPREHENSION SCORES AND ESTIMATES

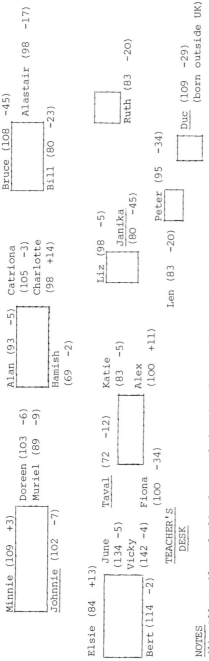

Minnie (109 +3)

Johnnie (102 -7)

Doreen (103 -6)
Muriel (89 -9)

Alan (93 -5)
Hamish (69 -2)

Catriona (105 -3)
Charlotte (98 +14)

Bruce (108 -45)
Alastair (98 -17)
Bill (80 -23)

Elsie (84 +13)

June (134 -5)
Vicky (142 -4)

Bert (114 -2)

Taval (72 -12)
Fiona (100 -34)

Katie (83 -5)
Alex (100 +11)

Liz (98 -5)
Janika (80 -45)

Ruth (83 -20)

Peter (95 -34)

Len (83 -20)

Duc (109 -29)
(born outside UK)

TEACHER'S DESK

NOTES

(1) All pupils underlined are ethnic minority pupils completely schooled in the UK, except where otherwise stated.

(2) The first number in brackets denotes the pupil's IQ; the second number represents the number of months by which the pupil's reading comprehension is above (+) or below (-) his predicted reading age, not his chronological age.

(3) For IQ, the teacher's mean over-estimation for boys is .60 positions, compared to a mean over-estimation for girls of 0.01 positions (p= .860). For IQ, the mean over-estimation of ethnic minority pupils is 3.50 positions, compared to a mean under-estimation of 0.40 positions for white pupils (p= .619).

(4) For reading comprehension, the teacher's mean over-estimation of girls is 0.35 positions, compared to a mean under-estimation of 1.44 positions for boys (p= .503). For reading comprehension, the mean over-estimation for ethnic minority pupils is 1.50 positions, compared to a mean under-estimation for white pupils of 0.80 positions (p= .507).

> is. If you want to comment on the
> effect it has on the teachers - it
> might not be relevant here - but we
> come to expect a certain type of pupil,
> if you like.

DH: Do you find that your estimate of what
>   is 'good' is possibly pulled down a
>   little?

Mr. Lane: Oh it is. There's no doubt about it.

Mr. Lane tended to over-estimate slightly the girls
for reading, but not for intelligence. Further, a
similar, though negligible, over-estimation of ethnic
minority pupils for both reading and for intelligence
obtained, but not a significant one (Figure 12).
     In all of the classes so far discussed, there
has been at least one girl on the 'top' table who
appeared to be very much overrated by the teacher.
So it was in Mr. Lane's class, in the person of Elsie.
Her ability was far below that of her classmates on
her table, a finding which surprised Mr. Lane:

> This is a person that surprised me: Elsie. Her
> ability - I've always believed that she's able
> in the top group. I've since discovered - again
> I keep harping back to social problems - they've
> had a death in the family quite recently, but I
> don't know what the problems were when these
> marks were taken. She's a funny kid. She's
> moody - this kind of thing, but I expected much
> higher marks from her. Nothing wonderful, but
> higher than that.

He suggested that Elsie 'probably copied a bit from
Vicky', the most intelligent girl in the class.
There was the implication that Elsie was a somewhat
anxious girl; an anxiety, perhaps moodiness, which
came with the constant need to keep up with children
much more intelligent than she:

> As I said, she's a very moody sort of person, in
> fact - not huffy, but she doesn't smile very
> much for instance, so it's very difficult to
> decide when perhaps one day she's in a mood:
> another day she's worried. And whenever you
> talk to her - which is frequently - it's sort
> of sly answers, not cheeky. She doesn't like
> to communicate in any sort of way so it's
> difficult to say. I know for instance when she

came back from being ill not so very long ago.
She'd been off three weeks. She was in a state
for a day or two because she had fallen behind.
So she's a conscientious girl. I think you
could definitely say that. She does want to
keep up.

Fiona was also over-estimated by some 14 positions
for reading comprehension:

Well, Fiona for instance. I would have expected
a wee bit higher, the reason being that she has
a home environment where everybody is much older
than her and I would have thought the language
experience would have been that much more.

As with Alison in Mr. Houston's class, Liz, a 'quiet'
girl, was very much under-estimated, both for IQ and
for reading: she was expected to achieve ranks of
23 and 14 respectively, but she actually achieved
ranks of 12 and 1 respectively.

There were few children in the school whose
measured intelligence was high. When such children
were recognised, and when they achieved on a par with
their ability, there was much favourable, even awe-
some, discussion of them. Again, the explanation of
the pupil's achievement was the home. Vicky in
Mr. Lane's class is a case in point. Both her parents
were teachers:

She's the brightest kid I've ever had and unfor-
tunately she's a pain in the neck too. So there's
no danger of her being the teacher's pet or
anything like that, you know. It stretches me
a bit. You get into all that and you enjoy it
because sometimes they pick you out - find
faults, you know. You've got to be on your toes
and it's good. I think it's really good; it
wakes you up a bit.

Sat beside Vicky was June. Again the home was
supportive, if not too much so:

It's really interesting that these two,
especially June ... June more so is interesting
than Vicky because of Vicky's background -
parents, etc., but so does June get the same
kind of back-up. The father is very into doing
work with June. In fact, he's a bit of a pest
sometimes. And it's interesting that they
(Vicky and June), especially in reading if you

like, have achieved quite a high mark and I
believe that the back-up that they get at home
has a lot to do with it.

Finally, in Mr. Houston's, Mrs. Scott's and
Mrs. Reid's classes there were some boys of poor
behaviour who were under-estimated in their ability
and in their achievement. So it was in Mr. Lane's
class. Bruce, Alastair and Duc were under-estimated
for IQ by 15, 10 and 11 positions respectively.
Alastair's unexpectedly high IQ mark was not disputed
and Mr. Lane tried to explain why he had been under-
estimating Alastair's ability. Again, the 'home'
background and his classroom behaviour provided the
explanation:

> Mr. Lane: I think he's (Alastair) got a lot of
> problems. Home, whatever. Social
> problems that obviously affect how he
> performs at school, and possibly the
> results that you've got have highligh-
> ted this fact - you know, that they
> really brought it to the surface in
> some ways if you like. His ability is
> greater; he is more able than myself
> or any teacher has given him credit
> for. But it's very difficult to draw
> things out of a person when they've
> got a lot of complex problems going on
> at the same time.

> DH: Does he have trouble getting along
> with other children?

> Mr. Lane: None at all. He's very normal, if you
> like - average kid in terms of rela-
> tionships with other kids. He's no
> hang-ups there. I think it's at home
> that's a problem.

> DH: Can he concentrate in class?

> Mr. Lane: Oh no, he can't concentrate ... He's
> very nervous. If you ever watch him
> you'll see his hands literally shake
> all the time, not through fear ... I
> under-valued his ability but it's
> been hidden through other problems,
> I think.

Duc, an ethnic minority pupil, was fourth in the

FIGURE 13

MRS. CARTER: SEATING PLAN

IQ AND READING COMPREHENSION SCORES AND ESTIMATES

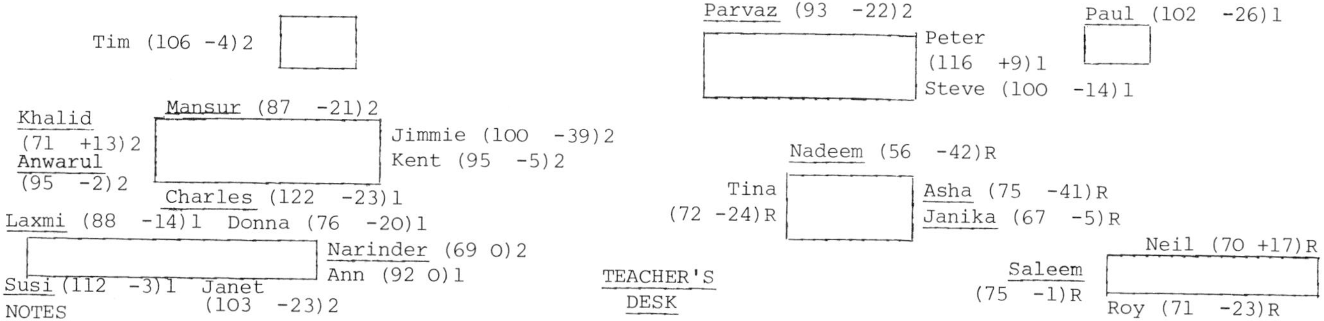

Tim (106 -4)2   Paul (102 -26)1

Peter (116 +9)1
Steve (100 -14)1

Parvaz (93 -22)2

Nadeem (56 -42)R

Asha (75 -41)R
Janika (67 -5)R

Neil (70 +17)R

Roy (71 -23)R

Khalid
(71 +13)2
Anwarul
(95 -2)2

Mansur (87 -21)2

Jimmie (100 -39)2
Kent (95 -5)2

Charles (122 -23)1
Donna (76 -20)1

Tina
(72 -24)R

Saleem
(75 -1)R

Laxmi (88 -14)1

Narinder (69 0)2
Ann (92 0)1

Susi (112 -3)1   Janet
(103 -23)2

TEACHER'S
DESK

NOTES

(1) All pupils underlined are ethnic minority pupils completely schooled in the UK, except for Anwarul who arrived from Bangladesh in 1976.

(2) The first number in brackets denotes the pupil's IQ; the second number represents the number of months by which the pupil's reading comprehension is above (+) or below (-) his predicted reading age, not his chronological age. An 'R' after the brackets denotes that the pupil received remedial reading instruction each day. A '1' after the brackets denotes that the pupil is in the top reading group, as defined by the teacher. A '2' after the brackets denotes that the pupil is in the second reading group.

(3) For IQ, the teacher's mean over-estimation of girls is 0.09 positions, compared to a mean under-estimation of boys of 0.46 positions (p= .785). For IQ, the teacher's mean over-estimation of ethnic minority pupils is 3.16 positions, compared to a mean under-estimation of 3.34 positions for white pupils (p= .001).

(4) For reading comprehension, the teacher's mean over-estimation of girls is 3.09 positions, compared to a mean under-estimation of boys of 2.53 positions (p= .066). For reading comprehension, the teacher's mean over-estimation of ethnic minority pupils is .58 positions, compared to a mean under-estimation of 0.79 for white pupils (p= .507).

235

class on the basis of his IQ test score; Mr. Lane
had assigned him to fifteenth place. His previous
teacher, Mrs. Carter, had called him 'a bright
button'. But Duc had a poor staffroom reputation
and was known as 'Wailer', a nickname which rhymed
with his real name and described his behaviour. He
sat alone in a corner of the classroom.

Mrs. Carter

Finally we come to Mrs. Carter's Primary 4 class,
which had the highest proportion of ethnic minority
children. Revealed in her class are the difficulties
which are posed to teachers at Rockfield, perhaps in
a more extreme form than in other classes.
Mrs. Carter's summation of the class admits the
problems:

> This class is immature in many ways: in reading
> maths and other subjects, as well as in basics
> such as toilet training (at the end of Primary 4).
> They have, however, been very easy to handle as
> regards behaviour, and have been on the whole
> truthful and honest. They seem on the whole a
> happy and well-integrated lot, in spite of
> difficulties at home, and in many cases depriva-
> tion. A reading test taken in Primary 3 gave
> poor results for this class.

The class had previously been taught by Mrs. Preece
whose ideology, discussed earlier, was one of pushing
the children, not tolerating them. Mrs. Carter had
not changed the reading groups from what they had
been with Mrs. Preece:

> When the class came into Primary 4 they contin-
> ued to work in the same reading groups as they
> had at the end of Primary 3.

As with other teachers, Mrs. Carter - and Mrs. Preece
before her - had mistakenly inflated the ability and
achievement of two girls in the top reading group on
the basis of their performance in reading, and
Mrs. Carter expressed surprise at their scores.
Donna, for example, was placed fifth for reading by
Mrs. Carter, but achieved 23rd place. On the other
hand, as in Mrs. Reid's class, there were other
pupils who were very much under-estimated. For
example, Tim and Kent (the younger brother of
Willy Scott of the 'nutter' category) were under-
estimated in reading by 11 positions respectively.

Mrs. Carter's class had a long 'tail'. Indeed, the need for further remedial instruction in Mrs. Carter's class was considerable: Mansur, Jimmie, Charles, Laxmi, Donna, Janet, Parvaz, Paul and Steve were all below their predicted reading ages by more than twelve months, but did not receive remedial help, even in Primary 4. As for those in receipt of remedial instruction, they had only just begun to have it, despite the poor reading results which had been obtained in the previous year.

If the top and remedial groups are considered, there is no obvious correlation between the teacher's perception of the 'home' and the performance of the pupil in the school. All groups had 'stable' and 'deprived' families. Take group 1: Susi, of mixed parentage, had a Pakistani step-mother, had lost a year's schooling in Pakistan, and had been taken into care: Laxmi, the fourth girl in her family, came from a 'stable' home; Donna, the youngest of five children, had been cared for in her early years by a relative, had a history of 'sulks' and 'huffs', had been referred to an educational psychologist, was 'very insecure and needed encouragement'; Ann had 'caring parents' and though a 'very subdued girl in school was a firebrand at home'. Charles came from a 'stable' home; Steve came from a 'broken home' but was 'well informed', 'well behaved' and had a 'caring mother'; Paul also came from a 'broken home' but was 'doted on and spoilt', his affections being 'the object of rivalry between mother and father'. Although there had been complaints from the public, he was 'likeable'.

Consider now the remedial group. Neil when a baby:

> ... had not been expected to live. He had still been in nappies when he started school. He is still frail, has poor coordination and has a speech defect. His greatest handicap is his poor vision: he wore specs then contact lenses, but has had neither for months.

Neil's parents were seen as being 'unable to cope'. Roy had begun his schooling at the age of seven in South Africa and, on arrival at Rockfield, 'had shown severe learning difficulties' and had been refused remedial help by Mr. McLean because it would have been 'wasted'. Since obtaining remedial help in Primary 4 he had improved markedly. Tina had a 'history of bed-wetting' and had had ear, throat and kidney infections. Her parents were 'concerned'.

The remaining pupils in the remedial group were
'immigrant' children. Asha had two handicapped and
disabled brothers; another was at a school for the
mentally retarded. Her youngest brother was
'normally in a day-care establishment where the
mother is supposed to learn the type of care required'.
Her 'father works long hours in a shop, and mother
has no English and little idea of schools, or the
children's requirements'. Asha's classmates had
provided her with a P.E. uniform. Tayra also had
'learning difficulties'. Her relationship with her
mother had not been ideal, Tayra having 'given her a
bad time, swearing at her'. Nadeem's parents were
not known to Mrs. Carter. Saleem was of mixed parentage - the marriage had broken up and he lived with
his mother. Overall, the categorization of
Mrs. Carter's pupils in the lowest ability group
closely approximate their actual performance. Like
her colleagues, Mrs. Carter was not sceptical of the
low reading score in general but, in some individual
cases, expressed surprise. Her frustration turned on
what was seen as an inadequate provision of remedial
instruction. This was regarded as one of the few
ways in which the school could 'compensate'. It
could not deal with the causes of the pupils' difficulties; it could not intervene in the ethnic
minority home to compel parents to speak English; it
could not effect structural change in society to
remove the material and psychological conditions
which rendered some of her pupils less educable; it
could not alter the genetic make-up of very low
ability pupils. The teacher had to cope, to balance
pragmatically an educational ideal against the
perceived situational realities.

'The Good Ones Will Make it Anyway'?

It was noted earlier that the functionalist analysis
of the school argues that future educational and
economic success will be commensurate with the talent
of the child, and not with the cultural milieu of
which he happens to be a part. Thus the claim turns
on the view that it will be the individual properties
of the pupil, not those which are socially conferred,
that will predict success. Academic and economic
status will rest with the individual's talents and
efforts, not with his social attributes of, say,
social class, ethnicity or gender. It will be the
role of the school to identify talent and to trans-
late it into educational credentials which will
represent the realisation of that talent to the full.

In short, it is the notion of meritocracy which
underpins the school and which legitimates the social
hierarchy beyond it.

The consideration of the five classrooms above
calls into question the functionalist rhetoric. In
some instances, the social attributes of the pupil
have been confounded with his intellectual attributes,
thereby serving to produce a pupil identity which is
in error. That is, the subjective opinion offered
by the teacher in respect of a pupil's talent is not
confirmed by an objective measure of that talent.
Further, this sometimes associates with an academic
performance by the pupil which is more at one with
the subjective view of him than with the objective
'predictor'. Moreover, the erroneous opinion of the
pupil by the teacher may be given spatial and tempo-
ral reinforcement. That is, the pupil may be
assigned to an ability group which gives organisational and manifest representation of his teacher's
mistaken view; and this allocation may persist from
year to year. The hierarchy of pupil identities may
be a consequence of undeclared criteria and the
teacher may be unaware that her actions perpetuate
them and their consequences for the pupil.

The detailed classroom-based analysis suggests
that this misrepresentation of individual pupils is
not uncommon and nor is it consciously in the
teacher's mind. If, however, the estimations made
by teachers of pupils' ability and performance are
viewed socially, not individually, then it is
possible to indicate some social attributes of the
pupil which may be auspiciously regarded by the
teacher, often unwittingly so. The social attribute
of gender appears to be a particularly powerful basis
for differentiation within classrooms, more so in
some than in others. That said, however, differentiation on the basis of gender does not appear to be a
conscious practice of teachers. For example, the
higher expectations which teachers have of girls
compared to boys is not something which teachers
publicly discuss. They do not explain pupils' work
and behaviour simply by citing the sex of the pupil.
Rather, teachers articulate other categories of
differentiation which have nothing to do with gender -
'ones that spark' and ones that are 'dim'; 'nutters'
and 'nice kids'; the 'top' and the 'tail' are
examples.

The detailed analysis above shows that girls
do not meet their teachers' expectation of them
whilst boys better it. This is in respect of ability
and reading achievement levels, not behaviour. The

pupil identity of girls is better than boys. Moreover it was shown in an earlier chapter that the
academic status of girls is seen by the girls themselves to be higher than that of boys, though only
among white pupils. This higher status of white
girls within the working class is not confirmed by
the status of women vis-a-vis men in the wider
structure. If the primary school is said to structure the identities of the sexes in a manner accordant
with the identities of the sexes beyond the school,
then, in functionalist terms, the role of the primary
school may be 'dysfunctional', or, in Weberian terms,
it reveals indications of institutional autonomy.
Functionalist cause for concern, however, diminishes
because the academic performance of working class
girls in the secondary school declines, whilst that
of boys improves (King, 1971). The reasons for this
are not easy to discern, but a number of comments may
be made. In the primary school, the gender role of
the girl is given greater academic recognition than
that of the boy. The pedagogic relationship between
the working class boy and the teacher is not easy.
He is physically more aggressive outside the classroom but is expected to curb this within it; the
sedentary behaviour expected of him in school is not
his preferred mode of play beyond it; he is less
used to conversing with an adult, especially a woman.
On the other hand, the transition from home to school
for the girl in the primary school may be easier.
Her more docile and compliant behaviour is rewarded
by parent and teacher; it is therefore doubly
reinforced.

The institutionalization of female docility in
the primary school and in the family may serve the
'needs of society' in a delayed manner. That is,
when the working class girl reaches adolescence, the
family influence which had previously aided her
success in the primary school may now serve to lessen
it in the secondary school, pointing her to early
marriage and a 'good job for a girl'. As a result,
girls may be more likely to 'drop out' than boys and
may do so before their ability warrants it. The
forces prevailing upon the working class girl to
respond to these influences are powerful and they are
not lessened by the omission of some secondary
schools to counter them. All this may apply with
greater force to the girl whose family is Moslem. At
Rockfield it has been indicated that such a girl has
a restricted social life, and, if Sharpe's (1976)
study of teenage 'Asian' girls has wide applicability,
this restriction may extend into adolescence. In the

home, compliance, even timidity, is required. In the
classroom the same behaviour may be defined as a lack
of interest or 'spark'. In this study the teachers
rated ethnic minority girls as the most 'withdrawn',
and they ranked them as the lowest achievers. Added
to this was the suspicion held by some teachers that
'immigrant parents' were also not interested in the
school, as 'revealed' by their objections to the
school dress code, and by their non-attendance at
parent-teacher meetings. But despite this emerging
view of Moslem girls being seen as disinterested and
bereft of 'spark', it is important to note that there
were exceptions to the 'wee mice' typifications of
some of these girls, as witnessed in the persons of
Susi in Mrs. Carter's class, Tayra in Mrs. Reid's
and Nighat in Mr. Houston's, all of whom were members
of the 'top' table in their respective classrooms.
Furthermore, we have been dealing here with a small
number of girls drawn from only one school and we
should therefore be wary of lending weight to a
potentially damaging typification which may not
obtain in other schools.
      We turn now to boys. At the aggregate level of
analysis, and in a number of classrooms, the ability
and the reading comprehension of boys is defined
incorrectly by teachers: it is under-estimated,
sometimes markedly so. Whilst the meritocratic ideal
in the primary school may obtain for the well-behaved
girl, it may not for the 'difficult' boys of above-
average ability. They may be consigned to low ability
groups from which it is difficult to leave. These
'failed' identities may be accepted by the boys
themselves and carried through to the secondary school
where they may come to be included in 'non-academic'
streams, or tracks. Only on rare occasions does the
boy of low academic repute lose his 'failed' identity
and re-type himself in a more favourable light. The
case of Ron in Mr. Houston's class is an example.
Finally, although teachers expected less of boys, in
general they actually bettered that expectation.
Conversely, girls failed to meet their teachers'
expectations. Indeed, the actual measured ability
and reading comprehension scores revealed virtually
no sex difference. But, in particular cases, some
girls may have received benefits through being exposed
to the mental stimulation of others in 'top' groups,
whilst some intelligent boys placed in the 'tail' may
have been at a disadvantage through not experiencing
enough such 'stimulation', or enough 'push' and
'stretching' from the teacher.
      From a functionalist, meritocratic perspective,

it is assumed that the 'cultural capital' (Bourdieu, 1974) of all pupils is the same. It is common coin among educationists that this is not so: working class children tend to have less 'cultural capital' to 'invest', and their 'return' is accordingly lessened. Moreover, at primary level, the 'capital' of boys may be less than that of girls, especially in the working class. Further, as we have attempted to indicate here, different ethnic groups differentially 'prepare' their children for school. At Rockfield, this ethnic difference was recognised and measures were taken in the form of the Immigrant Department to compensate for it. Yet the data here show that the teachers at Rockfield tended to over-estimate ethnic minority pupils; that is, they score lower than their teachers expected, in terms of rank orders. This seems to contradict the 'teacher-expectancy effect' (Nash, 1976) and is probably more easily explained as the product of a number of factors combining to depress the measured ability of ethnic minority children. These factors would include the culture-bias of the IQ test and reading test; the children's difficulties, despite the Immigrant Depart- ment, with the English language; and an unwillingness by the teachers to assign academic worth to the 'cultural capital' of the ethnic minority children.

Compensation and Teacher Ideologies

Social class-based cultural 'discontinuities' between home and school have long been recognised as limiting the reali ation of the meritocratic ideal that only 'talent' derived 'naturally', not socially, shall predict success. The emphasis so far in this chapter has tended to dwell more upon the status considera- tions of gender and ethnicity than upon social class. No implication is intended, however, that would negate the consequences of the pupil's social class for his school career. The intention has been to refine the social class analysis, not to replace it. No between- social class analysis has been undertaken within the study here because the school was defined officially, and by its teachers, as virtually homogeneous in its working class composition. It is this very homogen- eity which has permitted the analysis to point to the effects of gender and ethnicity within a social class. Our discussion of the social class of the pupils must therefore be located at the between-school, not the within-school level. It is best undertaken by referring to the ideologies of the teachers and their reactions to the actual measures of ability and

performance produced earlier. We have argued that
the ideological constructions of the teachers can be
represented along a continuum, the extremes of which
are defined by 'stabilization' and by 'stretching'.
The former pursued a more therapeutic goal, the
latter an academic one. The teachers did perceive
their pupils as deprived but it was their interpretation of the educational consequences of that
deprivation which informed their interpretation of
what counted as 'compensation' in this urban school.
The earlier consideration of the teachers' ideologies
concluded that the 'stabilization' ethos, though the
official one, was held by a minority of teachers.
Thus when posing the question, 'Has the school
compensated?', it would be unreasonable to criticise
a teacher whose ideology was one of 'stabilization'
and whose pupils were very low achievers. That
teacher did not pursue academic goals and should not
be called into question if he did not expect to
realise them.

A case in point is Mr. Houston. For him the act
of testing pupils on cognitive matters was a redun-
dancy, as beyond the remit both he and his head
teacher had set for the school. Academic gains were
not what compensation was about. Rather it was seen
as an adjustment to an expected lifestyle for children
in a working class setting. These teachers were not
unwitting dupes said to be reproducing the social
class locations of their pupils; they were
consciously doing it, and for reasons they defined as
well-intentioned. Indeed, it may be argued that the
very low level of the academic performance of the
Primary 7 pupils was partly the consequence of their
having been taught for the previous two years by two
teachers, Mrs. Scott and Mr. Houston, whose practice
was not to 'stretch' the pupils. These results would
appear to offer some vindication of the 'stabilization' ethos. But if the 'non-stabilizers' in the
school were a majority why, even in the other classes,
were the academic results so low? Moreover, the
pupils in Mrs. Scott's and Mr. Houston's classes had
previously been taught by Mrs. Findlay, Mrs. Davie
Mrs. Preece, Mrs. Letham, Mrs. Carter and Miss Darby,
none of whom practised 'stabilization'.

The apparent realisation of the 'stabilization'
ethos in the face of a majority of teachers who were
opposed to it requires explanation. The reasons may
be divided between those located within the school
and those beyond it. In respect of the former, the
ideology of the head teacher was unsympathetic to
that of the 'stretchers' and the 'straddlers'. This

is not to argue that the head teacher resorted to
somewhat forceful measures to have his views and
practices accepted; rather it is to state that he
devised certain administrative procedures which
limited the realisation of ideologies not at one with
his own. For example, the number of pupils requiring
remedial instruction far exceeded the capacity of the
school to give it; indeed, the efficacy of remedial
instruction as a policy was doubted by the head
teacher. Recalcitrant pupils whom the teacher found
hard to control were not brought to book by the head
teacher. There were other reasons. The work of the
'stretchers' might be 'undone' by 'stabilizers' who
later taught their pupils. The very label of the
school might have been internalised in the thinking
and practice of the teachers. That is, as a teacher's
time in this urban school increased, it was admitted
that her expectations of the pupils decreased. There
was an imperceptible drift from the cognitive. There
was also little opportunity for teachers to compare
their practice with that of other teachers, either
within their own school or in other schools. Furthermore, there were external pressures. The socialization of the pupil was regarded as deficient in a
majority and sufficient in a few. Pupil failure and
success were attributable to the home, regardless of
the teacher's ideology. Moreover, different home
backgrounds allegedly produced different deficiencies:
the ethnic minority home was regarded as emotionally
stable but as educogenically and linguistically
wanting. On the other hand, many white homes were
not emotionally stable and were thought to be the
scenes of deprivation, both emotional and material.
All this had to be coped with. The low performance
of the pupils in the school was therefore not thought
to be remarkable: the 'stabilizers' had not been
striving for high performance; the 'stretchers' and
'straddlers' were able to identify some of the
constraints which emanated from a permutation of
'pathologies' associated with the class and status
milieux of their pupils.
    Finally, if the expectations and wishes of the
'stabilizers' were realised in the academic performance of the pupils, the 'stretchers' could claim
some solace from an analysis of the pupils' occupational aspirations. In contrast to the belief held
by Mr. McLean that his pupils would not and should
not aspire to middle class occupations, the actual
career aspirations of the pupils reveal a greater
wish for upward mobility than might be expected. The
most ambitious of the four ethnic/gender groups was

white girls. Fifty-three per cent aspired to social
class levels I and II, as defined by the Registrar
General's classification of occupations, the majority
wishing to become teachers, nurses and veterinary
surgeons. White boys, on the other hand, were far
less ambitious in conventional terms. Some thirty
per cent chose to be a professional footballer, whilst
only fourteen per cent aspired to social class levels
I and II. As for ethnic minority pupils, they were
twice as likely to be undecided on their career
aspirations as whites, nearly one-third of them not
having made up their minds. As might be expected,
ethnic minority boys were more ambitious than girls,
with nearly a quarter aspiring to social class I,
mainly as doctors. Ethnic minority girls, however,
were more ambitious than might have been expected by
their teachers, twenty-seven per cent aspiring to
social class II, though none to social class I. The
occupational aspirations of the ethnic minority
children lend further doubt to the teachers' views
that neither the children nor their parents were
interested in education. Clearly, they seemed more
interested than the teachers had thought, though
they had not made that interest manifest to the
teachers. However, given the levels of under-
achievement in the school, it is doubtful if many of
those who aspired to professional occupations would
be able to remedy their under-achievement in time to
ensure placement in the stream preparing for higher
education at the end of the second year of secondary
school. The social order was being reproduced,
consciously so by the head teacher, reluctantly and
frustratingly so by some teachers who did not share
his purpose.

CONCLUSION

This study is of one school during a short three-year
period of its existence. Not all of the events which
occurred during that time were observed and interpreted. No completely accurate perception of those
events which were observed is claimed, or could ever
be claimed. The interpretation of the events which
I observed was influenced by my theoretical perspective, one based on Weber's concepts of ideology,
domination, power, social class and status group.
The Weberian approach is attractive for two reasons.
Firstly, it questions the extreme determinism of
structural functionalism and some strands of Marxism.
Both of these tend to reduce the individual's identity and ideology to external forces. That is,
functionalism subsumes individual consciousness
within the collective consciousness and its Parsonian
central value system. It assumes a consensus on
society's needs. It reduces action to the mere
acting out of roles legitimated by authority. The
power of the individual or of groups to resist is a
neglected issue. A similar determinism holds for
structural Marxism. Here the social order is effected through ideological control. Teachers are said
to misrepresent reality to themselves and to their
pupils. They are 'immersed' in a world-view, a
commonsense, which is really amenable to the interests
of capitalism but which is falsely thought of as
being in the best interests of teacher and pupil,
and therefore of 'society'. Whilst Weber does not
deny the force of external pressures on consciousness
and action, he does not see these constraints as
evoking a total passivity on the part of individuals.
Individuals interpret the same structure differently,
and are often in conflict over those definitions and
interpretations.
     The second reason, therefore, for adopting a

Weberian perspective is that Weber requires sociology to pay heed to the interpretations which individuals make of their situation, and to the extent these are shared and imposed upon others. It does not regard social action as the passive compliance with institutional roles, or as the result of false consciousness. The former stance obviates the need to go beyond official statements of roles in order to find out what goes on in institutions; the latter obviates the need to do empirical research at all because individuals cannot give the 'real' intentions behind their actions. A Weberian conflict theory of education and society allows the focus to be brought to bear upon either education systems in general (Ringer, 1979), or upon the organizational level of the school in particular. Our concern has been with the latter. Just as the former approach shows that education systems manifest a good deal of autonomy in respect of other social institutions, especially the economy (Collins, 1979; Anderson, 1961; Ringer, 1979), so the organizational approach reveals that teachers and pupils interpret their respective positions in dissimilar and often conflicting ways.
        It is now important to re-state the main findings which the study has generated, to interpret them within our theoretical perspective and to state their relevance to the current sociological analysis of the primary school. In this exercise it is important to stress that due caution in extending the interpretation here, that of a single school, to wider contexts is appropriate. We begin with the empirical findings.
        Much of the study has been to do with the educational ideologies which the teachers in the school expressed and how they put them into practice. We were further concerned with the extent to which such ideologies were shared and imposed upon others. In particular, the willingness and ability of the head teacher to realise his 'ethos' was analysed. The Weberian approach to the sociology of the school does not agree that the ideologies and practices of teachers can simply be 'read off' from the official role prescriptions stated by the head teacher. It does not agree that within schools there will be a consensus of purpose amongst its members. Rather, it argues that ideologies will differ and that some may seek to impose their ideologies upon others, to dominate them. The ideologies of the teachers could be found at various locations along a continuum typified at the extremes by 'stabilization' and by 'stretching'. The official ideology, that of the head teacher, was the former, but it was not one

shared by a majority of his teachers. He did not,
however, bring his dissenting teachers into line;
he did not impose his ideology in any overt way,
mainly because, had he done so, he would have
disturbed the very surface tranquility of staff
relations which he wished to preserve. If the
teachers followed his dictates on administrative
matters, then he afforded them what they regarded as
considerable professional discretion in the classroom.
In this regard the head teacher was effective. There
was little manifest 'unrest' among the staff. Two
exceptions to this were reported: that when
Mr. Alexander, the deputy head, arrived; and that
between 'immigrant teachers' and classroom teachers.
In respect of Mr. Alexander, he came to a school
whose teachers had long since made sense of it. His
ideology accorded with nobody's: the 'stretchers' in
his view did not 'stretch' the pupils enough; the
'stabilizers' were well nigh incomprehensible to him,
so great was their perceived 'slackness' in respect
of punctuality, preparation and academic standards.
In the end he withdrew to his classroom and took
stock of the situation. After an initial and much-
discussed clash of views, Mr. Alexander recognised
the power of ideological inertia to resist his
endeavours. As for the more pervasive discontent
between 'immigrant' and classroom teachers, not only
were they subjectively at odds, but objectively as
well; that is, their different ideologies were
realised in separate and distant parts of the school.
Where they came together was over the ethnic minority
pupils and what to do with them. The classroom
teachers thought that some or all of the so-called
'immigrant teachers' could be 'freed' to teach 'our
children' who were in need of remedial help, a view
vehemently resisted by the 'immigrant teachers', who
argued that they were not 'remedial teachers'.

Aside from these two sources of manifest ideological conflict, the only kind of professional conflict
which was visible was that within teachers, of
dilemmas they faced in effecting their educational
goals. Whilst others might have been seen as instrumental in causing these dilemmas, they could not be
confronted because they were either too powerful, as
in the case of the head teacher, or too distant and
beyond the beck and call of the teacher, as with many
parents who did not prepare their children properly
for school. Two strategies for easing the dilemma
were used: the expression of humorous analyses of
the school - the 'black comedy' theme - or a more
pragmatic revamping of their ideology so that it

accorded with circumstances. In practice, some of
the 'stretchers' admitted their drift from the
cognitive in the face of constraints beyond their
control. Others did not and were perhaps the most
frustrated as a result. They sought to resist the
'nutters' and the 'dead horses'; they coped with
the 'tragedies'; they ignored an unsympathetic
head teacher and they came to terms with 'unsupport-
ive' parents.

A further set of findings revealed how the
different social attributes of pupils associated with
the differing expectations of them held by teachers.
Girls, especially white girls, were highly thought
of by their teachers; ethnic minority girls much
less so. In the teachers' estimation, there was
little to choose between white and ethnic minority
boys. Both were ranked below white girls, but above
ethnic minority girls. Whilst teachers were aware
of the difficulties posed by the social class and
ethnic locations of pupils, they did not seem to
recognise that the regime of the school posed considerable problems for boys, both white and ethnic
minority, and that the continuing reinforcement of
compliant behaviour in girls, especially 'Asian'
girls, might render them unable later to resist
pressures on them to leave school as soon as possible,
to acquire 'pin money' jobs and to marry young. Thus
our concern was not solely with the effects of the
social class membership of the pupil; it was further
concerned with the consequences of his ethnicity and
gender, and how these interrelated with each other
and with the class factor.

To return to the ideologies of the teachers, how
may these be interpreted sociologically, and how may
they be related to the ways in which teachers defined
the ability and achievement of pupils from different
class, ethnic and gender locations in society? We
turn now to the first part of this question: that is,
what are the implications for the sociology of the
primary school of these ideologies?

There is an argument that not too much store
should be set on the ideological differentiation
indicated at the school. Both extremes of the ideological spectrum at Rockfield focus attention upon
the individual pupil, not his social location and the
explanation of it. Take the 'stabilizers'. They
took the Durkheimian view that the school should
foster social equilibrium by adjusting the individual
child to what was seen as his pre-specified destiny
within the manual working class. The individual was to
be integrated into society as it is, not what it might

be otherwise. Moreover, the head teacher did not
espouse a multicultural policy in respect of ethnic
minority pupils - they were to be assimilated into
white, working class culture. Their ethnic 'deficit'
was to be corrected, but their social class location,
as with white pupils, was to be preserved. On the
other hand, the ideology of 'stretching' was clearly
a less romantic strand of liberal educational thinking, but it still averred the notion of meritocratic
individualism, of helping the 'good ones make it',
regardless of the frustration incurred by teachers
and of the effort and strain to be endured by their
pupils. But like the 'stabilizers', the 'stretchers'
simply interpreted the needs of their pupils, albeit
differently. They did not ever address the question,
'What are the reasons behind the consciousness and
culture of these children?'. In short, their ideological differences turned on different meanings
assigned to the concept of 'compensation'. Did it
mean an emphasis was to be placed on therapy, or did
it mean an emphasis on instruction? Both 'functions'
were intent upon dealing with the symptoms of their
pupils, not with the causes of those symptoms which
were located at the wider structural level. In this
sense, therefore, their ideological differences share
a common, if unexpressed, basis.

It is this very failure of teachers to go beyond
what is essentially a social pathology model of
education that is said to indicate the permeability
of teachers to hegemonic forces which structure their
consciousness. Such teachers are locked into a funda-
mental tautology: that is, class causes class. Or,
put another way, they believe that social class
cultural differences cause class differences in
academic achievement which, in turn, produces the
class structure, as defined occupationally. Very few
teachers, so this argument goes (Grace, 1978), are
able to break out of conventional modes of educational
thought within a liberal democratic set of parameters.
They treat the class structure as a given, immutable
independent variable. However, Hargreaves (1978) is
correct in saying that just because teachers do not
express radical analyses of education, it does not
necessarily mean that they do not privately conceive
of such analyses. But the presence of what Hargreaves
(1981) refers to as 'extremist talk' in schools does
not seem to be widespread. This is perhaps because
most teachers are concerned with the practicalities
of getting through the school day and preparing for
the next one, all of which is not conducive to
embarking upon a detached criticism of teachers'

CONCLUSION

commonsense thinking.
   The difficulty for teachers in developing deeper
structural criticism is, as the ideological differentiation at Rockfield suggests, that they may regard
themselves as already critical. They can and do have
ideological differences. This is entirely in keeping
with their perceived view of themselves as professionals who are minimally supervised within 'loose'
bureaucracies. These ideological differences may be
articulated at 'in-service' sessions and 'professional
development' workshops. Moreover, the increasing
trend towards school-based curriculum development
seems to further the teacher's professional discretion.
But much of this criticism is, literally, located in
service, not outside of it. For Weber, 'getting out'
of the everyday, bureaucratised, rational world which
typifies capitalism (and, for him, socialism) is no
easy task:

      Bureaucracy is distinguished from other
      historical agencies of the modern rational order
      of life in that it is far more persistent and
      'escape-proof'. (Weber, 1978:1401)

This 'iron cage' of bureaucratic subordination - an
iron cage which itself is a human construction but
seems beyond human attempts to control it - is an
apparatus which suppresses the liberty of the individual. Teachers, as others, are constrained by it:

      Caught in the limited milieux of their everyday
      lives, ordinary men often cannot reason about
      the great structures - rational and irrational -
      of which their milieux are subordinate parts.
      (Mills, 1967:238)

Unlike Marx, who is concerned with both the analysis
of capitalism and with removing it, Weber confined
himself to understanding its 'spirit'. However, he
seemed very pessimistic, regarding specialised
officialdom and its power as 'practically indestruc-
tible' (Weber, 1978:1401). In Weber's analysis the
individual must somehow make space for himself within
the 'iron cage'; that is, he must interpret it for
himself, but from within. For Marx, however, it was
not a question of all this being unavoidable - both
the division of labour and capitalism were not
inevitable. Whilst Weber was reluctantly prepared to
subordinate the individual to 'rationality', Marx was
not prepared to condone the continuing 'alienation'
of man.

CONCLUSION

As discussed earlier, however, Weber doubted
that a pre-revolutionary class consciousness could
emerge. And he doubted that socialism could bring
about the end of bureaucratic institutional forms -
if anything, it would further them (Weber, 1978:225).
Although Weber was indebted to Marx for pointing to
the affinity between material existence and consciousness, he was not prepared to explain consciousness
ultimately on the basis of class alone. What some
Marxists ignore is that social differentiation is not
only class-based. Within a social class, status
groups serve to fragment it. Indeed, it would appear
that it is status groups, such as those based on
ethnicity, which are the more assertive. These groups,
by definition, share a subjectivity which itself may
be given objective distinction on the basis of a
common biology, skin colour or language. The sociological study of education, both from functionalist
and neoMarxist perspectives, has tended to ignore
this status dimension, preferring to concentrate only
on social class. The present study, however, has
sought to highlight status differences, but without
ignoring the dimension of class.

One of the central findings of this study has
been that teachers differentiate their working class
pupils on the basis of ethnicity and gender. It is
important to stress, however, that whilst they are
aware of their ethnic differentiation, they are less
aware of the fact that they differentiate on the
basis of gender, and in favour of girls. Thus these
teachers do recognise that the culture of their
pupils emanates both from their membership in the
working class and from their membership of ethnic
groups within it. They fail to recognise that the
gender background of their pupils differentially
prepares them for the regime of the classroom,
although they do seem conscious of the difficulties
which ethnic minority girls face. Therefore, in the
teacher's analysis, we are dealing here with social
pathologies, not just a single pathology based on
social class location. Thus these teachers are partly
aware that the gender, ethnic and class locations of
their pupils differentially prepare them for the
regime of the classroom. They have not, however,
explained these class, ethnic and gender structures
and, in that sense, their pathology theory does not
go beyond a superficial symptomatic level. But nor
can a Marxist interpretation offer a complete explanation. Whilst it does offer an analysis of social
class cleavages in society, it fails to account for
those based on ethnicity and gender, save to argue

that capitalism exploits for its purposes whatever status differences already exist. But patriarchy and racial discrimination are not derivatives of capitalism; they ante-date it (Weber, 1978:385-398; 1006-10). They will not necessarily disappear with the onset of socialism anymore than hierarchy itself will (Weber, 1978:225). Analyses of school and society which merely subsume status group consciousness to that of social class impose a spurious simplicity upon the social world. A Weberian perspective allows for a class dimension but does not hold to a mono-causal, economistic explanation of consciousness and institutional forms.

We have argued that although Weber's analysis of capitalism is very penetrating, and refines the materialist thesis, it did not offer more than an understanding of capitalism - it did not advocate social change along socialist lines. To have done so would have been to erect an even more formidable 'iron cage' of bureaucratic rationality than that which obtains under capitalism. Weber regarded our ability to go beyond our institutionalised frameworks as extremely doubtful, just as neoMarxist critics of education see the difficulties teachers face in combating capitalist ideology. That said, however, it would be wrong to say that no change is possible. But before change can occur we need to have new ways of seeing; that is, we need to go beyond conventional staffroom wisdom(s). As teachers, our focus is quite properly on our pupils in our classrooms; and, as professionals, we must ensure that we maintain and improve our pedagogical skills. Much of in-service education, therefore, is classroom-based; 'society' is kept at bay. Thus the analysis of <u>education</u>, as opposed to the fine-tuning of pedagogy and assessment, tends to be given short shrift in the continuing education of professional teachers. This imbalance should be corrected. At a time when the political nature of education is never far from the headlines, the trend towards 'teacher effectiveness' and 'accountability' seems to omit the crucial and contentious matter of 'effective' for what, and 'accountable' to whom.

This omission will lead to what Hoyle (1974) has called 'restricted professionality'. It is restricted in the sense that an undue emphasis on pedagogical skills training will cause the teacher to think that her role is only to teach individuals; that is, she will see her role as dealing with pedagogical techniques administered to this and that pupil. But education is very much a social, and therefore

political, process. The dilemmas which beset many
inner city teachers are expressed by them as
essentially pedagogical issues, and pedagogical and
technical solutions are sought, often to very little
avail. But the source of many of these dilemmas lies
in the social and political structures of society.
It is within those structures that solutions to the
inner-city's educational problems may reside.
However, many teachers and administrators seem unable,
or unwilling, to pose critical questions about those
structures, perhaps because they are locked into a
conceptual apparatus which does not allow for it.
Teacher education, therefore, should seek to widen
the analytical framework which teachers bring to bear
on educational issues. The consequence may be that
teachers will see education in a more political light.
They may then proceed to act politically on behalf of
the inner-city pupil in a manner that may improve his
rather limited chances within our 'meritocratic'
school system and society.

APPENDIX A

BEING THE RESEARCHER

Two problems beset the intending 'case study' researcher once decisions about the nature, theory and methodology of the investigation have been made. The first is gaining access to the research setting; the second is deciding upon how to manage the impression he conveys to those whom he observes. In respect of the first issue, the school I sought access to was a multiracial school. Although it was not my intention to do research on 'racism', the local education official with whom I had preliminary discussions thought that it was. It was, he said, a 'sensitive' area and, quite understandably, he did not wish to take any chances. He finally accepted that I simply wished to investigate a primary school within an inner-city, 'deprived' area which just happened to be racially mixed. Satisfied that I had no sinister, undeclared research purpose, he agreed to co-operate and introduced me to the head teacher who made me more than welcome, and so did his staff. I was not introduced to the assembled teachers so that I would have to justify publicly my existence in their midst; rather I was left to introduce myself in my own time to individual teachers. I was given 'coffee rights' and any chair I could find in the staffroom. I could come and go as I pleased. The staff treated me like a human being and I endeavoured throughout to treat them in the same way, not as 'subjects'. During the research no attempt was ever made to 'manage' my reseach activities. No teacher, for example, refused me access to her classroom or to her pupils. It was agreed that I could tape-record all my conversations with the pupils and that the teacher would not have the right to listen to them, although she could, and did, ask the pupils what they had told me.

Inevitably, a researcher affects the situation of which he becomes a part. The demeanour I sought

255

to portray to the teachers and to the pupils was one
of detached involvement: 'detached' in the sense
that in classrooms I adopted the role of nonparticipant observer; 'involved' in that I exchanged
pleasantries in corridors and hallways with pupils
and teachers, and in the staffroom I was at pains
not to obviously play the researcher role at all: I
was participant observer. When in the staffroom, I
tried to circulate as much as possible and I avoided
what might have appeared to be any excessive discussion with the head teacher. I did not wish the
teachers to think I was more 'with' him than them.
When the bell rang to signal the beginning of classes
after the morning and afternoon break, I got up promptly
and left the staffroom even if I did not need to - I
did not wish to give the impression that I was sitting
around the staffroom when others had to return to
their classrooms. If I had arranged to see someone,
I let her know in good time if I was unable to attend.
If, on the other hand, a teacher was unable to meet
me as arranged, I did not press for an explanation.
After about a year I was invited to play on the staff
badminton team but I respectfully declined. On a
number of occasions I was asked out to lunch with a
small group of teachers but I again declined. I did
so because throughout the study I became party to
many confidences about both the professional and
personal lives of teachers and pupils. I did not
wish to be seen to be 'friends' with a particular
group of teachers for fear that other teachers might
think that I was in a position to disclose what they
had told me in confidence. During the second year
of the study I was usually addressed and referred to
as 'Dr. David'. I was both amused and pleased at
this because it seemed to capture the right mix
between formality and friendliness which I had wanted.
   Naturally the teachers wanted to know what I was
doing, and why. Despite the cordiality of their
welcome I sensed that they did not make too fine a
distinction between research and espionage. Indeed,
during the early days of the study I overheard one
teacher say, 'Talking to the children is just a
cover'. Another teacher said to me, 'You must be
getting a marvellous picture of teacher watching'.
And another teacher was overheard to say, 'I'm sure
he's here to watch us'. As Rist has noted, an
association with a university is something of a
liability in schools. University teachers may be
seen as long on theory and short on classroom
practice. More than anything else, it was the fact
that I had taught in both secondary schools and in an

infant school which legitimated my presence in those
early days.

There are always ethical problems in school-
based research of this type. For example, by simply
listening to one teacher berate another, does one
implicitly condone her view? Similarly, does one
give tacit approval of theft and bullying when pupils
recount their part in them? What does one say when,
in response to the question about parental occupation,
a six year-old tearfully replies that his father is
in prison? Or what does one say to a pupil who tells
you her nickname is 'smelly bum' because her parents
fail to keep her clean? If one suspects that a child
has been subject to 'non-accidental' injury, what
does one do? Some of the things I have written about
particular teachers may, from some perspectives, seem
very critical. They are not meant to be. I have
only tried to understand the actions of these teachers,
not to evaluate them. Weber's maxim, to which I
subscribe, is appropriate here:

> All knowledge of cultural reality, as may be
> seen, is always knowledge from <u>particular points
> of view</u>. (Weber, 1949:81) (emphasis in original)

We turn now to the chronology of the research,
prefaced by a brief note on the need for an eclectic
methodology. There are occasions when a methodology
is inadmissible to a particular theoretical perspective. For example, an ethnomethodologist could not
embark upon the statistical analysis of a large data
set. Nor could a functionalist undertake an ethnomethodological study of a classroom. However, some
theoretical perspectives admit to both quantitative
and qualitative methods. For example, compare the
quantitative approach of Bowles and Gintis (1976)
with the qualitative methodology of Willis (1977)
both of whom, whilst not being completely at one, do
subscribe to a broadly Marxist perspective. Similarly,
both functionalists and Marxists may produce very
similar kinds of quantitative data but interpret them
differently, as the work of Wright (1979) and Halsey,
Heath and Ridge (1980) suggests. Weber's sociology
is particularly appropriate for both qualitative and
quantitative methods. It admits the qualitative
approach because it begins with the interpretation
of social action, or verstehen, and it seeks to
establish the extent to which individual ideologies
and actions are shared, and therefore social, thereby
requiring some form of quantification. An eclectic
approach is therefore both admissible and necessary.

It supports Glaser and Strauss' (1967:65) call for the collection of 'slices of data' and how these quantitative and qualitative methods may be used in a complementary manner.

The research spanned the period between December 1978 and March 1981. Between January 1979 and June 1979 I spent at least three days a week in and around the school. During this period I was concerned with three matters: collecting whatever 'facts' were to be had; becoming accepted by the staff, getting to know their routines, what they took for granted and what their 'shop talk' was; undertaking classroom observation of teachers and pupils. In respect of the 'facts', I obtained class lists and addresses and plotted the geographical distribution of the children's homes in the city. Using an orally administered questionnaire, I obtained details on the following matters: name, age, birth order, birth-place, language spoken at home, parental occupation, car ownership, garden access, type of dwelling inhabited, the taking of free meals, library membership, club membership and occupational aspiration. In respect of occupational aspiration, I was more concerned with the broad range of jobs - whether or not they were manual, nonmanual or professional - than with the particular job itself. In respect of getting to know the staff, I spent many lunch-hours and break-times in the staffroom listening to and talking to them. I also had one formal interview with Mr. McLean, the head teacher. Aside from chatting to the children during playtime, I had very little to do with them during the first six months of the study. As for classroom observation, I adopted a strictly nonparticipant observer stance and, after the initial curiosity of the pupils had waned, I was able to sit down in a corner and observe without interruption, a finding also reported by Hilsum and Cane (1971) and by King (1978). In most instances I spent three full days with each classroom teacher - thirteen in all - and I spent two days with the 'Immigrant Department'. Not in every case was it possible to observe a teacher continuously for three days. Although I began with the notion of trying to employ a more structured and systematic observation schedule (so as more easily to compare classrooms), I had to forgo this because ethnic minority children and 'remedial children' (in primary 4 and 5) were continually to-ing and fro-ing from the classroom. Finally, during this period I collected whatever documents I could. These comprised mainly notes to and from parents, the pupils' written work and the school 'prospectus'.

During the second academic year, from August 1979 until June 1980, I was mainly concerned with the children, talking to them during class time (with the teacher's permission) and out of class time. I usually recorded our conversations on a small, hand-held tape-recorder. Whenever possible I spoke to them in small groups of four. (Previously I had undertaken a sociometric study of preferred friendship choices so that I could talk to them as groups of friends.) As might be expected, some children were more forthcoming than others. Some were prepared to discuss 'school'-related matters at great length whilst others were not. Although I spoke to nearly every pupil, I cannot say that I have every pupil's view of school. Those accounts which I have selected for inclusion are representative of those accounts which were offered on this or that issue. It was also during the second year that some of the 'immigrant' families were visited by Sharon Lowe whose observations were recounted to me immediately after her visits. She also asked each pupil in Primary 4 to 7 inclusive to rank-order himself and his classmates according to perceived 'best pupil' status in the class. At this time, too, each teacher rank-ordered her pupils on the same criterion.

The final year was mainly devoted to obtaining measures of the ability and reading achievement performance of pupils in five classrooms, and with comparing those objective indicators with the subjective estimations given by the teachers. The testing was undertaken by Felicity Merchant. The results of these tests were made known to the teachers involved and their reactions to them were tape-recorded. During this final year I made fewer visits to the school. I did, however, observe Mr. Alexander's class (he had been a new arrival to the school), and I had a formal interview with the incoming headmistress, Mrs. Watt, who replaced Mr. McLean. I also continued to converse with teachers in the staffroom. Finally, on eight occasions I went to the local high school to which most of the outgoing Primary 7 pupils had gone during the first two years of the study. There I had informal conversations with some of them about their recollections of Rockfield School and its teachers. I also obtained details of their academic performance whilst at their new school. The fieldwork ceased in the spring of 1981.

Teachers and Pupils at Rockfield School: 1978-1981

years	Average monthly enrolment (1)	Classroom teachers (inc. 3 teachers in the Immigrant Department)	Teachers with administrative responsibilities
	n	n	n
1978-79	322	16	head teacher (Mr. McLean) assistant head teacher (infants) Mrs. French
1979-80	316	$15^{(2)}$	head teacher (Mrs. Watt)
1980-1981	283	$14^{(3)}$	head teacher

NOTES:

(1) Includes nursery section.

(2) Mrs. Preece left at Christmas and was replaced by Mrs. French. Mrs. Rogers also left during the year, and Mr. Alexander came on staff. He served as deputy head replacing Mrs. Reid.

(3) Mrs. Davie and Mrs. Letham left, and were replaced.

(4) In 1978-79 there were four male members of staff, including Mr. McLean. For the remaining years, there were also four male teachers, all in the junior school. This includes one male 'immigrant teacher'; that is, a teacher in the Immigrant Dept.

(5) Only one teacher was of ethnic minority status.

(6) The figures for classroom teachers do not include nursery staff/teachers.

NOTES

Notes to Chapter 1:
The Sociology of the Primary School

1   For more detailed analyses of theoretical shifts
     in the sociology of education, see, for example:
     Karabel and Halsey (1977), Hurn (1976), Reid
     (1978) and Davies (1981).

2   This assertion has been criticised by Murphy
     (1981) and by Musgrove (1979). On Musgrove, see
     Heath (1981).

3   A recent large-scale survey, the ORACLE project
     at the University of Leicester, has also employed
     systematic observation techniques (Galton, Simon
     and Croll, 1980).

4   Schutz was much concerned with refining Weber's
     method of verstehen by providing a detailed
     elaboration of the philosophical issues which
     arise between the apprehension of an event through
     the senses and the imputation of the subjective
     meaning of that event for the individual who
     performed it.

5   See also Smith and Geoffrey (1968), Henry (1963)
     and Hamilton (1977).

6   Relevant here are Stebbins (1975), Barakett (1981)
     and Nash (1973). Nash's claimed symbolic inter-
     actionist perspective has been questioned,
     however, by Hargreaves et al. (1975).

7   An introduction to the Weberian perspective on
     education is King (1980).

8   This is Zeitlin's (1968) opinion. For a Marxist
     critique of Weber, see Lewis (1975). On Weber's
     interpretation of Marx, see Mayer (1975). For
     a comparison between Marx and Weber, see Löwith
     (1982). For a Weberian analysis of American
     society, see Tiryakian (1976).

9   There is some doubt about the theoretical affili-
     ation of Bourdieu. Kennett (1973) defines him as
     a Marxist, but Swartz (1977) and Sharp (1980)
     regard his approach as more Weberian. However,
     Bourdieu's concern with ideology has prompted
     King (1980) and Jenkins (1982) to see aspects of
     both Marx and Weber in Bourdieu's writings.

10   Further methodological matters connected with the
     present study are discussed in passing and in the
     Appendix.

11   For a discussion of verstehen, see Leat (1972)
     and Outhwaite (1975).

12   This is developed more fully in Collins (1981).

Notes to Chapter 2:
The Pupils and Their Social Background

1   Mrs. Carter's analysis had some basis. Using
     data from the National Children's Bureau surveys,
     Wedge and Prosser (1973) noted that 1 out of 10
     children in Scotland were 'disadvantaged' (the
     criteria included family size, income and housing),
     as opposed to only 1 out of 47 in the south of
     England.

2   See also Sharpe (1976:278). In her study in
     Ealing, she reports that 80 per cent of the mainly
     Indian girls would have preferred to have been
     boys, given the choice, implying that this would
     have reduced the restrictions on their social
     lives.

Notes to Chapter 3:
Rockfield School: 'The Only Stable Part of Their Lives'

1   These illusory motives serve the interests of
     particular groups which seek to preserve their
     authority. See, for example, Apple (1979) and
     Harris (1979).

2   Schutz (1964:101) also uses the term 'half

conscious' to refer to habitual acts.

3   His view of 'just' was not, for example, that
     wealth, dignity, opportunity and income should be
     equally distributed (see Rawls, 1972); rather it
     seemed to mean that he advocated a 'just so'
     society, but one into which his pupils should be
     contentedly allocated.

4   There was no evidence of political radicalism,
     right or left, in Mr. McLean's analysis. That
     is, he accepted society for what it was, not
     what had caused it to be so.

Notes to Chapter 4:
'You're Here to Work'

1   A similar finding is reported by Sharp and
     Green (1975:186) in their account of the head
     teacher at Mapledene.

2   These three infant teachers - Mrs. Findlay,
     Mrs. Letham and Mrs. Davie - revealed none of the
     'invisible pedagogy' which Bernstein (1975) specu-
     lates is infiltrating the infant school through
     'new' middle class mothers. Indeed, in Scotland,
     the didactic style of teaching was seen to be adop-
     ted by 'most teachers' (at Primary 4 and 7 levels)
     by a team of inspectors from the Scottish Education
     Department (SED 1980). The following extract is
     appropriate:

     'Didactic and other expository styles require the
     close direction of pupils' work, to ensure that
     instructions are carried out, and teachers adopted
     forms of class organization and management to
     that end. Methods varied little from classroom
     to classroom. Teachers expounded and then gave
     directions for pupils to follow, whereupon the
     latter, usually as a class, did what they had been
     told to do. Differentiated group work, the use of
     audio-visual aids, and discussion were not common
     and when they did occur they were still employed
     in an essentially didactic form.' (pp 42:43)

     The Report continues:

     'Teachers are still sceptical of methods that
     encourage pupils to work by themselves from first-
     hand experience of evidence and sources. They
     are reluctant to foster too much pupil indepen-
     dence and responsibility.' (p.49)

3   Although the children sat around hexagonal and
     square desks - a physical arrangement implying

and facilitating collaboration - they worked as individuals, page by page, through structured, sequentially ordered workbooks. They did not collaborate.

Notes to Chapter 5:
'Stabilizers', 'Straddlers' and the 'Poor Relations'

1   This accords with the notion that infants are 'innocent', a second-order construct which King (1978) generated from his study of three infant schools in England.

2   Linked with note 1 above is the notion that young children should preserve something of their own reality, rather than have it 'corrected'.

3   See note 2 above, and Keddie (1971).

Notes to Chapter 6:
'Nutters', 'Tragedies' and 'Dead Horses'

1   The use of corporal punishment was taken for granted as an option to be exercised by some teachers. During my stay at the school, I never witnessed its use, nor did I hear it raised as a matter for staffroom discussion.

2   The expression 'poor stock' was sometimes used in this context.

Notes to Chapter 7:
'Status Differentiation: Ethnicity and Gender'

1   A recent elaboration upon the relationship between the Marxist definition of class and occupation is Wright (1980).

2   On this, see Figueroa (1984):

>   So, although the term 'race' has little validity as a socio-biological reality, 'races' as actually 'constructed' through social interaction constitute important structural features of a stratified (or divisive) social system, and are character- ised by differential access to power.'(p.21)

3   A similar point is made by Mullard (1983:143).

4   A useful analysis on this is in Heitlinger (1979).

264

Notes to Chapter 9:
'The Good Ones will Make it Anyway'

1 The validity of IQ tests is open to question.
   What counts as intelligence will vary in time
   and space (Squibb, 1973), and may be related to
   particular political interests (Lowe, 1980).

   The majority of IQ tests stress verbal ability
   and a particular cultural awareness. The IQ
   scores here should be treated very cautiously,
   especially in respect of the ethnic minority
   children's performance. My concern, however, was
   less with the actual scores and more with the
   rank which the pupil received in his class, the
   rank being derived from the IQ itself. Some of
   the difficulties experienced may be illustrated
   here. For example, one of the WISC questions
   asks, 'What does hazardous mean?' One pupil
   replied, 'Bad weather.' The logic behind his
   answer, entirely convincing, was as follows:
   On the day he took the test it had been snowing;
   a weather-warning had been broadcast on local
   radio which stressed the 'hazardous road conditions.' The pupil had associated 'bad weather'
   and 'hazardous', defining the latter in terms of
   the former. Consider another example. To the
   question, 'How are wine and beer alike?', three
   answers are cited:

   (i)   'We don't drink them. My mum doesn't;
          my dad does.'

   (ii)   'Wine's red and it's awful strong;
          beer isn't strong.'

   (iii) 'Something that mum and dad drink.'

   The correct answers require answers far more
   abstract than those offered here. Indeed, the
   evaluation of the answers might well be affected
   by the sense of humour of the tester. In short,
   the somewhat low mean scores at Rockfield may
   well turn on the children's habit of responding,
   not in the abstract, but in relation to a
   particular context, the nature of which is
   assumed by the pupil to be known to the tester.

2 Tables 8 and 9 are reproduced from Hartley (1982).

ANDERSON, A.C. (1961) 'Access to higher education and economic development'. in A.H. HALSEY, J. FLOUD and A.C. ANDERSON (Eds.) Education, Economy and Society, Free Press.

APPLE, M. (1979) Ideology and Curriculum. Routledge and Kegan Paul.

ARON, R. (1967) Main Currents in Sociological Thought, volume 2. Penguin.

BARAKETT, J. (1981) 'Social typing in an inner-city school: a case study of teachers' knowledge of their pupils'. Research in Education no. 26.

BECKER, H.S. (1953) 'The teacher in the authority system of the public school'. Journal of Educational Sociology vol. 27.

BECKER, H.S. et al. (1961) The Boys in White. Chicago University Press.

BERGER, P. and LUCKMANN, T. (1966) The Social Construction of Reality. Penguin.

BERLAK, A. and BERLAK, H. (1981) Dilemmas of Schooling: teaching and social change. Methuen.

BERNSTEIN, B. (1975) 'Class and pedagogies: visible and invisible'. Educational Studies vol. 1.

BIDWELL, C.E. (1965) 'The school as a formal organisation' in J.G. MARCH A Handbook of Organisations. Rand McNally.

BIRKSTED, I.K. (1976) 'School performance viewed from the boys'. Sociological Review vol. 24.

BLISHEN, E. (1973) 'Pupils' views of primary teachers'. Where no. 84.

BLOOM, B. (1956) Taxonomy of Educational Objectives: the classification of educational goals: Handbook 1: Cognitive Domain. David McKay.

BOURDIEU, P. (1974) 'The school as a conservative force: scholastic and cultural inequalities.' in J. EGGLESTON (Ed.) Contemporary Research in the Sociology of Education. Methuen.

BOURDIEU, P. and PASSERON, J-C. (1977) Reproduction in Education, Society and Culture. University of Chicago Press.

BOWLES, S. and GINTIS, H. (1976) Schooling in Capitalist America. Routledge and Kegan Paul.

BRAHA, V. and RUTTER, D.R. (1980) 'Friendship choice in a mixed-race primary school'. Educational Studies vol. 6.

BRANDIS, W. and BERNSTEIN, B. (1974) Selection and Control. Routledge and Kegan Paul.

BUCHER, R. and STRAUSS, A.L. (1961) 'Professions in process'. American Journal of Sociology vol. 66.

CASTLES, S. and KOSACK, G. (1973) Immigrant Workers and Class Structure in Western Europe. Oxford University Press.

CICOUREL, A.V. et al. (1974) (Eds.) Language Use and School Performance. Academic Press.

COLLINS, R. (1972) 'A conflict theory of sexual stratification' in H.P. DREITZEL (ed.) Family, Marriage and the Struggle of the Sexes: recent sociology no.4. MacMillan.

COLLINS, R. (1976) Review of: S. Bowles and H. Gintis (1976) Schooling in Capitalist America. Routledge and Kegan Paul in Harvard Educational Review vol. 46.

COLLINS, R. (1979) The Credential Society. Academic Press.

COLLINS, R. (1981) 'On the microfoundations of macro-sociology'. American Journal of Sociology vol.86.

CROLL, P. (1981) 'Social class, pupil achievement and classroom interaction'. in B. SIMON and J. WILLCOCKS (Eds.) Research and Practice in the Primary School. Routledge and Kegan Paul.

CROMWELL-COX, C. (1959) Caste Class and Race: a study in social dynamics. Monthly Review Press.

DAVEY, A.G. and MULLIN, P.N. (1982) 'Inter-ethnic friendship in British primary schools'. Educational Analysis vol. 24.

DAVIES, B. (1981) 'The state of schooling'. Educational Analysis vol. 3.

DAVIS, K. and MOORE, W.E. (1945) 'Some principles of stratification'. American Sociological Review vol. 10.

DELAMONT, S. (1980) Sex Roles and the School. Methuen.

DOUGLAS, J.W.B. (1964) The Home and the School. MacGibbon and Kee.

ELLIOTT, P. (1975) 'Professional ideology and social situation' in G. ESLAND and G. SALAMAN (Eds.) People and Work. Holmes McDougall.

FIGUEROA, P.M.E. (1984) 'Race relations and cultural differences: some ideas on a racial frame of reference'. in G.K. VERMA and C. BAGLEY (Eds.) Race Relations and Cultural Differences. Croom Helm.

FLANDERS, N.A. (1970) Analysing Teachers' Behaviour. Addison- Wesley.

FLOUD, J. and HALSEY, A.H. (1957) 'Intelligence tests, social class and selection for secondary schools'. British Journal of Sociology vol. 8.

FLOUD, J. and HALSEY, A.H. (1961) 'Introduction' in A.H. HALSEY, J. FLOUD and A.C. ANDERSON (Eds.) Education Economy and Society. The Free Press.

FORD, J. (1969) Social Class and the Comprehensive School. Routledge and Kegan Paul.

FREUND, J. (1968) The Sociology of Max Weber. Allen Lane.

GALTON, M.J., SIMON, B. and CROLL, P. (1980) <u>Inside the Primary Classroom</u>. Routledge and Kegan Paul.

GARFINKEL, H. (1967) <u>Studies in Ethnomethodology</u>. Prentice-Hall.

GIDDENS, A. (1981) <u>A Contemporary Critique of Historical Materialism</u>. MacMillan.

GLASER, B.G. and STRAUSS, A. (1967) <u>The Discovery of Grounded Theory</u>. Aldine.

GOFFMAN, E. (1971) <u>The Presentation of Self in Everyday Life</u>. Penguin.

GOODACRE, E. (1968) <u>Teachers and their Pupils' Home Background</u>. NFER.

GRACE, G. (1978) <u>Teachers, Ideology and Control</u>. Routledge and Kegan Paul.

GRAMSCI, A. (1971) <u>Selections from the Prison Notebooks of Antonio Gramsci</u> edited and translated by Q. HOARE and G.N. SMITH. Lawrence and Wishart.

GRAY, J., McPHERSON, A.F. and RAFFE, D. (1983) <u>Reconstructions of Secondary Education</u>. Routledge and Kegan Paul.

HALL, S. (1981) 'The whites of their eyes - racist ideologies in the media' <u>in</u> G. BRIDGES and R. BRUNT (Eds.) <u>Silver Linings</u>. Lawrence and Wishart.

HALSEY, A.H. (1980) 'Education can compensate for society' <u>New Society</u>, January 24.

HALSEY, A.H., FLOUD, J. and ANDERSON. A.C. (1961) <u>Education Economy and Society</u>. Free Press.

HALSEY, A.H., HEATH, A. and RIDGE, J. (1980) <u>Origins and Destinations</u>. Clarendon Press.

HAMILTON, D. (1977) <u>In Search of Structure</u>. Scottish Council for Educational Research.

HARGREAVES, A. (1981) 'Contrastive rhetoric and extremist talk: teachers, hegemony and the Educationist Context'. <u>in</u> L. BARTON and S. WALKER (Eds.) <u>Schools Teachers and Teaching</u>. Falmer Press.

HARGREAVES, D.H. (1967) Social Relations in a
Secondary School. Routledge and Kegan Paul.

HARGREAVES, D.H. (1972) Interpersonal Relations in
Education. Routledge and Kegan Paul.

HARGREAVES, D.H. (1978) 'Whatever happened to
symbolic interactionism?' in L. BARTON and
R. MEIGHAN (Eds.) Sociological Interpretations of
Schooling and Classrooms: a reappraisal. Nafferton
Books.

HARGREAVES, D.H., HESTER, S.K. and MELLOR. F.J. (1975)
Deviance in Classrooms. Routledge and Kegan Paul.

HARRIS, K. (1979) Education and Knowledge: the
structured misrepresentation of reality. Routledge
and Kegan Paul.

HARROP, M. (1980) 'Popular misconceptions of mobility'
Sociology. vol. 14.

HARTLEY, D. (1978) 'Sex and social class: a case
study of an infant school'. British Educational
Research Journal vol. 4.

HARTLEY, D. (1980) 'Sex differences in the infant
school: definitions and 'theories'. British
Journal of Sociology of Education vol. 1.

HARTLEY, D. (1982) 'Ethnicity or sex: teachers'
definitions of ability and reading comprehension
in an E.P.A. primary school'. Research in
Education no.28.

HEATH, A. (1981) Review article: 'Does social class
make a difference?' Research in Education no.26.

HEITLINGER, A. (1979) Women and State Socialism.
MacMillan.

HENRY, J. (1955) 'Docility, or giving teacher what
she wants'. Journal of Social Issues vol. 77.

HENRY, J. (1963) Culture Against Man. Random House.

HILSUM, S. and CANE, B.S. (1971) The Teacher's Day.
NFER.

HOPPER, E. (Ed.) (1971) Readings in the Theory of
Educational Systems. Hutchinson.

HOSELITZ, B. (1968) 'Investment in education and its political impact'. in J. COLEMAN (Ed.) Education and Political Development. Princeton University Press.

HOYLE, E. (1974) 'Professionality, professionalism and control in teaching'. London Educational Review vol. 3.

HURN, C.J. (1976) 'Recent trends in the sociology of education in Britain'. Harvard Educational Review vol. 46.

JACKSON, P.W. (1968) Life in Classrooms. Holt, Rinehart and Winston.

JACKSON, P.W. and LAHADERNE, H. (1967) 'Inequalitites of teacher pupil contacts'. Psychology in the Schools vol. 4.

JELINEK, M.M. and BRITTAN, E.M. (1975) 'Multiracial education: 1. Inter-ethnic friendship patterns'. Educational Research vol. 18.

JENKINS, R. (1982) 'Pierre Bourdieu and the reproduction of determinism'. Sociology vol. 16.

KARABEL, J. and HALSEY, A.H. (1977) 'Educational research: a review and an interpretation'. in, by the same authors, Power and Ideology in Education. Oxford University Press.

KEDDIE, N. (1971) 'Classroom Knowledge' in M.F.D. YOUNG (Ed.) Knowledge and Control. MacMillan.

KENNETT, J. (1973) 'The sociology of Pierre Bourdieu'. Educational Review vol. 25.

KING, R. (1969) Values and Involvement in a Grammar School. Routledge and Kegan Paul.

KING, R. (1971) 'Unequal access in education- sex and social class'. Social and Economic Administration vol. 5.

KING, R. (1978) All Things Bright and Beautiful? John Wiley.

KING, R. (1979) 'The search for the 'invisible' pedagogy'. Sociology vol. 13.

KING, R. (1980) 'Weberian perspectives and the study of education'. British Journal of Sociology of Education vol. 1.

KOUNIN, J.S. (1970) Discipline and Group Management in Classrooms. Holt, Rinehart and Winston.

LACEY, C. (1970) Hightown Grammar: the school as a social system. Manchester University Press.

LEAT, D. (1972) 'Misunderstanding verstehen'. Sociological Review vol. 20.

LEWIS, J. (1975) Max Weber and Value-Free Sociology: a Marxist Critique. Lawrence and Wishart.

LOWE, R. (1980) 'Eugenics and education: a note on the origins of the intelligence testing movement'. Educational Studies vol. 6.

LÖWITH, K. (1982) Max Weber and Karl Marx, translated by H. FANTEL. George Allen and Unwin.

LYMAN, S.M. and SCOTT, M.B. (1970) A Sociology of the Absurd. Appleton.

McHUGH, P. (1968) Defining the Situation. Bobbs Merrill.

MacRAE, D. (1974) Weber. Fontana Modern Masters.

MARTIN, W.B.W. (1975) The Negotiated Order of the School. MacMillan.

MAYER, C. (1975) 'Max Weber's interpretation of Karl Marx'. Social Research vol. 4.

MEHAN, H. (1978) 'Structuring school structures'. Harvard Educational Review vol. 48.

MERTON, R. (1968) Social Theory and Social Structure. The Free Press.

MILLS, C.W. (1967) Power Politics and People. Oxford University Press.

MITCHELL, J. (1966) 'Women: the longest revolution'. New Left Review no. 40.

MULLARD, C. (1981) 'The social context and meaning of multicultural education.' Educational Analysis vol.3.

272

MULLARD, C. (1983) 'The racial code: its features, rules and change'. in L. BARTON and S. WALKER (Eds.) Race, Class and Education. Croom Helm.

MURPHY, J. (1981) 'Class inequality in education: two justifications, one evaluation, but no hard evidence.' British Journal of Sociology vol. 32.

MUSGROVE, F. (1979) School and the Social Order. John Wiley.

NASH, R. (1973) Classrooms Observed. Routledge and Kegan Paul.

NASH, R. (1976) Teacher Expectations and Pupil Learning. Routledge and Kegan Paul.

NEALE, M.D. (1966) The Neale Analysis of Reading Ability. MacMillan.

NEWSON, J. and NEWSON, E. (1976) Seven Years Old in the Home Environment. Allen and Unwin.

OUTHWAITE, W. (1975) Understanding Social Life - the method called Verstehen. Allen Unwin.

PALARDY, M. (1969) 'What teachers believe - what children achieve'. Elementary School Journal vol.69

PARKIN, F. (1982) Max Weber. Ellis Horwood and Tavistock Publications.

PARSONS, T. (1951) The Social System. Routledge and Kegan Paul.

PARSONS, T. (1961) 'The school class as a social system'. in A.H. HALSEY, J. FLOUD and A.C. ANDERSON (Eds.) Education Economy and Society. Free Press.

PLOWDEN REPORT (1967) Children and their Primary Schools (Report of the Central Advisory Council for Education (England). H.M.S.O.

RAMPTON, A. (1981) West Indian Children in Our Schools interim report of the Commission of Inquiry into the Education of Children from Ethnic Minority Groups. H.M.S.O.

RAWLS, J. (1972) Theory of Justice. Clarendon.

REID, I. (1978) 'Past and present trends in the sociology of education: a plea for a return to educational sociology'. in L. BARTON and R. MEIGHAN (Eds.) Sociological Interpretations of Schooling and Classrooms: a reappraisal. Nafferton Books.

RICHER, S. (1975) 'School effects: the case for grounded theory'. Sociology of Education vol. 48.

RINGER, F.K. (1979) Education and Society in Modern Europe. Indiana University Press.

RIST, R.C. (1970) 'Student social class and teacher expectations: the self-fulfilling prophecy in ghetto education'. Harvard Educational Review vol.40

RIST, R.C. (1973) The Urban School: a Factory for Failure. Massachusetts Institute of Technology Press.

RIST, R.C. (1978) The Invisible Children: school integration in American Society. Harvard University Press.

RIST, R.C. (1979) (Ed.) Desegregated Schools: appraisals of an American experiment. Academic Press.

RITZER, G. (1975) Sociology: a multiple paradigm science. Allyn and Bacon.

ROSE, A.M. (1962) Human Behaviour and Social Processes. Houghton Mifflin.

ROSENTHAL, R. and JACOBSON, L. (1968) Pygmalion in the Classroom. Holt, Pinehart and Winston.

ROWBOTHAM, S. (1973) Woman's Consciousness, Man's World. Pelican.

RUBOVITZ, P.C. and MAEHR, M.L. (1973) 'Pygmalion black and white'. Journal of Personality and Social Psychology vol. 25.

SALTER, B. and TAPPER, T. (1981) Education Politics and the State: the theory and practice of educational change. Grant McIntyre.

SCHOOL OF BARBIANA (1970) Letter to a Teacher. Penguin.

SCHUTZ, A. (1964) 'Collected Papers: volume II.' in A. BRODERSEN (Ed.) Studies in Social Theory. Nijhoff.

274

SCHUTZ, A. (1967) The Phenomenology of the Social World. Heinemann.

SCOTTISH EDUCATION DEPARTMENT (SED) (1965) Primary Education in Scotland. H.M.S.O.

SCOTTISH EDUCATION DEPARTMENT (SED) (1980) Learning and Teaching in Primary 4 and Primary 7. H.M.S.O.

SHARP, R. (1980) Knowledge, Ideology and the Politics of Schooling. Routledge and Kegan Paul.

SHARP, R. and GREEN, H. (1975) Education and Social Control. Routledge and Kegan Paul.

SHARPE, S. (1976) Just Like a Girl: how girls learn to be women. Penguin.

SHIPMAN, M.D. (1974) Inside a Curriculum Project. Methuen.

SHIPMAN, M.D. (1980) 'The limits of positive discrimination'. in M. MARLAND (Ed.) Education for the Inner City. Heinemann.

SHORTER, E. (1976) 'Women's work: what difference did capitalism make?'. Theory and Society vol. 3.

SMITH, G. (1977) 'Positive discrimination by area in education: the E.P.A. idea re-examined'. Oxford review of Education vol. 3.

SMITH, L.M. and GEOFFREY, W. (1968) The Complexities of an Urban Classroom. Holt, Rinehart and Winston.

SQUIBB, P.G. (1973) 'The concept of intelligence: a sociological perspective'. Sociological Review vol. 21.

STEBBINS, R. (1975) Teachers and meaning: definition of classroom situation. Brill.

STRAUSS, A.L. et al. (1964) Psychiatric Ideologies and Institutions. Free Press.

STREET, D., VINTER, R.D. and PERROW, C. (1966) Organisation for Treatment: a comparative study of institutions for delinquents. Free Press.

SWARTZ, D. (1977) 'Pierre Bourdieu: the cultural transmission of social inequality'. Harvard Educational Review vol. 47.

SZRETER, R. (1975) 'Some fads and foibles in today's sociology of education'. Educational Studies vol. 1.

TAYLOR, M.C. (1979) 'Race, sex and the expression of self-fulfilling prophecies in a laboratory teaching situation'. Journal of Personality and Social Psychology vol. 37.

THOMAS, W.I. (1928) The Child in America. Knopf.

TIRYAKIAN, E.A. (1975) 'Neither Marx nor Durkheim – perhaps Weber'. American Journal of Sociology vol. 81.

TURNER, R.H. (1960) 'Sponsored and contest mobility and the school system'. American Sociological Review vol. 25.

VAUGHAN, M. and ARCHER, M. (1971) Social Conflict and Educational Change in England and France 1789-1848. Cambridge University Press.

WALLER, W. (1932) The Sociology of Teaching. Wiley.

WEBER, M. (1949) The Methodology of the Social Sciences. translated by E.A. SHILS and H.A. FISHER. The Free Press.

WEBER, M. (1951) The Religion of China. translated by H.H. GERTH. The Free Press.

WEBER, M. (1978, original 1922) Economy and Society: an outline of interpretive sociology, edited by C. ROTH and C. WITTICH. University of California Press.

WEDGE, P. and PROSSER, H. (1973) Born to Fail? Arrow Books.

WILLIS, P. (1977) Learning to Labour. Saxon House.

WOODS, P. (1979) The Divided School. Routledge and Kegan Paul.

WRIGHT, E.O. (1979) Class Structure and Income Determination. Academic Press.

WRIGHT, E.O. (1980) 'Class and Occupation'. Theory and Society vol. 9.

WRONG, D. (1961) 'The over-socialized conception of man in modern sociology.' American Sociological Review vol. 26.

YOUNG, M.F.D. (1971) Knowledge and Control. MacMillan.

YULE, W. (1967) 'Predicted Reading Ages.' British Journal of Educational Psychology vol. 37.

ZEITLIN, I.M. (1968) Ideology and the Development of Sociological Theory. Prentice Hall.

ZELDITCH, N. (1956) 'Role differentiation in the nuclear family' in T. PARSONS and R.F. BALES (Eds.) Family: Socialization and Interaction Process. Routledge and Kegan Paul.

AUTHOR INDEX

Floud, J. and Halsey, A.H., 2, 3, 192, 206
Ford, J., 3
Freund, J., 11

Galton, M., Simon, B. and Croll, P., xi, 261
Garfinkel, H., 18
Giddens, A., 159
Glaser, B. and Strauss, A.L., 63, 258
Goffmann, E., 63
Goodacre, E., 206
Grace, G., 250
Gramsci, A., 153
Gray, J., McPherson, A. and Raffe, D., 3

Halsey, A.H., 3
Halsey, A.H., Heath, A. and Ridge, J., 257
Hamilton, D., 261
Hargreaves, A., 4, 250
Hargreaves, D.H., 9, 66, 124, 250
Hargreaves, D.H., Hester, S.K. and Mellor, F.J., 261
Harris, K., 153, 262
Harrop, M., 192
Hartley, D., 193, 197, 208, 265
Heath, A., 261
Heitlinger, A., 264
Henry, J., 79, 261
Hilsum, S. and Cane, B.S., 258
Hopper, E., 62
Hoselitz, B., 11
Hoyle, E., 120, 253
Hurn, C., 261

Jackson, P.W., 4, 79
Jackson, P.W. and Lahaderne, H., 4
Jenkins, R., 262

Karabel, J. and Halsey, A.H., 261
Keddie, N., ix, 193, 264
Kennett, J., 262
King, R., 4, 9-10, 110, 166, 197, 208, 240, 258, 261-2, 264
Kounin, J.S., 4

Lacey, C., 4
Leat, D., 262
Lewis, J., 261
Lowe, R., 259, 265
Lowith, K., 262
Lyman, S.M. and Scott, M.B., 8

McHugh, P., 8
MacRae, D., 11

Martin, W.B.W., 7
Mayer, C., 262
Mehan, H., 14
Merton, R., 205
Mills, C.W., 251
Mitchell, J., 159
Mullard, C., 158, 190, 264
Murphy, J., 261
Musgrove, F., 261

Nash, R., 160, 180, 201, 206, 242, 261
Neale, M.D., 218
Newson, J. and Newson, E., 41, 190

Outhwaite, W., 262

Palardy, M., 205
Parkin, F., 11
Parsons, T., 2, 47

Rampton, A., 18
Rawls, J., 263
Reid, I., 226, 261
Richer, S., 63
Ringer, F.K., 12, 246-7
Rist, R.C., viii, 7, 68, 193, 205, 208, 256
Ritzer, G., 51
Rose, A.M., 5
Rosenthal, R. and Jacobson, L., 204-5
Rowbotham, S., 159
Rubovitz, P.C. and Maehr, M.L. 206

Salter, B. and Tapper, T., 14
School of Barbiana, 76
Schutz, A., 5-6, 14-15, 48, 50
Scottish Education Department, xi, 263
Sharp, R., 262
Sharp, R. and Green, A., 8-10, 62, 145, 166, 193, 212, 263
Sharpe, S., 240, 262
Shipman, M.D., viii, 3
Shorter, E., 159
Smith, G., 23
Smith, L.M. and Geoffrey, W., 261
Squibb, P.G., 265
Stebbins, R., 261
Strauss, A.L. et al., 16, 162
Street, D., Vinter, R.D. and Perrow, C., 62
Swartz, D., 262
Szreter, R., 9

SUBJECT INDEX

anthropology of schools, 7
assessment, 56, 59, 68, 74, 80, 103, 109

bureaucracy, 251-3, see also Weber, M.
"busy books", 57, 70

charismatic authority, 94
child-centred education, xi, 89
classroom control, 69-73, 78, 97, 101-2, 106, 111,
    114, 167-72, 229
college of education lecturers, 67, 85
compensation, ix, 242, 250
curriculum, 171, 190

"dead horses", 57, 65, 113, 145
    see also remedial teaching
deprived children, 25-36
domination, 93-96
dress code, 39-41, 45

E.P.A., 3, 17, 23
educational sociology, 1, 17
entrepreneurs, 154
ethnic differences
    and classroom behaviour, 194
    and I.Q., 216
    and reading comprehension, 216
    and social relations, 161-171
    and teacher expectations, 206-208
ethnic minority
    pupils, 20-21, 23, 33, 36-45
    parents, 19, 33-35, 37-38
    girls, 41-45, 195, 240-41
    see also "Immigrant Department"
ethnicity, 155
ethnocentrism, 161